CAPITALISM AND
CHRISTIANITY,
AMERICAN STYLE

CAPITALISM AND CHRISTIANITY, AMERICAN STYLE

WILLIAM E. CONNOLLY

DUKE UNIVERSITY PRESS

DURHAM AND LONDON

2008

© 2008 DUKE UNIVERSITY PRESS
All rights reserved.
Printed in the United States of America
on acid-free paper ∞
Designed by Amy Ruth Buchanan
Typeset in Scala by Keystone Typesetting, Inc.
Library of Congress Cataloging-in-Publication Data
appear on the last printed page of this book.

CONTENTS

My relation to capitalism has long been ambiguous. When I was a boy in Flint, Michigan, I would observe my father returning from the auto factory, unclean, worn out, and somewhat short tempered. I was also acutely aware of men in our neighborhood who had worked in the auto paint shop. Several were wasting away from cancer in bedrooms with the shades drawn down, while General Motors assured everyone that it was safe to spray lead-based paint in small, enclosed spaces. At the age of eleven I stood on a few picket lines with my dad, absorbing the wisecracks and idealism of the men with whom we stood. I attended several union meetings, including one memorable national meeting of delegates to the UAW in Detroit, where five hundred men roared in unison as Walter Reuther, their president, regaled them with the difference between "trickle-down economics"—which "management," newspapers, and the Republican Party celebrated—and the "trickle-up economics" of the union. The delegates roared, stamped their feet, and laughed from the gut when Reuther spoke. They participated in a vibrant movement.

The drive back to Flint after Reuther's speech was interesting too, with six local leaders and me squashed into a large, old Chevy. On the way to Detroit, prodded by my dad (who was president of local 598), they had scoffed at Reuther for opposing "wildcat strikes"—local strikes called on the spur of the moment to protest a speed-up or firing. On the way home there was embarrassed silence, as these no-nonsense men doubtless gauged the gap between that skepticism so recently expressed and their rampant enthusiasm when Reuther spoke. "Too bad Emile Mazey" (the secretary-treasurer of the UAW) "can't deliver a speech for the life of him," one guy finally said. "Reuther seemed good, though," I intoned, listening with delight as they broke into guilty laughter. They loved the charismatic leader they purported to disdain, remembering his courage during the sit-down strike in 1937 in which my dad and a couple of others in that car had participated as young men, remembering too how that strike—aided by lucky breaks—had forced General Motors to recognize the UAW and set the table for a period of union advance.

We took this trip when the welfare state was on the upswing, as achievement and projected future. A relatively high proportion of blue-collar workers were organized, they typically voted Democratic, wages were rising, workers' rights and job security received decent protection, the union supported racial integration, community colleges were sprouting up, retirement programs were improving, a "committee man" could be called on the spot when a worker had a "grievance," the GI Bill was in full swing, and above all, union families imagined a future democratic capitalism in which these achievements would grow. Indeed, the distance between the dominant meaning of "welfare state" then—as a symbol of economic programs for both citizens in general and those who had hit a bad spot—and now—as the sign of programs aimed at the permanently unemployed—shows how successful the evangelical-capitalist resonance machine has been in recoding its meaning and substance. I admired these worker-activists, forgiving them for the occasional heavy drinking, carousing, and neglect that punctuated their commitments to work, family, activism, and education.

My relation to Christianity harbors similar ambiguity. As a youth I heard radio programs in which Christian leaders called for equality and justice. But alongside the white families in my neighborhood who had lived in Michigan for sometime was a large cohort of white families who had recently migrated from Tennessee, West Virginia, and Kentucky. Union supporters sometimes called them "hillbillies" behind their backs. Few displayed positive feelings about the union. Their kids talked a lot on the street about Jesus and the Bible. Between the ages of six and twelve I heard repeatedly that you must be baptized or go to hell, that hell was a place of fire and brimstone, that "the Jews" killed Jesus, that Catholics were headed for eternal agony, and that Christ would return very soon to judge us all. Since my parents had broken with Catholicism and Protestantism respectively, it troubled me to think that we—and several members of our extended family—were on the road to hell.

We left that neighborhood when I was twelve, and I lost touch with those kids. I would love to meet a couple of them again, seeing how they have come to terms as adults with the actual deaths of relatives and acquaintances they once consigned to hell. They were already inhabited by Proustian layers, nooks, and sparks that exceeded the stories they recited. Our differences often dissolved in the dust kicked up by the neighborhood street games that provided the center of life for many of us. Nor did they disrupt the little bands we formed to steal candy bars from local stores: one guy buying a pack of gum, another chatting to the owner, and the third loading his pockets. There were no pear trees in that neighborhood.

The intensity of these neighborhood exchanges along with the inspiration of my parents doubtless helped to forge the nontheistic outlook in me that has lingered and evolved. I was a proud atheist as a teenager, impressed with the power of reason to dissolve religious superstition and prepared to test its power at a moment's notice. I now confess nontheism: it is not proven by reason or evidence, though impressive considerations can be advanced on its behalf. It is one creed among others, a minority stance to express in public as you also acknowledge the contestable elements in it. Each layer of the self is loaded with a deposit of faith. And faith—same as it always was—is a many-splendored thing.

One afternoon, when I was six or seven and my father had recently returned home from a two-year stint in the navy, he was yelling loudly at my mother. "Why don't you just kick her in the belly, dad?," I blurted, staring up in defiance and fear at this large figure who darkened the horizon. The two adults laughed, and that little crisis dissipated. My father regaled his brothers with this story, spicing it up in the Irish style loved by them and annoying to others. Those who enjoyed the story are now dead, dispatched to hell or oblivion as the case may be. Apparently I was more identified with my mother at that time than my father, a feeling no doubt filtered through an oedipal screen. My mother frowned on jokes about other creeds, even as she assured me that neighborhood announcements about baptism, hell, Jews, Negroes, Catholics, and a second coming could be taken with a grain of salt. She hoped that I would not forgo college to follow my father into the factory out of loyalty, the prospect of decent wages, and the desire to be a labor activist. It turned out that my dad agreed with her.

Now, when I recall the sermons at neighborhood churches that I occasionally attended with friends, I feel again the passions circulating through those assemblies. These devotees expressed in different tones many of the grievances they shared with union loyalists. The union and the church set two poles of attraction around which factory families were organized, with many folding bits and pieces from each into their lives.

None of the evangelical families with whom I was acquainted was "political" in a secular sense of the word. They avoided union meetings, seldom voted, and dedicated their extra-familial life to their congregations. They accepted the "right to work" doctrine peddled by editorialists, corporate leaders, and the Republican Party. This doctrine did not hold that every adult had the right to a job, but rather that it is theft to compel union dues even when the worker rights and seniority you have gained are protected by a union. These families were ripe to be picked by the George Wallace movement of the late 1960s. General Motors made its contribution too: every time an advance in pay, job security, or benefits was wrestled from it by the threat or fact of a strike, GM would issue a glossy brochure about the benefits it "gives" to members of "the company family." Capitalism seemed tolerable as long as corporations and the media were balanced by a strong labor movement.

Retrospectively, it is easy to detect seeds of the contemporary evangelical-capitalist resonance machine in the conjunctions between white migration, menial work, segregated neighborhoods, union priorities, evangelical hope, and church and corporate images of the self-made individual. But no union leader, left-leaning publicist or liberal secularist of the day, of whom I am aware, anticipated that movement. Nor did any expect a "New Left" to arise even earlier to oppose a horrible war, demand new rights, and foment an evangelical-capital reaction. I do not blame intellectuals for these omissions. My philosophy of time, emerging from the lived experience of the unexpected and from theoretical study, suggests that time is punctuated by surprise, not only because of limitations in our ability to know the world but also because the world itself contains an element of volatility. This book addresses elements of volatility in capitalism and Christianity, as it also addresses resonances between them.

I regret the demise of the welfare state and of the labor movement upon which it was based. But it seems impossible to reinstate either that particular movement or the image of secular politics in which it was set. Today "religion"—a flat word collapsing creed, liturgy, and spirituality into one compass —surges into the pores and pulsations of politics. And a new movement on the democratic left, if it emerges, will be organized *across* religious, class, gender, ethnic, and generational lines without trying to pretend that citizens can leave their faiths entirely behind them when they enter public life. It will take the shape of a complex assemblage, both mirroring and outstripping the evangelical-capitalist machine that it challenges, divides, and displaces. Its participants will bring a degree of self-modesty into their diverse faiths when they draw them into public life, forging an assemblage which combines care for equality, the earth, and the future in public presentations of interests, fears, hopes, principles, obligations, and responsibilities.

This book attempts to diagnose the evangelical-capitalist machine, to propose concepts appropriate to its diagnosis, to show how its themes resonate across lines of creedal and class difference, and to identify incipient energies from which a more positive resonance machine might be forged. The goal is to place egalitarianism and ecological integrity more actively onto the political agenda in ways that protect the virtues of a pluralist society. In pursuing these ends I neither seek to eliminate religion from public life nor pledge to hold my breath until capitalism collapses. The idea is to form an *interim vision*, one which must be *visualized* by many in order to be felt, and *felt* in order to energize action in interwoven institutions and individuals, including labor unions, churches, the news media, political candidates, writers, investors, government at all levels, educational institutions at all levels, consumers, professional associations, international organizations, and the courts. To build a new political assemblage it is necessary to go beyond both liberal secularism and some traditional notions of solidarity on the left—not by heaping contempt on either but by incorporating the two into larger imbrications between spiritual life, economic practice, and state politics.

The Introduction makes the general case for exploring the ethos insinuated into capitalist practices of investment, work, consumption, and state action. And it reviews two contending tendencies in Christianity with respect to that ethos.

Chapter 1 frames this study. It places Marx, Weber, and Deleuze into a discussion about the capitalist "axiomatic"; it invites Weber to clarify the relation between Calvinism and capitalism in early northern Europe; it engages evangelical-capitalist publicists in the United States who seek to shape the spirituality of contemporary capitalism; and it suggests adjustments in the academic division of labor needed to expose and resist those pressures. If the politics of identity both infiltrate and nudge the expression of self-interest, the media-savvy publicists examined in this chapter have helped to redefine many white working- and middle-class identities. They also vindicate the extreme sense of entitlement advanced by a powerful section of the capitalist class.

Just as chapter 1 delineates the political formula of Christian-economic publicists, chapter 2 explores how the evangelical-capitalist "resonance machine" on the right actually works, how it deploys the media, churches, electoral campaigns, and financial reporting to infiltrate the cultural unconscious, and how a spiral of resonances between evangelism and cowboy capitalism embeds a distinctive spirituality into these institutional practices, one larger than the sum of its parts. This chapter also seeks to come to terms with how existential resentment can infiltrate any constituency, doctrine, or creed, including the one I embrace. One question is how to ward off such a possibility, particularly when you have become—as I have—disaffected from the domestic policies and global priorities of the regime in which you live. The chapter then reviews a minority report within the evangelical movement—reports from other sectors of Christianity will be heard in later chapters. "Open Theism" dissents from a couple of beliefs in the dominant doctrine. But it resists even more the ethos that has gained hegemony in it. Participants in a counter movement must listen closely to those teetering on the edge of the evangelical-capitalist resonance machine as we seek to forge connections with them. Finally, the political advance of an ethos of cultural revenge suggests a need to establish an affirmative attachment to this world. Chapter 2 closes with a reflection on this issue, treating the evangelical-capitalist resonance machine both as a danger in itself and as a sign of larger pressures to withdraw affection from this world. A counter political movement, if it is forged, will unite criticism of specific economic priorities with a vigorous attachment to the larger world in which mortality, human diversity, and severe limitations upon human agency are set. Critique is indispensable, but the energy to promote positive achievements depends upon more as well: it requires cultural amplification of our attachment to this world. To ignore this register of being is to expose large sections of the populace to either resignation or recruitment by a resonance machine of the radical right.

Chapter 3 begins by comparing the method of reading the Bible prescribed by Augustine for his church to methodological injunctions governing the churches of empiricism, rational choice theory, and neoliberalism in the academy today. The idea is to show how method, problems, ethos, and findings are loosely interwoven, forming a "problematic." The last half of the chapter articulates the problematic governing this book. It advances a concept of "emergent causality," applying it to "rogue waves" roaming around the oceans and to the birth of Geneva in the sixteenth century as a rogue, proto-capitalist city. The latter engagement hearkens back to Weber's account of imbrications between Calvinism and early capitalism, seeking to weave a concept of emergent causality into his historical analysis. One intention is to show how the relations of resonance explored in chapter 2 between capitalism and evangelism have counterparts in other domains, including those between aspects of nature and culture. The concept of resonance, I contend, is not simply a metaphor. It, and the family of ideas associated with it, carry us closer to nature-culture processes than the concepts against which it competes. Behind the desire to avoid coming to terms with the phenomenon of resonance may be a strange line of convergence between two contending cultural drives: the desire for consummate human agency apparent in some versions of secularism and the quest to surrender to an all-encompassing God apparent in others. I do not, however, claim that the problematic advanced in this chapter is incontrovertible. I do claim that it is both defensible and capable of engaging complex patterns of becoming discounted by some other modes of investigation. Chapter 3 closes with a discussion of changes needed in the ethos of academic life, seeking to add another element to a counter-resonance machine.

Chapter 4 asks to what extent "Eco-Egalitarian Capitalism" is possible, let alone probable. It proceeds through a critique of established priorities to an interim image of a possible future. By an *interim future* I mean one close enough in time and shape to enable us to think about its possible details, even if the image is apt to be disturbed by surprising events. By *image* I mean the actual visualization of such a future, a visualization filled with positive affect. Visualization helps to mobilize the energy and insight needed to challenge the evangelical-capitalist resonance machine at multiple sites. This chapter reviews a theory of consumption in market societies developed by Fred Hirsch in the 1970s. He showed how the established infrastructure of consumption creates severe obstacles to formation of a political will to equality and ecological integrity, partly because it locks producers and consumers into self-defeating patterns. Hirsch, brilliant in his analysis of the micro-rationality and macro-irrationality of consumption in a market economy, is less so in his account of how things got out of hand. He thinks that early capitalist consumption was constrained by a religious ethos, and that the modern economy has become "disembedded." In effect, he inverts the assumptions of economists who visualize market self-sufficiency when they blame most economic failings upon religious "altruism," state "interference," and labor "stickiness." Hirsch discerns economic autonomy and yearns for its containment by a traditional Christian ethos. But I will have argued in earlier chapters that capitalism—and every political economy—always has an ethos embedded in it. It is never disembedded. An urgent need today is to reload the ethos of investment, consumption, work, and state priorities. This chapter closes with elaboration of several additional elements needed in a counter resonance machine.

In contrast to the affirmative possibilities reviewed in chapter 4, chapter 5 explores the tragic potential that inhabits the spirit of capitalism today. It begins with the strategic role played by Tiresias in *Antigone*. Tiresias hovers over the rest of the chapter: over the account of a tragic element in violent struggles between Arian and Trinitarian Christians that absorbed much of the fourth century in the Roman Empire; over delineation of the positive power of a tragic vision through engagements with Christians such as Paul Ricoeur, Karl Jaspers, Catherine Keller, and William James, who address this tradition; over an elucidation of Friedrich Nietzsche's modernization and respiritual-ization of the tragic vision; and over exploration of the tragic potential in the contemporary conjunction between cowboy capitalism, evangelical Chris-tianity, and a providential image of history.

A tragic vision renders vivid by contrast implicit assumptions about provi-dence that inhabit theories of a self-sufficient market. While a tragic vision can foster resignation, the version embraced here *affirms* a world without divine providence, a self-regulating market, or consummate capacities of human mastery of the world. It seeks to activate positive political energies in such a world. There is no expectation that everyone will accept this creed, and the partial separation between creed and ethos that we have already examined shows why universal acceptance is not necessary. Rather, the idea is to *contest* the providential image of being, while soliciting relations of agonistic respect toward those who adopt it without infusing an ethos of revenge into it. It is, however, to *challenge* more militantly implicit and explicit images of market providence. One way to do this is to show how smooth assumptions about market self-equilibration are sustained by abstracting it from multiple, un-ruly forces to which it is intrinsically connected. Another related way is to allow a tragic vision to compete with faith in the "incalculable providence" of capitalism advanced by George Gilder in *Wealth and Poverty*. Because the first image was criticized in chapters 1 and 3, I allow Albert Hirschman's critique of market optimism to fend it off in chapter 5. I concentrate on the theological supplement that Gilder provides to shore it up under unfavorable conditions, bringing out, I suggest, a residual theological element that has been slumber-ing in market theory all along. His study renders more transparent some of the assumptions governing benign secular conceptions of the capitalist mar-ket; it discloses how these images require a supplement to sustain popular support today; and it lends critical support to the evangelical-capitalist ma-chine. Again, I do not suggest that everyone must embrace the tragic wisdom embraced here. I say rather that it provides an important counter to explicit and implicit assumptions about the interplay between nature, capital, state, and spirituality in play today. That is why it is encouraging when Christian thinkers incorporate pieces and chunks of tragic wisdom into their eschatology—as key figures engaged in chapter 5 do—or respect it as a contending tradition—as yet others do.

———

I am indebted to my parents and neighborhood for the spirituality that informs this book. I am equally grateful to my (still) younger sister, Judy Beal, who lives in Flint and regularly forwards internet materials about the issues in this book to me. This book is also written for my children and grandchildren. It is important to join them in responding militantly to the losses and damage caused by outrageous American policies of torture, reckless military violence, huge deficits, growing inequality, evasion of global warming, and spending down of the social, cultural, and economic capital heretofore accumulated. A more immediate debt is to Mark Blyth, a political economist at Johns Hopkins. In the fall of 2005 we taught an exploratory seminar together on capitalism and Christianity. We read the Books of Luke and John, as well as texts by Calvin, Marx, Weber, Jürgen Habermas, Gilles Deleuze, and Linda Kintz, with the changing contours of the capitalist-Christian nexus at the forefront of our attention. I also thank Adam Culver, Bill Dixon, Stefanie Fischel, Dorothy Kwek, Mabel Wong, Simon Glezos, Jake Grear, Jairus Grove, Jeremy Arnold, and Filip Wojciechowsky for contributions they made in and around that seminar.

Three decades ago Michael Best and I wrote *The Politicized Economy*. I remain indebted to him for that collaboration and the work he has since done in political economy. Published in 1976, revised in 1983, the book warned the democratic left to incorporate the white working class more actively into the noble agendas of affirmative action and ecology. Such inclusion, we thought, was both important in itself and essential to ward off threats from the right. We also explored the relation between the market and self-defeating patterns of consumption, a discussion renewed and updated in this book. While we worried about gathering threats from the right, we did not see how important the evangelical movement would become to it.

I gratefully acknowledge permission to reprint, in revised and substantially expanded form, two essays originally published elsewhere. Chapter 2 initially appeared in the winter 2005 issue of *Political Theory*, 869–86; it is republished with the permission of Sage Press. An earlier version of chapter 3 appeared as "Method, Problem, Faith" in *Problems and Methods in the Study of Politics*, ed. Ian Shapiro, Rogers Smith, and Tarek Masoud (Cambridge University Press, 2005), 332–50.

Earlier drafts of these chapters have been delivered at conferences and symposia in England and the United States. Several suggestions and criticisms on these occasions have found their way into these pages. I note in particular comments by Kathleen Skerrett, a professor of religious studies; John Buell, an independent scholar of political economy; Tom Dumm, Melissa Orlie, Samantha Frost, Mort Schoolman, and Steve Johnston, political theorists; Danilyn Rutherford, an anthropologist; Lauren Goodlad, a professor of English; and David Campbell, a geographer. I also note with thanks responses from the floor to talks at the University of Durham in the fall of 2005, a paper at the APSA in the fall of 2006, a fall 2006 paper at the University of Chicago, a winter 2006 symposium at Columbia University, my time as a visiting Mellon fellow at the University of Illinois, a set of lectures in the spring of 2007 at the universities of Nottingham and Durham, and an enlivening conference on my work at Swansea University in the spring of 2007. Courtney Berger, an acquisitions editor for Duke University Press, has gone beyond the call of duty in working with this book, helping to make it more sharply defined than it would have been. And Fred Kameny has served as a superb copy editor, smoothing out rough spots in this book as he did in my previous book with Duke.

The results of a seminar that Jane Bennett and I taught on the politics of nature find expression in this book. Each time Jane reads the draft of a chapter I am grateful for the insights that she brings. Besides, she has been chairwoman of the Hopkins department during the writing and production of this book, and I am told by savvy academics that it is wise to curry favor with the chair.

INTRODUCTION

THE SPIRIT OF CAPITALISM

assemblage, A bringing or coming together; a meeting or gathering, the state of being gathered or collected. The joining or union of two things; conjunction; a work of art consisting of miscellaneous objects fastened together.

imbricated, Formed like a gutter tile or pantile. Covered with or composed of scales or scalelike parts, *overlapping* like roof tiles. Aestivation (or vernation) with overlapping.

intercalated, *Inserted* or introduced between the members of an existing series; *interpolated*. Of material things, especially geological strata, e.g., "The *liquefaction* of underlying or intercalated snow and ice," 1876. To insert (an additional day, days or month) into the calendar in order to bring the current reckoning of time into harmony with the natural solar year. *Interstratified, interembedded* with the original series, "Marine mud and sand, accumulated bed upon bed, intercalated here and there with strata of limestone," *Phys Geography*, 1878.

infused, L. *infus-us*, a *pouring in*. To introduce as pouring; to *instill, insinuate*, as the work of God in the *imparting* of grace, and of nature in *implanting* innate knowledge. To pour, to shed, *diffuse*. To affect . . . a liquid by steeping some soluble substance in it; hence to *impregnate, pervade, imbue* (with some quality, opinion, etc.).

incorporated, To combine or unite into one body; to *mix* or *blend* thoroughly together. "Equal parts of oat, wheat, barley and bean meals, and the whole incorporated by stirring," *Cassells, Techn Educ*, 1879. *Transfigured*, "An Atheist and a Wit are incorporated, and like man and wife become one flesh," Lacy, *Sir H. Bufoon*, 1875. "To *embody*," "The religion of that age was not merely allied to the state; it was incorporated into it." Paley, *Evid*. 1817.

—*OED*, italics added

The Contending Spiritualities of Christianity

Christianity is a many-splendored thing. It is both a long-term, shifting constellation of existential experiments and a set of contending spiritual dispositions informing to various degrees the lives of about one third of the world's
population. By spirituality I mean individual and collective dispositions to
judgment and action that have some degree of independence from the formal
creeds or beliefs of which they are a part. The relation between creed and
spirituality is real but loose. Thus, you might confess the Trinity and fold
either a punitive or generous disposition into that confession. Similarly, you
might harbor doubts about the divinity of Jesus and be inspired by the generous spirituality that Jesus advanced in his ministry. The relation between
creed and spirituality contains a variety of possible nuances.

A large cultural constellation can also emphasize one spirituality over
another. I call a shared spirituality an ethos. An ethos of engagement is a set
of constituency dispositions that informs the shape and tone of its relations
with others. And it is more than shared: once a few elements are in place, the
parties act upon each other through church assemblies, neighborhood gossip, TV programs, electoral campaigns, casual sports talk, films, and so on, to
amplify, dampen, or modulate that ethos. A central theme of this book is that
every institutional practice—including economic practices—has an ethos of
some sort embedded in its institutions. The institutions would collapse into a
clunking hulk if the ethos were pulled out. Of course the ethos might display
considerable ambivalence, uncertainty, and points of contestation. With these
preliminaries in place let's look at two spiritual orientations that have set the
bookends of the Christian tradition.

Stephen Mitchell, in *The Gospel According to Jesus*, collects sayings that
many biblical scholars in "The Jesus Project" conclude were spoken by Jesus
himself. These scholars isolate probable sayings by reading the earliest extant
texts in which they are found, attending to the language in which they were
written, and applying accumulated knowledge of the historical context in
which they were spoken. Mitchell also brings his own touch to bear, trying to
identify those statements which seem most authentic, in light of others reliably made by Jesus. Given this method, some inclusions and exclusions are
inevitably controversial, as indeed are the decisions that the church fathers
made about which texts to include within the New Testament and which to
exclude. (We will review Augustine's guide to reading the Bible in chapter 3.)
In Mitchell's gospel, though, it is fascinating how noble, inspirational, and

perhaps uncomplicated Jesus is. No saying that survives Mitchell's tests conveys a mood of generic revenge against other people or existence as such. Most convey the opposite, a care for the richness of life and the density of the earth that may exceed the reach of any tightly defined religious doctrine. Consider a few examples:

> Blessed are the poor in spirit, for theirs is the kingdom of God.
> Blessed are those who grieve for they will become comforted.
> Blessed are those who hunger and thirst for righteousness, for they will be filled.
> Blessed are the merciful, for they will receive mercy.
> Blessed are the pure in heart, for they will see God.
> Blessed are the peacemakers, for they will be called sons of God.
> Don't judge, and you will not be judged. For in the same way that you judge people you yourself will be judged.[1]

At least one American Founding Father received the word of Jesus in a way that corresponds remarkably well to *The Gospel According to Jesus*. Thomas Jefferson retranslated the gospels in the early nineteenth century, excluding formulations that he took to have been added later by scribes to fit a doctrine formulated after the untimely death of Jesus. Jefferson's version is longer than *The Gospel According to Jesus*, but its spiritual content meshes well with it.[2] About his relation to Jesus and Christianity Jefferson writes, "To the corruptions of Christianity I am indeed opposed; but not to the genuine precepts of Jesus himself . . . The whole history of these books is so defective and doubtful . . . In the *New Testament*, there is internal evidence that parts of it have proceeded from an extraordinary man, and other parts are of the fabric of inferior minds. It is as easy to separate those parts, as to pick out diamonds from a dunghill."[3] It thus turns out to be as American as the Declaration of Independence, manifest destiny, and apple pie to seek the historical Jesus. Jefferson, indeed, calls upon readers to undertake such a project themselves, even in the face of the existential stakes involved and the fervent opposition that the project will encounter from some Christians: "Do not be frightened of this inquiry by any fear of its consequences . . . If it ends in a belief that there is no God, you will find incitements to virtue . . . If you find reason to believe that there is a God . . . you will find a vast, additional incitement . . . The truth is that the greatest enemies to the doctrines of Jesus are those calling themselves expositors of them, who have perverted them . . . Of this band of dupes and impostors, Paul was the first . . . corrupter of the doctrines of Jesus."[4]

About Jesus himself Jefferson writes, "his parentage was obscure, his condition poor, his education null, his natural endowment great, his life correct and innocent . . . When we have done away with the incomprehensible jargon of the Trinitarian arithmetic . . . we shall have knocked down the artificial scaffolding."[5] Later we will review the century-long, violent dispute between "Arians" and "trinitarians" over whether Jesus was a man who later became divine or was divine from birth. Clearly, Jefferson is closer to the former view, perhaps taking it another step.[6]

It would be difficult to square a punitive or vengeful ethos with the Jesus received by Jefferson. Jefferson solicits a generous ethos of engagement, as he calls upon American citizens to make room for a plurality of creeds about Jesus in keeping with the uncertainties in the texts from which each creed is drawn. Beyond that he resists efforts to attach the legacy of Jesus to a culture of revenge.

By an ethos of existential revenge, I mean one in which underground resentments against the human condition or your place in it circulate through life. An ethos of this sort is seldom articulated explicitly. Rather, it finds expression in punitive orientations toward others outside the fold: in a bellicose orientation to other faiths, states, and civilizations, in patterns of scandal and gossip, in an extreme sense of entitlement for your constituency, and in a tendency to devalue the claims and needs of other constituencies. It finds expression in the *style* of what you do, say, and write as well as the substance—hence the word "style" in the title of this book. Above all, an ethos of existential revenge, to the extent that it circulates in a culture, becomes *embedded* in a variety of institutions, including those of work, investment, church assemblies, educational practices, modes of consumption, voting habits, electoral campaigns, and economic theory. It does not control each institution; rather it infects and inflects each in its relations to the others. An ethos of existential revenge thus *could* coexist with the profession of Jesus as a noble prophet embraced by Jefferson. For words and sayings are porous; they can be twisted by drives and inclinations at odds with them; and hypocrisy makes it possible to cover hostility to diversity in unctuous phrases. But if this ethos were to become extensive its opponents could also find ample textual resources to draw upon in pushing back against it.

One sign of an ethos of revenge inside a variant of Christianity is the insistence by a sect that its reading of Jesus is the only one acceptable, that all other readings should be castigated (or worse). Jefferson and Mitchell both resist a spirit of cultural revenge, though there are troubling zones of omission in Jefferson's application of the ethos that he embraced.

I will define the tendencies toward presumptive generosity and presumptive bellicosity as two end points on a long line of possibilities, with most of us having bits and pieces of each in our souls. It is a simplification because life is more complex than a line. The relational dispositions within and between us assume the shape of a bush more than a line, with stinginess, generosity, bleakness, revenge, self-regard, suspicion, care for the future, desperation, ebullience, gratitude, trust, and decency entering into shifting relations of resonance and dissonance. Nonetheless, this simplification may have some value, since it allows us to explore how spiritualities occupy the creeds and institutional complexes of the day and what turns on these occupations. Let's consider, then, an expression at the other end of the line within the New Testament.

The Revelation to John, composed eighty to ninety-five years after the crucifixion, was written by a devotee who lived in the western section of present-day Turkey. It was addressed to followers facing extreme persecution from Rome. John (not the author of the Book of John) embraces faith in resurrection, the second coming, and the day of final judgment, themes not prominent in the Jesus sayings but present in the official gospels and accepted by most Christians for centuries.[7] Revelation, however, situates these articles of faith in a vitriolic story of divine revenge. Let's bypass the seven seals and seven trumpets to move to its image of divine wrath. Here is a formulation, embodying John's *visualization* of the day Christ returns to inaugurate a thousand-year reign of peace against the devil and his cast of earthly consorts: "Then I saw heaven opened, and there was a white horse! Its rider is called Faithful and True, and in righteousness he judges and makes war . . . He is clothed in a robe dipped in blood and his name is called The Word of God . . . From his mouth comes a sharp sword with which to strike down the nations . . . Then I saw the beast and the kings of the earth with their armies gathered to make war against the rider and the horse and his army. And the beast was captured and with it the false prophet who had performed in its presence the signs by which he deceived those who had received the mark of the beast . . . These two were thrown alive into the lake of fire that burns with sulfur. And the rest were killed by the sword of the rider on the horse" (19:11).[8]

These acts of vengeance by the "King of Kings and Lord of lords" are followed by a thousand-year reign of Christ. At the end of this period Satan, somehow, is released again; and the divine war recommences. Christ again speaks directly to John in his vision of the future: "Those who conquer will inherit these things and I will be their God and they will be my children. But as for the cowardly, the faithless, the polluted, the murderers, the fornicators, the sorcerers, the idolaters, and all liars, their place will be in the lake that burns with fire and sulfur, which is the second death" (Rev. 21:5).

John closes this report on his vision with a fateful statement: "I, John, am the one who heard and saw these things." And "I warn everyone who hears the words of the prophecy of this book, if anyone adds to them, God will add to that person the plagues described in this book; if anyone takes away from the words of the book . . . , God will take away that person's share in the tree of life" (22:8, 22:18).

Many devotees of Christianity treat Revelation as an allegory rather than a prophecy of divine events yet to come. Some even draw sustenance from its opposition to Rome to resist the imperial drives of America today. Even so, one worries about the kind of sensibility that this image of divine wrath encourages among those who incorporate its spirituality into their faith. In the United States today, another reading attaches these events to the collective future of the world. This reading is advanced by many—but not all—evangelical Christians. They anticipate the time of divine revenge promised in the Book, and many plan to participate in it. Not everyone, again, who is so inducted into the Book is imbued with a will to revenge against more casual believers and nonbelievers. Some noble souls rise above vengeful themes in the text they honor. Nonetheless, Revelation provides textual sources, pretexts, and vindications to integrate an ethos of selective revenge and special entitlement into political and economic practices. Those within a congregation who dissent from this temper may have to tread softly or face the risk of exclusion. For they have been forewarned not to add to or subtract from any of "the words of prophecy of this book," on pain of facing the plagues vividly described therein.

Revelation taps heterogeneous drives to revenge against others and demands for compensatory entitlements that often circulate in life, as people absorb a host of grievous losses, existential anxieties, illnesses, defeats, persecution, and economic exploitation. If these drives develop a momentum of their own, the Book is ready to fill them with moraline righteousness and divine vindication. It also invites its followers to identify contemporary personifications of "the cowardly, the faithless, the polluted, the murderers, the fornicators, the sorcerers, the idolaters, and all liars of today," and to take righteous revenge against them. It even prepares them to condemn those who shy away from the virulence of these injunctions, who are identified in advance as couriers of the Antichrist. The Book identifies its critics as destructive agents and dangerous tempters. It is unfortunate that this book made its way into the Christian Bible, while a series of other texts were excluded.

We will explore how revenge themes have become incorporated into one wing of Christianity today and how they resonate with exclusionary drives and claims to special entitlement running through the cowboy sector of American capitalism. The spirituality of each constituency amplifies that of the other, even as their creeds vary. One point of this inquiry is to gauge what it would take to counter the resonance machine of right-wing evangelism and crony capitalism with another machine. It is to pursue a noble ethos of engagement between Jews, Muslims, Christians, nontheists, and secularists who disagree in their existential *beliefs* while incorporating respect for the earth and care for the future into their religious creeds, political priorities, and economic practices. The agenda is to engage key elements in the spirit of capitalism and Christianity together.

Is there a way to test ourselves on the shape of our own spiritualities? It is not easy, since this domain is rife with potential for self-deception. But here is one test to run in a country where a majority of the populace confesses Christianity. According to it, the most compelling differences are *not* always between those who affirm and those who deny that Christ promises eternal life. An even more potent difference is between affirming without resentment the profound *contestability* in the eyes of others of the creed embraced and condemning such an acknowledgment of contestability as weakness or blasphemy. The hypothesis is that those who, through good fortune, the positive example of others, or self-cultivation scale back resentment of the obdurate facts of human mortality and cultural diversity may incline toward a generous ethos of engagement even in the face of counter-pressure from their own creed. And those who, through fortune, example, and imbued habit, bitterly resent the terms of existence may incline in the other direction, even in the face of creedal pressure. This spiritual difference cuts into differences of creed, class, age, region, sexual affiliation, gender, and ethnicity, without erasing them. It may be important enough to be schematized:

    1. those for whom resentment of human mortality and diversity has been surmounted to a considerable degree, who identify the kingdom as eternal bliss after earthly death;

2. those for whom resentment of the obdurate facts of human mortality and diversity of creed has been surmounted to a considerable degree, who identify the kingdom of heaven as a blessed state of the self on earth;

3. those who bitterly resent the obdurate facts of mortality and diversity, and who deny an afterlife;

4. those who resent the facts of mortality and diversity, confess faith in divine salvation, and adopt punitive orientations to those whose different beliefs threaten confidence in their own.

It is easier to present the schema than to measure one's place on it. "Belief" is a marvelously complex condition, with a belief in one nook of the self often competing with belief in others, with significant variations in the intensity of specific beliefs, with social pressures to appear serene when you are actually bitter, and so on and on. But it is still pertinent to read ourselves symptomatically through the schema, regardless of which religious and economic doctrines we embrace. It is ethically advisable, since our behavior may express intensities we officially deny; and it is difficult, because those very intensities will influence the reading we give of our own symptoms. This kind of complexity is replicated in other dimensions of life too. The schema speaks to a responsibility to others that we have—to cultivate acceptance of the obdurate facts of mortality and diversity, either through faith in life after death or through acceptance of death as oblivion. For on the hypothesis adopted here, the *spirituality* that we cultivate is as important to the quality of political, legal, and economic life as the shape of the formal *creed* adopted. One of the burdens of this book is to show how this is so, not only in the life of the individual but in the ethos of political and economic life.

Today it is imperative for those who incline toward zones 1 and 2 to cultivate even more affirmative orientations to being, to align together on some critical issues of the day, and to forge larger political assemblages. The parties don't share doctrines but are linked by spiritual affinities.

How can this be accomplished? I am not sure. But some clues are provided by discerning how what I call "the evangelical-capitalist resonance machine" on the right is organized. Its leaders differ among themselves in creed and doctrine. Those who accept a secular version of economic theory often do not share the religious doctrines of their allies. But they are connected across those differences by bonds of spirituality. These affinities make a real difference to the priorities of the spiritual-economic machine without forming *the* difference. It is important to explore how the differences are amplified and mobilized politically and how they become embedded in institutional life.

But is this religious, spiritual stuff *really* pertinent to the operations of capitalism? Isn't capitalism an autonomous system that either determines the ethos it needs or works behind the back of the ethos that mystifies it? I doubt it. Nor is it sufficient, in my view, to hope that the current evangelical-capital machine on the right will collapse after one or two electoral defeats. It has been defeated electorally a couple of times already, only to reassemble on slightly different terms. What is essential today is to consolidate a counter-resonance machine, linking multiple constituencies across differences of creed, class, ethnicity, age, and gender. Do I nonetheless exaggerate the importance of ethos and spirituality? Perhaps. If I do, it is to underline the importance of an element that the democratic left ignores at its peril, particularly when it comes to the texture of economic life.

Capitalist Assemblages

It is redundant to probe connections between capitalism and Christianity if you treat capitalism either as an autonomous system or as a mode of production that determines its own superstructure. I do not suggest that all neoliberal economists do the former and Marxists the latter. We will encounter instances where the pattern does not hold. But drawing upon both Max Weber and Gilles Deleuze, I push this envelope further. To probe the complex and shifting relations between capitalism and Christianity we need to show how the defining characteristics of capitalism display a degree of indeterminacy, room to be stretched, and evolutionary potential. Doing so can also help to identify potential means by which to usher in new configurations. Modern history is already replete with laissez-faire capitalism, fascist capitalism, the capitalism of social democracy, the capitalism of neoliberal finance and neoconservative culture, the capitalism of corporate paternalism and intimate state involvement, and other types yet. The latest incarnation of the capital-Christian complex, finding active expression in the United States, is distinctive and fateful in the dangers that it presents. That is the premise, the drive and the anxiety informing this book.

The idea is not that if you identify elements of openness and uncertainty in the trajectory of capitalism you therefore show how to control, move, or manage it smoothly. No, the idea is that by coming to terms with the periodic volatility and messiness of capitalism you can better discern both how tragic binds *could* unfold to capture it and identify experimental actions that *might* help to move it in more positive directions. That is what I mean by the volatility and contingency of capitalism, the topic of chapter 1. To accept a messy conception of the world is to emphasize simultaneously its capacity for surprise, its tragic potential, and possible lines of creative action to take. Capitalism is too messy and volatile to fit either the romantic ideal of a self-regulating market or the instrumental model of human mastery. You must act experimentally upon it, and then step back to see what the fruits of those actions have actually been.

Through all its numerous historical variations, though, capitalism does differ from feudal, state-socialist, and mercantile systems. This general set of differences amid significant internal variation can be captured by speaking of a capitalist *axiomatic*. An axiomatic, you might say, is a set of institutional knots with dense tangles and loose ends. The axiomatic twists and turns through time as it absorbs the shocks and additions created by previously exogenous forces. The capitalist axiomatic includes the priority of private profit, a significant role for market pricing mechanisms, the contract form of labor, and the primacy of the commodity form. The relations among these elements are more than random but less than structurally determined. Specific variations incorporated into an axiomatic might include the selective practice of slavery, exclusion of women from the workforce, child labor, significant racial inequality, indentured servitude, the relative independence of managers from stockholders, well-organized labor unions, extensive state regulation of contracts, a flourishing underground economy, a relatively flat curve between the highest and lowest incomes, effective job security, disaffection by lower classes from the opportunities available to them, intimate ties between religiously inspired disciplines and productive-consumption practices, state regulation of consumption, a state-church focus on sustainable growth, or the inverse of each of these. It is not that any combination can fit together—rather, it often takes historical experiments to ascertain which combinations mesh and which do not. There has never been a *pure* capitalist axiomatic consisting of abstract elements alone. The abstract character of the axiomatic reveals how much must be added, incorporated, imbricated, implanted, and consolidated before it becomes a specific, ongoing assemblage.

A capitalist axiomatic must be at least loosely coordinated with an educational system, though that system may retain considerable autonomy. It then infiltrates into what capitalism becomes. Similarly, historically variable practices of science and technology are loosely or tightly coordinated with operational modes of finance, production, marketing, and consumption. There is the presence or absence of electoral institutions. There are variations in state policies of support or reform of the infrastructure of consumption, as well as variable modes of state taxation, corporate subsidy, market regulation, and compensatory programs for orphans, the poor, the infirm, the old, and the mentally distressed. There is the ethos or spirituality—uniform, stratified, or contested—impregnated into these practices, itself drawn from intersections between market practices and religious institutions, aspirations and resentments collected from the past, the habit-forming mechanisms of family, school, TV, and neighborhood, and the periodic shock of definitive events. There are contested orientations to the past and future embedded in these practices, expressing underlying images of God, nature, culture, and time. There are variations in the extent to which the order strains the absorptive capacities of the earth. And so on. Capitalism is a many-splendored thing.

An ongoing capitalist *assemblage* consists of the ways that state policies, educational institutions, media practices, church proclivities, class experiences, and scientific practices relate to the axiomatic, stretching the axiomatic in this way and contracting it in that. The axiomatic and these other elements are essentially interinvolved in a way that may seem paradoxical at first. Neither is entirely reducible to the others. Yet the axiomatic would collapse into a rusty hulk if all these practices were subtracted from it, and specific practices of currency regulation, investment, work, faith, consumption, etc. would fluctuate ("uselessly" or "freely") if they were not incorporated into some axiomatic or other. The relation between axiomatic and the other elements is not that of a base determining a superstructure, or organic inclusion, or full identity, or efficient causality between separate factors. It is an *assemblage* composed through relations of imbrication, infusion, and intercalation between heterogeneous elements that simultaneously enter *into* one another to some degree, *affect* each other from the outside, and generate residual or torrential *flows* exceeding the first two modes of connection. An assemblage is composed of such complex temporal movements. Complexity, interactivity, and an uncertain degree of temporal openness compose its mode of being.

When I was in graduate school, an authoritative question often posed to a guest speaker was, "Is the relation you are portraying empirical or conceptual, contingent or analytic?" The question is an invitation to force thought into a straitjacket. You can't address the complexity of the world by decomposing it into "analytic" relations in which two items are definitionally equivalent and "synthetic" relations in which they are discrete before entering into a contingent or causal relation. An assemblage is a temporal complex in which numerous coexisting elements are simultaneously interinvolved, externally related, and jostled by flows that exceed these two modes of connection. Examples include the flow of illegal immigrants into the United States, the creation of offshore havens for tax evasion and for drug and weapons traffic, and microeconomic experiments that stretch the established contours of capitalism in one way or another. A capitalist assemblage is a historical contrivance, with knots, tangles, loose energies, and uncertain experiments that may stretch its established terms. Its complexity is manifold.

But is the world really that complex? Even if it is, would it not be wise to construct simple models of the world in order to govern it effectively? Yes. And no. The world is that complicated, as numerous historical failures to predict or control the future suggest. And it is unwise to simplify models radically in order to master the world. That strategy draws attention away from multiple levers of strategic influence that might be engaged, and it also exudes a sense of potential mastery that easily leads to dangerous overreaching. In its extreme form, it reminds one of the statement that the news media attributed to Richard Cheney, with results now available for all to see: "We don't negotiate, we dominate."

The terms italicized at the beginning of this introduction disclose that many of us already possess an operational sense of the manifold complexity of the world. The problem is the methodological straitjackets that professionals often impose upon it. They should consult dictionaries more often to appreciate the complexity of being already inscribed in our language and to contain the hubris that too often stalks corporations, the state, and the academy.

The complexity, volatility, and messiness of a capitalist assemblage mean that reflective engagement with it must draw upon multiple skills: these include *interpretation* of its current operation, *visualization* of new possibilities, microeconomic *experiments* that stretch established limits, and political *interventions* into its knots and flows. Each of these skills must be acquired in relation to the others. Such a medley of activities is already in play, of course, but awareness of it needs to be integrated more actively into the agendas of academic inquiry and critical politics.

Capital-Christian Assemblages

There is certainly capitalism without Christianity. But my focus is on Christian-capital assemblages, particularly as they operate in the United States. Christianity and capitalism have formed multiple assemblages, composed partly of elements that impinge *upon* one another, partly of those that are differentially incorporated or infused *into* each other, and partly of those that *exceed the reach* of such connections. To address capital-Christian imbrications at any historical moment is also to address the ethos or spirituality—drawn from multiple sources—that enters into the institutional practices of work, consumption, investment, saving, income distribution, media life, voting, and state action. To pursue this inquiry, however, it is necessary to rethink the ideas of causality, secularism, and nature operative in much of social science today. The inquiry may even challenge aspects of interpretive or narrative theory as it proceeds. But I am running ahead of myself . . .

In this book I use the United States as a touchstone, delineating some knots and experiences in its state-capital-spiritual organization. To pursue this project we need to explore shifting state agendas, changing modes of religious inspiration, contemporary structures of consumption, and a larger cultural ethos that leaves its imprint upon these practices. I am particularly concerned with the extent to which the current assemblage stymies the ability to reduce income inequality and turn back the threat posed by global warming. What orientations to the future infuse it? What are the existential sources of these orientations? How do these disparate sources amplify or dampen one another? What entitlements, condemnations, and calls to sacrifice are invoked by strategic actors in the assemblage? To what constituencies is each call addressed? What assumptions and intensities sustain their claims? What possesses others to accept or contest them?

Max Weber and Gilles Deleuze are two thinkers, differing significantly, who understand how the axiomatic and the operational ethos of capitalism are interinvolved. Weber explores the interplay between early European capitalism and Calvinism. Deleuze advances a theory that supports a similar inquiry today, though he himself does not carry out the assignment. I use each theorist to inform and complicate the other. I agree with Weber that something like a capitalist axiomatic emerges when a set of heretofore floating elements become knotted together by hook and by crook. But I doubt that there is only one such set of knots, or even one way to tie them. Japanese, Danish, Chinese, Russian, and Indian capitalism display significant variety.

The focus today by many publicists on the globalization of capital contains much truth. But these formulations may be inflated somewhat by an unconscious desire to insist that capitalism is the gift (or imposition) of western civilization to the rest of the world. At any rate, drawing upon the early Marx to supplement Weber, I use the distinctive ethos that Calvinism helped to bestow on the early capitalism of northern Europe as a starting point to engage the ethos of capitalism in the United States here and now.

I concur with the John of the Book of Revelation in one respect. It is necessary today to *visualize* an interim future that departs significantly from the shape of the present, and then to work back from that image to see what changes are needed and possible today. To do less is to allow those who implicitly visualize a continuation of the present into the future to control the terms of debate. It also concedes too much to a significant minority of Americans who look forward to the collapse of the world in a fiery cataclysm of divine justice. It even concedes too much to a smaller minority who contend that nothing positive can be accomplished until capitalism collapses of its own weight. A counter image, linked to contemporary practices by interim proposals to action, is a step on the way to renegotiating the contemporary capital-state-Christian assemblage. Would success, were it to occur, set the stage for a world beyond capitalism? That question stretches my powers of imagination too far, though the decision to treat "capitalism" as a specific historical assemblage does leave it open.

There are several things this book does not do. I do not examine how neoliberal theory has penetrated international institutions such as the World Trade Organization and the International Monetary Fund, though I am indebted to those who have.[9] My prime focus is on a set of Christian-capital-state imbrications in the United States, imbrications that affect the priorities of international institutions too. An advantage of this focus, amid its obvious limitation, is that it points to the stickiness and braking power of large states in the global economy and to their corollary ability to accelerate some global tendencies. Both things are present in spades of the United States, even as it spends down the capital that made it a world power. Some trends and tendencies commonly identified as global receive much of their impetus from the priorities of the United States.

A more extensive account of spiritual elements in American capitalism would address relations between the major world religions. But I am not qualified for that task. The assignment I have accepted is already big enough. Weber, were he alive, might undertake such a large investigation again. Today he would need to collaborate with people in postcolonial studies, anthropology, regional studies, comparative religion, and comparative political theory.[10] I have tried to profit from such studies but am not expert in them. The more limited operation pursued here may have some utility, however, in its efforts to cross lines of division between theological, political, ethical, and economic analyses, to gauge the power-infused ethos of economic life in one state influential throughout the world, and to craft concepts appropriate to those tasks.

The concluding chapter of this book draws together elements discussed in earlier chapters to identify a potential resonance machine of the democratic left. Critical to its consolidation is a negotiation of alliances between Christians, Jews, Muslims, nontheists, and secularists who resist the destructive ethos of the evangelical-capitalist resonance machine. Equally critical is recapture of a segment of the white working and middle classes neglected by the otherwise noble movements of pluralization in the 1970s and 1980s. We cannot promote equality and defend advances in cultural diversification without them, and they cannot reverse the effects of the evangelical-cowboy juggernaut without us.

It is important to translate demands for "solidarity" and "unity" on the democratic left into the agenda of constructing a complex, multi-tiered assemblage. The demand for unity too often issued in authoritarian tendencies in the 1970s, making its own contribution to the demoralization of the left. It is also pertinent to see that one or two electoral defeats will not suffice to roll back the power of the evangelical-capitalist resonance machine. A counter machine must be forged. We need a political assemblage composed of multiple constituencies whose diverse experiences resonate together, finding expression in churches, schools, factories, neighborhoods, the media, occupational groups, the electorate, a segment of the capitalist class, state policy, and cross-state citizen movements.

Is the academic, media, church, and think tank machine of the right correct on a critical point? I think it is. For at least forty years its theorists, publicists, religious figures, and media cheerleaders have insisted that the ethos embedded in individual habits, family dynamics, economic priorities, work practices, consumption decisions, TV dramas, constitutional decisions, electoral politics, media news reports, and governmental policy helps to define an entire civilization. They have worked in numerous venues, with considerable effect, to change that ethos. It is just that they pursue a bellicose, unitary culture, disconnected from responsibility to future generations, stingy about diversity, uncaring about urban poverty, and supportive of a system of extreme economic inequality. I concur that an ethos is important, even as I contest the ethos that they support. A counter-ethos too must find expression in the work that we do upon ourselves as individuals and in a variety of collective processes such as state policies, inventive films, media life, church sermons, investment movements, work life, family life, consumption habits, modes of advertising, state laws, judicial appointments, electoral politics, and constitutional decisions. It must secure a foothold in several venues to establish a solid grip in any.

The struggle today is thus partly existential and partly institutional. Better, it is both in their relations of imbrication, infusion, and interdetermination. For example, the state-funded infrastructure of consumption and the ethos of consumption must be reconstituted together, and that goes for the institutions of investment, income distribution, market competition, and the organization of work life as well. To participate together in an affirmative ethos of economic life does not mean that we must all adopt the same creedal *beliefs*. It involves, as will become abundantly clear, crafting an ethos of egalitarianism, diversity, and care for future generations from diverse creedal beliefs, class perspectives, and generational experiences.

Those who continue to think that the existential dimension of life is merely personal, or only private, or unsusceptible to cultural dissemination, or irrelevant to economic life, or wholly determined by other forces, still don't get it.

CHAPTER ONE

THE VOLATILITY OF CAPITALISM

Capitalism and Christianity

Max Weber defines "a capitalist economic action as one which rests on the expectation of profit by the utilization of . . . (formally) peaceful opportunities of exchange." For these transactions to carry the reliable promise of profitability, you need the "rational . . . organization of (formally) free labor."[1] So, four conditions: expectations of profit, socially sanctioned spaces for exchange, free labor, and the rational organization of business and labor. "Free labor" is the labor of those who have been lifted (or torn) from a relation of service (or servitude) to a feudal lord. Rational organization involves a complex set of institutional arrangements: "the separation of business from the household," "rational bookkeeping," the "regular discipline" of labor, the penetration of market arrangements into new areas of life, the recruitment of the natural sciences for production, and the formation of a populace whose livelihood and survival depend upon the purchase of consumption goods.[2] Weber thinks that a strategic shift enabling traditional economic life to be transfigured into capitalism was the Calvinist formation of disciplinary individuals. When this spirit is plugged into other conditions the pursuit of riches becomes capitalism.

Weber may overplay his hand some in focusing on the spirit of Calvinism. For as Hans Blumenberg argues convincingly in *The Legitimacy of the Modern Age*, pressures internal to Catholicism in the thirteenth and fourteenth centuries also helped to create conditions of possibility for the formations of the Enlightenment, secularism, the state, and capitalism. Nominalist theology (*via moderna*) emphasizes the omnipotence of God so stringently that it extracts faith in divine providence from nature and history.[3] While its proponents sought to drain providence from nature and history to nurture Christian piety, that withdrawal in fact increased the sense of existential insecurity in many, a sense reinforced by plagues, the discovery of a New World full of "pagans," massive earthquakes, and other surprising events.

Blumenberg's amendment of Weber is notable, partly because it calls into question the claims of conservatives who say that modern Europe broke unwisely with a time that was intact in itself, partly because it also questions secular theories that represent modernity as marking a clean break with medieval authority, and partly because it points to disputes internal to Catholicism that set the stage for the Protestant Revolution. But Blumenberg and Weber contend together that religious doctrines, rituals, and struggles both penetrate secular practices in some ways and interact with them in others. While Weber sometimes talks as if it is the beliefs of the devotees which inspire a specific mode of conduct, a closer reading of his text reveals that a complex set of beliefs, habits, techniques of induction, and larger institutional processes complement each other, creating a complex reducible to no single element alone. This becomes most clear when old habits of conduct continue for a time after the beliefs to which they were attached are superseded. These habits will eventually wither unless they become attached to other disciplinary techniques. Thus Ben Franklin, the son of a Calvinist, was himself a "colorless deist." Nonetheless a set of Calvinist dispositions to thriftiness, efficiency, punctuality, and pecuniary shrewdness that "his father drummed into him again and again" were integral to Franklin's business activities, keeping them alive in a new context.[4]

In playing up the encoding of spiritual forces neither Weber nor Blumenberg is an "idealist"—contending that ideas and beliefs alone are the motor of history. The emergence of the Calvinist individual as a type involved the mixing of doctrinal themes—the priority of salvation, divine omnipotence, predestination—into materialized disciplines such as prayer, ministerial drumming, bodily revulsion against the "magical" practices of Catholicism, local regulation through recognition, gossip and informal punishments, and sufficient religious capture of the state to incorporate several of those strictures into criminal codes and police enforcement.

These town and church disciplines are eventually carried over into the regularities of economic life, and the latter, reworked, also flow back. The distinction between "materialist" and "idealistic" theory rests upon a dubious dichotomy—fueled by some Protestants and secular academics—between economic *roles* determined by autonomous structures and floating *ideas* and *spiritual beliefs* disconnected from disciplinary practices. But this is a difficult division to sustain after the work of Michel Foucault, and before that of Augustine, John Calvin, Jean-Jacques Rousseau, Karl Marx, and Max Weber. It is true that Weber, by comparison to, say, Marx, Werner Sombart, and Edward Said, underplays how the pursuit of empire generated unexpected conditions of possibility for capitalism. But to factor in that element still does not vindicate a division between materialism and idealism.

We will return to the shifting role of Christianity in econo-political life, but let's note first another Weberian theme. After claiming that a series of contingently assembled elements helped to engender capitalism—crowned by a Calvinist calling toward diligent labor, delayed consumption, and the conversion of surplus into profit—Weber closes his classic text by subtracting the element of contingency from mature capitalism: "The Puritan wanted to work in a calling; we are forced to do so. For asceticism . . . did its part in building the tremendous cosmos of the modern economic order. This order is now bound to the technical and economic conditions of machine production which today determine the lives of all the individuals who are born into this mechanism . . . with irresistible force. Perhaps it will do so until the last ton of fossilized coal is burnt . . . material goods have gained an increasing and finally an inexorable power over the lives of men as at no previous period in history . . . ; victorious capitalism, since it rests on mechanical foundations, needs its support [i.e., Protestant asceticism] no longer."[5]

The contingent assemblage out of which the capitalism of northern Europe was composed eventually contracts into a mechanism in mature capitalism. Weber's aristocratic lament about the "mechanized petrification" of capitalism has also become that of part of the critical left today. The irony is that the most active presentations today of the contingent, creative, and unpredictable dimensions of capital come from liberal corporate élites and right-wing Christian prophets who endow *only* God and capital with those characteristics. Critics who bond a closed mechanism to political despair meet those who celebrate Christianity, economic uncertainty, and creativity together. I wonder who wins that debate.

The leftish reduction of capitalism to a mechanism is understandable during hard times. But it may also hinder the democratic left from exploring proximate strategies to infuse egalitarianism, ecological protection, and cultural diversity into economic life, from exploring contacts with Christians eager to challenge the corporate-evangelical right, and from identifying sore points and tensions in the current capital-evangelical configuration that belie the promises of its most confident defenders. It may be timely to attend to the contingency of contemporary capitalism.

By the volatility of capitalism I mean several things: that the contingency and elasticity of its constituent elements render its range of variation significant over time; that the force of these elements eludes enclosed models of explanation in much of economic theory; that "externalities" of climate change, religious upheaval, natural disaster, resource emergency, state failure, war, civil strife, and political overreaching periodically become internalized because of the deep ties between the operation of capitalism and the stabilization of these forces; and that it periodically foments dangers and potential binds that could recoil back upon the world in a devastating way. Volatility as the element of unruliness, temporal uncertainty, explanatory indeterminacy, creative possibility, and mortal danger that inhabits capitalism essentially. Weber in his classic text at least attends to the last, the contingency that capitalism may face "when the last ton of fossilized coal is burnt." But he tends to downplay the others.

In a brilliant piece (written before he composed a labor theory of value) Marx explains why eighteenth- and nineteenth-century capitalism produces pauperism. Replying with acerbic irony to a comrade on the left who thinks that the king of Prussia could curtail pauperism by edict, he ties the essence of capitalism to the type of politics found in the English state, the "most advanced" state of the day:

> The state is the organization of society. So far as the state admits the existence of *social evils*, it attributes them either to *natural laws*, which no human power can change, or to *private life*, which is independent of the state, or to *the inadequacy of administration*, which is dependent on it. Thus England finds poverty rooted in the *natural law* according to which the population continuously exceeds the means of subsistence. From another side, England explains *pauperism* as a consequence of *the ill will of the poor*, just as the King of Prussia explains it by the *unchristian spirit of the rich* . . .
>
> The state cannot transcend the *contradiction* between the aim and good intentions of the administration on the one hand and its means and resources on the other without transcending itself, for it is *based* on this contradiction . . . If the modern state would want to transcend the *impotence* of its administration, it would have to transcend the present

mode of *private life* . . . [But] *suicide* is unnatural. Thus the state cannot believe in the *innate* impotence of its administration, that is, of its
own self.[6]

The mobilizing power of these formulations rests on Marx's outrage at the
suffering of the poor and his demand to pursue a post-capitalist alternative
around which the "proletariat"—as he later calls it—can unite. His defining
insight is that the capitalist state oscillates between treating poverty as an
effect of the ill will of the poor and of defects in state programs to curtail
poverty. This oscillation in state policy between welfare and punishment—
and indeed the tendency of the state to integrate each into the other—is
familiar to anyone who participates in a capitalist state today. But what are the
sources of that oscillation? It comes, Marx writes, from the contradiction
between general interests that exceed the state's power of recognition and
action and accumulated private interests that cut against them, a contradiction which the state cannot resolve because it itself forms the pinnacle of
private life. Part of this division is lodged in "sanctimonious Christian antith-
eses" associated with the English capitalism of Marx's day.[7] Part resides in a
putative logic of capital not yet formulated closely by Marx.

I wish to linger for a moment on Marx's insight into assemblages between
private life, embedded spirituality, and the state. What if it is true that the state
cannot stretch far beyond the ethos of private life also infused into it, but at
the same time that spiritualities help to shape the internal workings and
intersections between labor processes, profit mechanisms, market competition, investment priorities, and electoral priorities? The plausibility of these
imbrications is already suggested by the impossibility of neatly dividing the
people who participate in a cultural ensemble into distinct roles consisting of
spiritual dispositions, work habits, consumption proclivities, wage needs,
investment priorities, and state preferences, even though each role does ex-
hibit a degree of viscosity. The idea that capital treats labor as a disposable
commodity while the living, breathing, loving and needy worker exceeds the
commodity form trades on this irreducibility.

This is a point at which Weber and Marx meet. For the mature Marx never
did isolate a set of tight contradictions of capitalism; and, as Tawney has
shown, the ethos of Protestant Christianity incorporated into early state-
capitalism was strongly disposed to blame poverty upon the character of the
poor.[8] Marx intimates in "The King of Prussia" how capitalism, the state, and
Christianity are intercoded to a significant degree, with a change in any

finding some expression in the interior of the others. We have here a state-capital-Christian complex, with each coiling to some degree into the interior of the others and also pressing against them from the outside. There is an element of volatility in these patterns of resonance and dissonance. We don't know in advance precisely when a tipping point will alter the complex, just as urban cops don't know how far they can go on a given day before triggering a riot, or as medieval dissidents, parish priests, mercantile élites, Jewish traders in the diaspora, monarchs in need of credit, and devout Calvinists did not know when their conjunctions would tip into capitalism. That latter assemblage, for instance, did not even take the form of a clear concept before it became a historical reality.

The history of state-capital-Christian imbrications calls into question attempts by political scientists, economists, and theologians to define each autonomously. Each element forms a sometimes volatile force, variously surging into the others and containing energetic uncertainties within itself that might agitate its companion. The stability of each thus depends significantly upon the balance that each element maintains with several others; the emergence of disequilibrium in one is apt to bump or jump into the others too.

To the extent that Marx's mature understanding of capitalism underplays this volatility—absorbing the idea of periodic, uncertain volatilities into the more contained idea of contradictions—it is because after his flirtation with the Epicurean idea of the swerve in nature, he depreciated the element of volatility in nature and underestimated the potential for religious upheavals that affect everything else. We need analyses that attend to the sometimes volatile relations between the state, nature, capital, science, and Christianity, to currents of uncertainty opened up by the historically specific shape of these assemblages as they encounter new forces, and to the periodic dangers and possibilities that these dissonant conjunctions create. I hope someone can range so broadly. I will only scratch part of that project here by bringing the idea of a state-capital axiomatic advanced by Deleuze and Guattari to bear on the imbrications between Christianity, the state, and capitalism already suggested by Marx and Weber.

The Capitalist Axiomatic

In a dramatic formulation in "The Apparatus of Capture," plateau 13 of *A Thousand Plateaus*, Deleuze and Guattari write that the state came into being "in a single stroke" and that the state-capital "axiomatic" did too. Many historians conclude that capitalism " 'could have' developed beginning at a certain moment, in China, in Rome, in Byzantium, in the Middle Ages, that the conditions for it existed" but were "not effectuated or even capable of being effectuated."[9] It took a series of "decoded flows" from feudal society to create the conjunction of naked labor and wealth necessary to capitalism. "But it is their abstract conjunction in a single stroke that constitutes capitalism, providing a universal subject and an object in general for one another . . . However the different sectors are not alone in serving as models of realization—the States do too. Each of them combines several sectors, according to its resources, population, wealth, industrial capacity, etc. Thus, the states in capitalism are not canceled out but change form and take on new meaning: models of realization for a world wide axiomatic that exceeds them."[10]

The word "axiomatic" is not, to my eye at least, closely demarcated by Deleuze and Guattari. It seems to be a set of elements knotted together in a way that resists capture by a formal analysis. Once so knotted, it creates constraints and possibilities as it bumps along, adding new components here, dropping others there, and facing unexpected obstacles at other moments. Capitalism consists of both knots and flows. Some elements carry nomadic possibilities, engendering new formations as they encounter unexpected opportunities, obstacles, and crises. The axiomatic ties together the priority of private profit, wealth applied to free labor, and commodities treated as consumption goods. Does it also include a state apparatus that fluctuates uneasily between regulating, contesting, and subsidizing priorities of the unruly machine? That is not perfectly clear, though it is clear that for Deleuze and Guattari, there is no capitalism without a robust state. I will confine the capitalist *axiomatic* to the elements listed above; the larger *assemblage* to which it is connected will include the state and a host of other institutions to be noted below.

The state provides the mandatory taxation that secures capital in the last instance and supports the legal-political-banking-civil processes by which a portion of capital can be generated through credit oriented to the future promise of return. The contingency of capitalism is anchored in part on confidence in promises about the future that it promotes.

How *could* such a complex axiomatic emerge "in a single stroke?" I am not sure. But I interpret this to be a useful exaggeration, designed to make a point. In Nietzsche—to whom these two leftists are profoundly indebted—"a moment" seems to mean any period of heightened disequilibrium out of which a new idea, faith, state, or species might emerge; it might last a short or long period in chrono-time, depending upon the event in question. So "a single stroke" may signify a period of accelerated disequilibrium from which a new assemblage occasionally emerges out of volatile exchanges between elements torn loose from previous constraints. It may last a minute, a month, or a few decades, as when the last ice age was fomented during a period of ten to twenty years of accentuated disequilibrium. This duration counts as "a single stroke" because during it the markers by which we recognize relatively durable things are under suspension. This is, for instance, what the biologist Brian Goodwin means when he speaks of a period "at the edge of chaos" from which a new species sometimes emerges.[11]

Thus I receive a single stroke as a series of reverberations back and forth between multiple elements which have attenuated their previous condition of relative interstabilization. To pursue the issue in the context of capitalism, consider what Weber says about a series of "capital*istic*" processes at one moment that do not assume the shape (or knots) of capital*ism*. He is writing about a textile "putting out" system in Germany that was in operation until the middle of the nineteenth century: "The form of organization was in every respect capitalistic: the entrepreneur's activity was of a purely business character; the use of capital . . . was indispensable; and, finally . . . the bookkeeping was rational. But it was traditionalistic business if one considers the spirit which animated the entrepreneur: the traditional manner of life, the traditional rate of profit, the traditional amount of work, the traditional manner of regulating the relationships with labor, and the essentially traditional circle of customers and the manner of attracting new ones."[12]

The ethos embedded in those intercoded practices—the practices of entrepreneurialism, profit, work, advertising, consumption habits—was noncapitalist. As the emerging ethos became embedded in them capitalism came into being in a single stroke. The situation forms a mirror image, in Weber's view, of the time when Ben Franklin and his admirers were imbued with a Calvinist ethos, without the other elements of capitalism available to capture that ethos. Deleuze and Guattari are less committed than Weber to the idea that the one element missing is always a Calvinist disposition to salvation, character, investment, work, saving, and profit. So am I. That would suggest, for instance, that capitalism could not be introduced outside Europe unless a Calvinist ethos preceded it or it was imposed by imperial power. But he and they do concur that since it takes several elements together to form a capitalist knot, the capitalist axiomatic could emerge rather fast once a key missing element were added to a complex in which several others are already present.

The process is comparable to that which E. L. Doctorow describes in *Welcome to Hard Times*. A down and out dirt farmer, a couple of defeated outlaws, two discouraged whores—all running from previous defeats and regrets—band together out of desperation on a small plot of barren land in North Dakota. The resident Native American coaxes a few vegetables from the dirt. At one moment a common well is dug. A feeble-minded guy is enlisted as sheriff to protect against marauding cowboys. The last act does the trick, in a single stroke. The differential elements now resonate together in a new way. Welcome to Hard Times.

Once a state-capitalist axiomatic emerges, it acquires a set of defining characteristics. But within a broad range that is not predictable with precision, any element can stretch out without being destroyed. For the hinges of the axiomatic are loose, and an addition of new elements might stretch or move it in new ways too. The axiomatic repeatedly encounters events, people, dispositions, faiths, natural events, and attacks that disrupt it, or threaten to defeat it, or give it new energy. Moreover, the larger assemblage produced from these encounters never exhausts its own world or other regions with which it is connected by multiple ties. It contains more pluripotentiality than a mechanism; it possesses no implicit end either. It is neither mechanism, nor organism, nor a system of tight contradictions. It is too messy and volatile to fit those images. As it becomes through crooked, uncertain encounters, drawing selective sustenance and challenges from contingent developments in the domains of science, natural resources, Christianity, the ethos of labor, wars, unexpected natural events, and noncapitalized peoples, it also generates a series of "decoded" flows. For the nomadic element of capitalism compromises its knot-like element. "Capitalism forms with a general axiomatic of decoded flows." And: "Today we can depict an enormous, so called stateless, monetary mass that circulates through foreign exchange and across borders, eluding control by the states . . . constituting a de facto, supranational power."[13] New capital is often generated by the state as it expands the money supply in the hope or faith that a new plateau of production will redeem that expansion in the future. Capitalism depends upon faith in the future. Because it depends upon faith in the future, when a previously "exogenous" force like global warming enters the picture, and there is no concerted collective response to it within the short time available, the resulting contraction of time projections will find expression in savings-to-spending ratios, investment priorities, work motivation, consumption choices, and state priorities. In a capitalist world organized around trust in the future, nothing remains reliably exogenous.

Capitalism often exceeds attempts by states to capture it. So at a certain point of success "it seems that there is no longer a need for a State," as "the economy constitutes a world wide axiomatic which overflows every restriction and bond."[14] But despite these pretensions capitalism continues to need the state. Money itself, while "overflowing" the state, still needs state taxation and national banks capable of securing interest and investment promises. The educational, consumption, civil, resource, and punishment infrastructure of capitalism is provided or guaranteed by the state. And the programs of welfare, discipline, and criminalization of the poor, oscillating from one moment to the next as Marx discerned, also depend upon the state. Finally, the state's capacity to wage wars of capture or defense is critical to the capitalist axiomatic, even as war making can easily backfire against the interests of capital. As Deleuze and Guattari write, "capitalism is never short of war cries against the state, not only in the name of the market, but by virtue of its superior deterritorialization."[15] What they don't say, but might, is that those war cries lean upon the state as an object of support and political displacement. The neoliberal story of the self-regulated market in a minimal state would fall flat on its face if there were no large state upon which to displace responsibility for each failure or excess of "the market." But there always is.

This, then, is the two-part harmony: "If it weren't for state interference, the market would flourish"; and, in a lower key, "Please give us more subsidies, support, criminalization and ideological cover so we can continue to sing our song." As Deleuze and Guattari put the point so inimitably, capitalist states are "immanent models of realization for an axiomatic of decoded flows."[16] In this, and in the other ways, Deleuze and Guattari draw attention to shifting imbrications between the axiomatic of capitalism and a variety of events and experiences that help to move, pull, and stretch it in this way or that. Deleuze and Guattari would not endorse Weber's statement that once the assemblage of capitalism was formed by contingent means it became a mechanism humming on automatic, but they could translate his warning about having the supply of coal run out into their own sense of the tragic *possibility* facing capitalism today. For the very contingency of its knots and flows in a world ungoverned by providence means that capitalism could run into a cul de sac. We must, however, defer until chapter 5 the tragic potential inhabiting contemporary capitalism.

Capitalist Assemblages

State capitalism has many faces and innumerable variations. There is Nazi capitalism; fascist capitalism; the capitalism of social democracy; post-Soviet runaway capitalism; a capitalism of minimal market regulation; supply-side capitalism joined to a punitive state; the global dimension of capitalism; the capitalism of invasion and empire; and a state capitalism infused with Catholicism, Judaism, Protestantism, Hinduism, Buddhism, atheism, or some mix thereof, with each creed assuming a number of variations. Several of these can appear together in various mixtures.

An economistic understanding of today's world might suggest that the themes of nationalism, multiculturalism, and pluralism operate on one track and the imperatives of the economy on another, with the former pertinent to the economy only when it poses advantages or problems in adjusting workers, scientists, and consumers for economically ordained roles. Here you first study capitalistic rationality—such as that proposed by neoliberalism—and then see to what extent the rest of "culture" measures up or down to that standard. Deleuze and Guattari, along with others,[17] see the relations between these elements to be both more intimate and more volatile. For example, the state-capitalistic axiomatic, as it has accelerated and extended, has given rise to a new world of interlocked "minorities." The capitalized nation-state, organized around a putative linguistic, religious, ethnic, and gendered center, has devolved into a world of interdependent minorities. Here "the national majority" increasingly becomes a symbolic center consisting of fewer people than the sum of the minorities. The capitalistic axiomatic thus contributes to effects that its most bellicose representatives often treat as foreign intrusions: the flow of illegal immigrants looking for jobs; the emergence of gay rights movements in cosmopolitan cities; the rise of feminism as education changes and the need for two breadwinners grows; the multiplication of ethnic minorities on shared territory as the (legal and illegal) mobility of capital, labor, managers, and legal immigrants accelerates; the proliferating drug trade (an old story in capitalism); mafia-like capitalisms; underground economies; money laundering; legal and illegal campaign financing; offshore banking; child slavery; and so on. The state-capitalistic assemblage proliferates minorities of many types, even as its neoliberal and neoconservative publicists see many minorities as external productions to be excluded, managed, punished, or exorcised by the state.

Between the 1930s and about the 1970s, social democracy gained a foothold in Euro-American capitalism. What were its sources? A world capitalist depression unanticipated by the most fervent defenders of capital; the spread of socialist and communist movements, tempting to many insecure workers in capitalist states; the emergence of state-command economies dedicated to suppressing civil liberties and providing social services; adjustments in the politics of individual aspiration as workers identified more with lifting up their own class than with the individual advance that publicists had promised them (or their children) through hard work, entrepreneurial dedication, and intelligent investment; and the retreat of the right edge of Christianity to private enclaves.

The social democratic movement has cascaded downward, even though its decline cannot be attributed to an ironclad necessity of state capitalism. My guess is that several elements are critical, each connected to some extent with the others: the extension of global capital, restricting the power of individual states to support social democracy in the old style; the upsurge of the right wing of Christianity into politics; the resurgence of the politics of individual aspiration in the working and middle classes; and the replacement of the Nordic model as something to emulate by an Islamic one seen as threatening the civilization of capitalism, democracy, and Christianity together.

This is the point at which we encounter limits of Deleuze's and Guattari's analysis. While their account draws attention to how porous and uncertain the state-capital dynamic is, as it outflanks, absorbs, resists, and runs over other forces, Deleuze and Guattari do not themselves focus on recent conjugations between state capitalism and right-wing Christian movements. Their hesitancy may proceed partly from a focus on European states and partly from a noble desire to encourage more constituencies to loosen the dogmatism of identity in a new world of multiple, interlocked minorities. But that focus, while laudatory, ignores the dangerous ways in which one wing of Christianity and the most predatory side of capitalism now work together.

A Christian-Capital Political Formula

It is time to return, with Marx and Weber, to the Christian dimension of the state-capitalist assemblage. Some may resist doing so by saying that Christian resurgence is concentrated in the United States. But three considerations count against that. First, the United States remains the dominant state in global capitalism; its conjugations and priorities set conditions to which others are compelled to adjust or resist. Second, there is a resurgence of public

Christianity in eastern European states as well. Third, the rise of Islamic movements, in conjunction with the European sense that Christianity is very much a minority faith in the world, could spread this American cultural disposition to other European states. The recent drive by the Vatican to define the Christian tradition as critical to the very constitution of Europe is one sign of that pressure. The campaign plays upon the sense of a traditional Christian territorial unity threatened by a growing Islamic minority and secular depreciation of the spiritual dimension of culture.[18]

We can track the direction of the new capitalist-Christian assemblage in the United States by noting a single fact. On the economic and cultural right nomadism is seen as restless, mobile, unreliable, parasitic, narcissistic, and egoistic, a reputation almost as bad as it had when European priests, puritans, and military conquerers encountered the nomadic peoples of the Americas. The new nomadism circulating through capitalist states—of atheists, prostitutes, non-Christian minorities, inner-city blacks, the media, illegal aliens, gays, lesbians, left-leaning Jews, and unmarried women—is authoritatively contrasted to the centered calmness of sites of tranquility: the family, the nation, the church, and heterosexual normality. Yet the most dramatic expression of nomadism in the history of the world escapes criticism. The nomadism of the capitalist axiomatic is treated as either the most beautiful site of uncertainty and creativity the world has seen since its creation by God, or as a civilizational necessity to be compensated by the calmness of the centered family, the Christian church, and the nation. Or both. Capitalist nomadism is exempted from critical engagement, while many of the minorities that it helps to create are defined as irregular, unreliable, restless, mobile, flip-flopping, and unsteady—that is, as feminine in the classic senses of that term.

The right edge of Christianity provides impressive energy to secure this distinction between legitimate and illegitimate nomadism. If the old capitalist war cry was to cut down the state that capitalism so urgently courts and needs, the evangelical supplement is to demonize constituencies engendered by the capitalist axiomatic while simultaneously repressing awareness of the internal links between the nomadic element in capitalism and the proliferation of minorities. The political formula is to expand the aggressive, punitive arm of the state (through drug wars, preemptive foreign wars, new modes of surveillance, torture, criminalization, the construction of prisons, repressive social legislation) while curtailing its democratic and pluralist activities (social security, minority rights, health care, public transit, unemployment compensation, recomposition of the infrastructure of consumption, a secure retirement, progressive taxation, urban development, experiments with worker ownership, and policies to conserve energy).

As I have argued elsewhere, one source of this dynamic resides in the historic hesitation of the noble social movements of the 1970s and early 1980s—in feminism, civil rights, gay and lesbian rights, affirmative action in education, and abortion rights—to build a class dimension into the counter-movements otherwise so brilliantly forged.[19] This combination of positive energy and implicit exemption intensified race and gender and class resentments among many white working class males closed out of the only dynamic in town. They were implicitly treated to be the one non-elite constituency undeserving of political pressure and state support to improve their lot. The political bind in which they found themselves was first exploited by the racist politics of George Wallace; given a new code through the production of Reagan democrats; and endowed with increased intensity through an alliance between the evangelical right, many working and middle class whites, and assorted people in other social positions whose resentments resonated with them.[20] We need to look at how this counter-movement draws support from the very classes social democracy was designed to mobilize.

In *Between Jesus and the Market*, Linda Kintz examines a constellation of media savvy, public intellectuals on the Right who forge close links between God the Creator, the creativity of capitalism, and the resentments and aspirations of white Americans, particularly men left in the lurch by social movements of the 1960s, 1970s, and early 1980s. The figures she examines include Beverly and Tim LaHaye, Rebecca Hagelin, Elizabeth Dole, Stu Weber, George Gilder, Newt Gingrich, Rush Limbaugh, Michael Novak, and Robert Timberg. These have been the most creative engineers of a political formula that seeks to bind a large portion of the capitalist class to white and middle-class workers by mixing family, gender, religious, and economic themes together. Two dimensions are particularly pertinent.

In a dazzling, unacknowledged rewriting of Christian theology, Tim and Beverly LaHaye—the latter a co-author of the "Left Behind" series modernizing The Book of Revelation—bind the future of the nation, Christian sanctity, the joy of sexuality, and the nuclear, heterosexual family. Sex outside the two-gendered family is dangerous and immoral; sex within it is joyous, adventurous, Christian, and contributive to the stability of the nation. The male must take the lead, since "God designed man to be the aggressor, provider and leader of his family."[21] And working-class women, perhaps overwhelmed by the load of resentment felt by the men beside them and an emerging class of professional women above them, are promised the security of the marriage contract. Beyond that, they receive the promise of a sexual fulfillment that draws secret sustenance from feminism while locking its space of propriety inside the nuclear family: "The strangest paradox in the realm of sexuality is the widespread idea that woman's orgasmic capability is less than a man's . . . Equally difficult to understand is why such a pleasurable and exciting experience has been hidden from so many women while their male counterparts almost universally have tasted the delight of ejaculation . . . Yet the tragic tale of female sexual frustration winds its way through almost every tribe and people, leaving literally billions of married women sexually unfulfilled. Fortunately there is no longer any reason to perpetuate this hoax on potentially one half of the world's population."[22]

"The strangest paradox"; "tasted the delight of ejaculation"; "this hoax." Slide over the Freudian slip, if you will. No mention of that Augustinian-Calvinist reserve—now to be treated as part of the hoax?—about sexuality. This reserve was expressed, for instance, in Augustine's reading of original sin, his command of chastity for nuns and monks, and his commendation that married couples aspire to chastity as the highest plateau of married life. Rather, the capitalist, secular pursuit of worldly happiness is now bonded to Christian marriage; and working-class male desire for a reliable site of authority and supply of sexual pleasure is bonded to a promise of sexual adventure and marriage security for their wives. The Christian, heterosexual family becomes the wondrous site of sexual excitement. All in a single stroke.

The Christian-family-eroticism formula is then joined, by George Gilder, Rush Limbaugh, and Michael Novak, to an insistence that capitalist creativity is *the one and only site in the mundane world that legitimately copies the creativity of God*. For capitalism, on their reading, does not conform to a set of knowable regularities:˙ it is the prime site on earth of risk, uncertainty, and creative action. These guys are Deleuzians of the right. God, creation, and capitalism; capitalism, creation, and God, a formula easier to sustain in a country where the news media ignore or misrepresent the achievements of social democracy in other places.

It is pertinent to see how the evangelical rendering of capitalist creativity resonates with the self-description of cutting-edge capitalist élites, some of whom participate in this movement while others adopt a more liberal perspective. This self-description is delineated by Nigel Thrift in *Knowing Capitalism*. He draws attention to the emphasis upon flexibility, innovation, and creativity by managers in experimental sectors. The gist is captured by one publicist who writes: "the development of the complex systems model that seems so salient to us . . . , the model that seems to underlie the organization of our bodies, our groups, our work settings, our world—this model repudiates the notion of a structure built on one foundation, an explanation that rests upon one principle . . . All is in flux, order is transient, nothing is independent . . . , and no one system is ever necessarily in charge."[23]

This self-description is at odds with the idea of automatic market self-regulation. It could even resonate with a Deleuzian understanding of capitalism, in which an element of creativity is discerned in "our bodies, our work settings," *if* its defenders also came to appreciate multiple sites of uncertainty and creativity in the world, including nature, and if they sought to redress the effects of the current capitalist assemblage on those at the bottom. There is a thread here to tug upon, though it has not been pulled far to date, partly because many on the left insist upon identifying "postmodernism" with the corporate right and partly because postmodernists too seldom carry their analyses into the heart of the capitalist axiomatic.[24]

Back to the right edge of the Christian-capital formula. The political formula of the Christian right is capped by defining men to be vulnerable, persecuted warriors in the capital-state system. They must receive special *compensation* for the ordeals that they undergo, if the most creative and godly economy the world has ever seen is to flourish. Defining (putative) natural differences between men as warriors and women as civilizers, George Gilder plays to the resentments that many white working- and middle-class men feel as they are caught between the success of a traditional male élite and the more recent entry of professional women into its lower reaches. The message is that men must receive deference and special compensations if they are to sacrifice the warrior mentality natural to them to the higher civilizational imperatives of risky capitalist enterprise and stable family life. This is the fraught context, perhaps, in which new intensities of male support for guns, hunting, military campaigns, public expenditures for prisons, football stadiums, the military, and heterosexual normality are to be placed.

The Christian-capital political formula helps to answer the question, Why do members of the working- and lower-middle-class males, often supported by loyal spouses and girlfriends, confine themselves to a politics of individual aspiration? That is, what seduces them to a politics grounded in individual identification with economic classes above them rather than a drive to lift the class in which they are located? Several elements can be identified, including

the absence of perceived social democratic alternatives, the successful binding of social democratic men to feminine (flip-flop) characteristics, the resentment that social movements of recent decades have fueled among working-
and middle-class white males, and the evangelical identification of unfettered
capitalism with the unlimited possibility of upward mobility. George Gilder
makes connections of this sort, albeit in a differently coded way: "The sex
drive of the young male is not only promiscuous; it also tends to merge with
the male impulse to affiliate upward to worship power. Since male sexual
power is embodied in physical endowment and prowess, young men with
sexual confusions and anxieties, fears of inadequacy primed by rejection
from women, can react passionately—and in a homosexual environment ad-
dictively—to the naked bodies of aroused and powerful men. Homosexuality
can therefore feel more natural to many men than their comparatively la-
borious, expensive, and frustrating pursuit of young women."[25]

This perhaps surprising enunciation is packed. It first solicits young work-
ing- and middle-class men locked in a sexual market that seems to be full of
liberated women; second, it points to homosexual desires that "naturally"
point to virile, assertive élites; third, it poses a civilizational imperative to
repress the sexual component of those desires; this leads, fourth, to vindication of a series of *compensatory entitlements* for these sacrifices and repressed
desires; and that entire ensemble becomes sublimated, fifth, into *identification* with the most visible models of prowess, creativity, and power available to
non-élite men in late modern capitalism: entrepreneurial agents and military
warriors. Translate Gilder's "male impulse" into the cultural pressure cooker
that generates it. Once this political formula has been digested—that is, incorporated into cultural resentments, virile identifications, and compensatory
entitlements—the politics of individual aspiration acquire a new intensity.

It may take only a bit more work to convince the men involved that unfettered capitalist creativity gives virile men or their children the best chance to
attain the station in life to which they aspire. The tipping point is provided by
publicists who admit that unfettered capitalist enterprise, treated as indispensable to the health of western civilization, always involves a large measure
of luck. *You too, with your invention, athletic prowess, lottery ticket, or TV booklet
on how to earn millions in real estate, just might hit the jackpot.*[26] Michael Novak,
Bill O'Reilly, Rush Limbaugh, and Newt Gingrich carry out this latter assignment, even as they stoke the resentments that prepare their constituency to
hear the message. If it is true that a near-majority of adults in their twenties

think that their income will place them in the upper 5 percent of the population by the time they are fifty, we can understand why these are some of the forces propelling *that* inflationary spiral.

The radical Christian right *compensates* a series of class resentments and injustices produced by the collision between cowboy capitalism and critical social movements by promising solace in the church and the family; it then cements (male) capitalist creativity to the creativity of God himself, fomenting an *aspirational politics* of identification by workers with men of prowess and privilege; these self-identifications and compensatory entitlements then encourage those sweltering in the pressure cooker to demonize selected minorities as nomadic enemies of capitalism, God, morality, and civilizational discipline. Once it starts to roll, the machine can be reinforced by intense attacks on the welfare state. The militarization of the welfare state proceeds apace, while its nonmilitary dimensions are dismantled.

If there is no place else to run, why not invest hope in economic gambles? It no longer matters so much that small-time investors run great risks as they play second fiddle to speculators who control the volume, displace much of the risk downward, and reap the highest rewards. For male identity has now been bonded to a politics of individual aspiration. Support for social democracy dies on the vine. And a series of positive feedback loops between masculine piety, compensatory entitlement, aspirational politics, and the feminization of degraded minorities threatens to devolve into a fascist movement.

I have condensed and schematized an emergent political formula to show how its parts fit together. The formula finds recurrent expression in popular texts, talk shows, sermons, Fox news reports, electoral campaigns, bumper stickers, and congealed habits of perception. The condensation, however, inevitably occludes sites of slippage and contact with other formulas. The formula does not always take with the constituencies at which it is aimed. Some may imbibe it fervently, others may absorb pieces and chunks of it while being touched by competing formulas, and still others may resist it in the name of union loyalty, Christian devotion, Jewish responsibility, secular decency, Muslim moderation, nontheistic love of the diversity of being, or a combination of such sources. We will return to this issue in chapter 2. For now it is important to note that between the construction of a political formula and its receipt by those whose life experiences it touches, many things can intervene.

The Plasticity of Christianity, The Contingency of Capital

The state-capital-Christian assemblage has shifted and swerved numerous times over the last few centuries. But the current trajectory courts disaster. The theo-economic resentments and entitlements that help to energize it may produce a level of resource depletion and global warming that limits its ability to meets its imperatives of investment, production, income security, consumption levels, and profit.[27] As it spends down public investments from the past, it may intensify resentments and a will to revenge among a growing number of citizens who experience new losses and insecurities without identifying a positive counter-movement in which to participate. State leaders may pursue policies that incite more participants in predominately Islamic states to conclude that the United States is waging a Crusade against them. And several of these conditions *could* meet in a perfect storm, as hurricane Katrina did when it hit New Orleans after a period of global warming, destruction of wetland buffers, racism, and state incompetence. Welcome to Hard Times.

What counter-strategy could turn the current state-Christian-capital assemblage in a new direction? I will speak here only to adjustments that the democratic left within the academy might pursue, reserving to later chapters the dicey question of how to foment a positive resonance machine as protean and energetic as the forces arrayed against it.

First, the liberal-radical distinction between secular public life and religious private life must be reworked. It has led academic liberals and radicals alike to ignore for too long developments on the state-capital-Christian right that they might otherwise address. As part of that process we must acknowledge actively and publicly the multifaceted role that faith plays in our own existential assumptions, identifications, and economic projections. Second, each time a particular theology and religious sensibility is engaged, specific cultural resentments, economic priorities, political programs, and constituency exclusions linked to it must be addressed. The relation between these elements is not one of simple determination. But they are loosely intertwined. It is mere intellectualism—the principal sin of the academy—to ignore these resonances.

Third, it is critical for those on the non-Christian left (left-leaning Jews, Muslims, Buddhists, and nontheists) to pursue active alliances with Christians in several walks of life who resist the contemporary evangelical-capitalist machine. At the outset, forging a connection requires those of us outside the three major monotheisms to acknowledge the element of faith in the nontheistic image of the world that we embrace. There is a corollary too. Christians who embrace the sayings of Jesus rather than, say, modernization of the revenge themes of the Book of Revelation face an urgent responsibility to criticize this vengeful movement militantly and articulate a positive image publicly. In a world of growing diversity and interdependence it may also be incumbent on those outside the Christian tradition to press upon them the importance of that task. In a different time it may have been noble to oppose the politics of human indignity in public while leaving the sources of that concern in the private realm. Today, several constituencies have left the private-public distinction behind, as they either invoke Christianity to support the politics of torture, suspension of due process, a unitary presidency, preemptive wars, and the extension of inequality in income, job security, workers' rights, and retirement or remain silent about these issues while celebrating publicly the virtues of their faith. So it is indispensable for dissenting Christians, Jews, Muslims, and nontheists to cite publicly the sources from which they find the inspiration to oppose these policies. We do not need to insist that the diverse sources we draw upon must be accepted by others—indeed, it is noble to invoke them while acknowledging their profound contestability in the eyes of others—but today it is our responsibility to publicize the links between these sources and our positive econo-political stances. And critical to seek lines of connection across significant difference with others.

Fourth, the hardest nut to crack may be the compensatory politics of individual aspiration in the working and middle classes. The task is not to stifle individual initiative but to connect it more actively to positive, collective identifications. Perhaps women who have tolerated cowboy capitalism out of loyalty to their men can be exposed more dramatically to the real cruelties and suffering that these practices engender, even as we join them in supporting modes of virility compatible with social justice. Academic proposals in favor of universal health care and retirement programs ring more true when they are joined to real affirmative action in education for the sons and daughters of working-class families. But these adjustments can only work to the extent that we also succeed in breaking the line of equivalence between capitalist innovation and divine providence that has been forged below our threshold of attention.

Fifth, the state-evangelical-capitalist right now draws upon the expertise and fervency of a massive think-tank and media assemblage that works simultaneously on the visceral and refined registers of cultural identity. It is much larger and more interconnected than its counterparts in the 1960s, 1970s, and 1980s were. This combination, while it repeats neoliberal slogans, presents itself as the defender of the family, stokes religious resentments, and fuels demands for compensatory entitlements, has done more than anything (except our own inertia) to exclude academics in the sciences, social sciences, and humanities from religious discourse, public life, and the media world. One way of putting this is to say that the difference between the Nixon and Bush eras is Fox News and the large network of right-wing think tanks attached to it. Academics remain word strong and image weak. We need to acquire new media skills to counter the political formula of the Christian-capitalist right.

Just as there is no such thing as a pure man, pure woman, pure nation, or pure culture—lessons the democratic left has learned rather well—*there is no such thing as pure capitalism either.* At each historical juncture, this or that ethos acquires a significant presence in a capitalist assemblage, and vice versa. Better, each periodically infiltrates the interior of the other as it also nudges and pushes it from the outside. To pretend otherwise is to reduce critical economic orientations to secular dreams of smooth economic management, revolutionary fantasy, or leftist resignation. We participate in a state-capital-spiritual assemblage replete with distinctive knots, open flows, modes of domination, compensatory entitlements, and uncertain sites of intervention.

CHAPTER TWO

THE EVANGELICAL-CAPITALIST
RESONANCE MACHINE

Resonance . . . to resound . . . ; a vibration of large amplitude . . .
caused by a small periodic stimulus of the same or near the same
period as the natural vibration of the system; the intensification and
enriching of a musical tone by supplementary vibration . . . ; the en-
hancement of an atomic, nuclear or particle reaction . . . by excitation
of internal motion in the system.

—*Webster's Ninth New Collegiate Dictionary*

What is the connection *today* between evangelical Christianity, cowboy capitalism, the electronic news media, and the Republican Party?[1] Is it a connection
that can be understood through the terms of efficient causality, in which you
first separate factors and then show how one is the basic cause, or how they
cause each other, or how they together reflect a more basic cause? Does, say, a
corporate-Republican élite manipulate the evangelical wing of this assemblage, leading it to subordinate its economic interests to spurious appeals to
faith? Or are leading parties to this coalition linked above all by economic
interests, with evangelical and corporate leaders together manipulating their
followers? Or, alternatively, do the two groups share a general doctrine or
creed, which defines common interests and allegiances? My sense is that none
of these explanations, nor others like them, adequately fills the bill. As I have
argued earlier, no political economy or religious practice is self-contained.
Particularly in politics these diverse elements *infiltrate* each other, metaboliz-
ing into a moving complex. Spiritual sensibilities, economic presumptions,
and state priorities slide and blend into one another, though each also retains a
modicum of independence from the others. Causation as resonance between
elements that become fused to a considerable degree. Now causality, as relations of dependence between separate factors, morphs into energized com-

plexities of mutual imbrication and interinvolvement, in which heretofore unconnected or loosely associated elements *fold, bend, blend, emulsify, and resolve incompletely into each other*, forging a qualitative assemblage resistant to classical models of explanation.[2]

It is impossible to approach the resonance machine to be interrogated in a mood of political neutrality. Any attempt to do so would defeat itself through the terms of description that it deploys. For descriptive terms already express the evaluative standpoint from which they are formed, as when the term "mistake" both includes the criteria through which to characterize an act and expresses the judgment that in meeting this description there are presumptive reasons to excuse the doer. So evaluation is infused into the very terms of description we adopt. I will not veil the critical disposition that animates this interpretation, but I will identify dissonant moments in it and will also explore what this movement can teach the rest of us about ourselves.

The capitalist-evangelical assemblage finds multiple modes of expression, each amplifying the others: in the market apologism and scandal mongering of the electronic news media, in mobilization drives by Fox News, the Republican Party, and campaign ads, in administrative edicts to roll back environmentalism, weaken labor, and curtail minority rights in the name of religious morality, in right-wing appointments to the Supreme Court, in support for preemptive wars, in tolerance or much worse of state practices of torture that negate the Geneva Conventions, and in propagating a climate of fear and loathing against the Islamic world. The resonance machine that results both infiltrates the logic of perception and inflects the understanding of economic interests. It is thus important to come to terms with the *affinities of spirituality* that fuel the machine across creedal differences, affinities that translate some economic interests into corporate greed and fill others with religious intensity, affinities that convert some articles of religious faith into vindictive campaigns to oppose those outside the faith and abrogate our collective responsibility to the future. A key idea is that affinities of spirituality—whether finding expression as devotion to a loving God, a disposition to tolerance, care for the future, love of this world, or a drive to revenge against the most fundamental terms of human existence—often jumps across different professions of creed, doctrine, and philosophy. The advocates of different creeds—secular in some cases, theological in others—are drawn together despite creedal differences, because of affinities or complementarities of spirituality.

Consider for instance an atheist who unconsciously resents the world for not containing the promise of redemption, and a God-fearing person who secretly resents his God for creating so many hurdles to salvation. Each set of feelings is tied to ideas, but we also find two dispositions to revenge lodged in different doctrines. These two parties might align together to support a set of punitive policies. Or, depending on the circumstances, they might define their opposition to each other through the same spirit of bellicosity. I am interested in the first possibility, exemplifying what happens when the spirit of evangelical and corporate leaders resonates together across a set of doctrinal differences. This combination sets the stage for consolidation of a movement larger than the sum of its component parts. At first, the parties sense preliminary affinities of sensibility; eventually they provoke each other to transduct those affinities into a political machine. The machine then foments new avenues of crossing and intensities of interinvolvement.

One way to challenge the machine is to focus publicity and protest upon the economic effects on ordinary people of the corporate and government practices that it promotes. Many attempt this strategy, and it is pertinent. Thus, to focus for a moment on the alliance between Enron and the Bush administration, you could show how Enron manipulated the energy market, Dick Cheney and Enron cooperated to stifle state regulation of the market, accounting firms and the SEC allowed the company to "mark up" income promised as income already received, the electronic news media ignored the emerging crisis, and media programming after exposure tended to treat the combination as a renegade event.[3] You could also review the effects of the debacle upon Enron employees, its retirees, and consumers of electricity in California and elsewhere. All that is highly relevant. But what type of sensibility drew Cheney, Fox News, the SEC, the Republican Party, and Enron to push these envelopes so hard? Is it simply that they all believed in the free market? Or, a bit better, that they supported deregulation in the name of a free market that also gives specific corporations the power to manipulate markets? Or, better yet, that they were linked by a history of economic ties, interests, campaign contributions, and so on? Yes, all those things. But again, how did those links become so overweening? And what separates the parties to this alliance from other parties with similar formal views about the market and the role of government? Would any party, company, CEO, or media outlet participate in this assemblage if given the chance? Perhaps so, to some degree. But still, what impelled this particular assemblage in some cases to push the envelope so relentlessly, and in others to look away so carefully? What escalated greed to its maximum intensity? Here as elsewhere, the degree of vehemence and ruthlessness is critical. What *else*, then, drew these parties together into such an aggressive constellation, *calling upon them* to manipulate the market without restraint, to stretch the law, and to defend the market interpretation of events so belligerently in the face of available evidence?

=====

One possibility is that amid some creedal linkages helping to define their sense of interests, the parties share a spiritual disposition to existence. Their ruthlessness, ideological extremism, readiness to defend neoliberal ideology in the face of significant counter-evidence, and compulsion to create or condone scandals against any party who opposes their vision of the world—all express a fundamental disposition toward the world. The interinvolvements between them then function to amplify the spirituality. To the extent that they succeed in installing new structures and legal avenues, the pressure to support these practices now becomes more imperative institutionally, even to those who do not share the spirituality.

Don't get me wrong. I am not saying that a particular existential ethos is "the cause." Rather, it is an element that enters into patterns of reverberation with others. It infiltrates, inflects, and intensifies a host of perceptions, institutionalized creeds, economic interests, alliances, loyalties, enmities, and political priorities. Each of these encoded elements in turn recoils back upon the ethos, modifying it in this way and intensifying it in that. The cumulative result is a resonance machine, not a windup doll. It is also pertinent to see that the term "resonance" is no more metaphorical than other terms through which cultural interpretation is organized. It is a real force. As will become clear in chapter 3, relations of resonance affect processes studied in neuroscience, climatology, and biological evolution as well as those in political economy. Further, we shall see that other political doctrines and economic movements are not entirely immune to the sort of contagion described here. They might become susceptible to it. Nor will I focus further beyond the speculations advanced in chapter 1 on what initially draws some constituencies more than others toward a theo-economic spirituality of this sort. It is fascinating that the markers of class, age, race, income level, education, religious creed, and gender, while pertinent, do not sufficiently demarcate those drawn into the machine from those who run away from it. That fact in itself supports the idea that an existential element is involved in the politics of attraction and avoidance, though it is not determinative by itself. Finally, I am not saying that everyone who believes in a deregulated market shares this bellicose ethos. Many do not. I am saying that the partners to the resonance machine in question have an existential orientation that encourages them to transfigure interest into greed, greed into anti-market ideology, anti-market ideology into market manipulation, market manipulation into state institutionalization of those operations, and the entire complex into policies to pull the security net away from ordinary workers, consumers, and retirees—some of whom are then set up to translate new intensities of resentment and cynicism into participation in the machine. Above all, individual and group bearers of this spirituality encourage each other to forge alliances with those in other walks of life who have the same spiritual affinities.

Given the *intensity* of the ethos binding the parties across variations in religious doctrine, economic creed, and life circumstances, any constituency or social movement that crosses them is subject to sharp castigation and accusation. This is the kernel of truth in Bill Clinton's assertion that the Republican Party possesses a "destruction machine" that the Democrats lack. He should know. What Clinton underplays, however, is how the machine extends well beyond a political party; it is as much involved in initiating new corporate practices as in character destruction.

I am confident that this account, as so far presented, will seem implausible to many, partly because it draws into the fabric of political economy itself existential elements that many take to be irrelevant to those structures. The account may become more plausible, however, when we shift gears, exploring the ethos of the evangelical side of this machine. As a preliminary to that turn, consider the political economist Mark Blyth's account of how Keynesianism, which had been hegemonic for a couple of decades in Europe and the United States, was overturned in the 1970s and 1980s by the doctrine of an unfettered market, supply-side economics, and state attacks on the social safety net. Blyth contends that the shift is insufficiently explained by either structural determinants or the fixed economic interests of those who adopted the doctrine. He looks through these elements to the emergence of a distinctive set of economic *ideas*, their publication through new think tanks on the right, their amplification through the media, their partial acceptance by President Carter, and their embrace by President Reagan.

In periods of economic uncertainty, Blyth suggests, the differential capacity that agents have to publicize their ideas plays a significant role in shaping the perception of political and economic interests. Do the unemployed need state job training and unemployment payments as the Keynesians said? Or should they support tax reduction for capital to promote new jobs, as neo-liberals say? The Keynesians, in this instance, lost the competition of ideas, even though the predictions and promises attached to their economic theory worked. Later in the same book Blyth asks why some economic ideas come to prevail over others during periods of uncertainty, even if their powers of explanation are relatively weak: "One possible answer is that in moments of crises when agents are uncertain about their interests, they resort to reper-toires of action that resonate with their core identities."[4]

Today too, identity plays a role in the second installment of the same movement. Identities are composed of a mixture of faith, doctrine, and sen-sibility, with each element entering to some degree into the fabric of the others. The affect-imbued ideas that compose them are installed in the soft tissues of affect, emotion, habit, and posture, as well as the upper reaches of the intellect. Once installed, these sensibilities trigger preliminary responses to new events, even before the respondents think consciously about the events. This is particularly so when complementary dispositions loop back and forth in a large political machine, with each constituency helping to crystallize, amplify, and legitimize one set of dispositions displayed by the others.

The element of identity most significant to this movement, I suggest, is the insistence by its leaders that they are being persecuted *unless* they are thoroughly in power, and the sense of special entitlement that accompanies the rise to power of a constituency that so construes itself. It remains to be seen whether these bellicose dispositions with respect to economic life ex-press a deeper existential orientation.

The right leg of the evangelical movement today is joined at the hip to the left leg of the capitalist juggernaut. Neither leg could hop far unless it was joined to the other. Some may explain the association between them in simple terms: corporate self-interest harmonizes with the economic interest of evan-gelical preachers, who manipulate poor and older citizens to pour money into church coffers to save their souls. True enough, to some extent. But again, why does one set of evangelical preachers give such intense priority to eco-nomic gain, instead of pressing the state and corporations to protect the weakest among us? And why are so many ready to follow? Why not preach the Social Gospel, as innumerable Christian believers have done in the past, giving the Jesus of Mark priority over the vengeful Christ of Revelation? We identified some pressures that encouraged a section of white lower- and middle-class males to migrate in this direction in chapter 1. Now we need to examine the shape of the ethos that has been forged. We deal with the right edge of evangelism first, turning to dissenting voices within it later.

The cutting edge of the evangelical right is organized around a vengeful vision of the Second Coming, modeled upon one reading of Revelation and dramatized in the best-selling series of novels "Left Behind." The series has sold over sixty million copies to date, and film versions are also in wide circulation. While Revelation itself protested the persecution of Christians by the Roman Empire, the new series maintains the ethos of revenge expressed in the book on behalf of American sovereignty and world hegemony. It is the ethos it promotes that I will examine, in relation to the doctrine professed.

In the first novel of the series, itself entitled *Left Behind*, millions of born-again Christians around the world are lifted suddenly to heaven during the Rapture. The rest of humanity is "left behind." The sudden departure of these millions creates thousands of accidents and traffic jams, interruptions in medical surgery, airplane crashes, government chaos, and grieving spouses who have lost partners and children. If you think the terrorism of Al Qaeda and the Bush torture machine has been traumatic, it is a tempest in a seaside resort by comparison to the global terror practiced by the Christ figure in this book.

A few of those left behind soon figure out what has happened and give themselves totally to the Christ of Revelation (as that Book is interpreted in the series). The conversion of Buck Williams in the film version is exemplary. A young, secular reporter who looks a lot like Luke Skywalker, he hears about the plan for global peace and the creation of ten new world centers of food production from Nicolai Carpathia—the young, recently crowned head of the United Nations, who speaks with a Romanian accent. Buck is dumbfounded by how the plan parallels the story of Revelation and how it also reminds him of the insidious international plot that a friend had just warned him about before being shot mysteriously. He retreats to a bathroom, where amid a great clamor of music he gives himself to God for the first time. Returning to the closed meeting of world leaders over which Carpathia presides, he now discerns how everyone else in the meeting is being manipulated by this charismatic leader. At a key moment, one of the men who had elevated Carpathia to his new post protests a change in the plan, asking Carpathia, "Do you know who you are dealing with?" Carpathia, with his eyes glowing strangely, responds in a voice from an echo chamber: "Do you?" He calmly shoots his erstwhile ally and then the ally's buddy too, eliminating the final competitors to his world supremacy. Carpathia immediately hypnotizes the room full of global leaders—who include idealistic people from Africa, Asia, Israel, and other Mideast countries. Everyone leaves the room remembering that the two renegades had committed suicide. But Buck, because of his pledge to God in the nick of time, is insulated from the Devil's hypnotic power. He remembers what actually happened, now realizing that the head of the UN and the Antichrist are the same person, one who has superhuman powers of seduction and manipulation. The music surges as Buck whispers, "Everything the Bible predicted is happening." The convert now commits himself fervently to follow God wherever He leads during the violent, fateful time to come. It is Carpathia, the UN, the Antichrist, professions of world peace, and duped world leaders versus Williams, the true Christ, a cadre of born-again Americans, a war against the Devil, and the promise of final judgment.

The book tracks this scene too, closing with a cadre of believers in America coming to see that they must fight to the death against the Antichrist, unbelievers, dupes, and the UN. The closing line of the book is, "The task of the Tribulation Force was clear and their goal nothing less than to stand and fight the enemies of God during the seven most chaotic years the planet would ever see."[5] Later, on the day of Judgment, Christ will heave the world's Muslims, Jews, agnostics, atheists, and many Catholics into everlasting fire. Looking back in a vision on this wondrous day to come, a crusader recalls that "Jesus merely raised one hand a few inches and they . . . tumbled in, howling and screeching."[6]

Is this an escape fantasy reminiscent of the *Star Wars* series and other films in that genre? Yes, in one respect. But it trumps them. For it purports to track future events and divine injunctions lodged in the divinely inspired Book of Revelation, a book to which millions of Americans are devoted. Its themes are regularly reinforced in radio talk shows, evangelical churches, and media events. This adventure story thus carries deadly implications for action and judgment in everyday life. It would be dangerous to disparage it as merely an escape fantasy, because of its connections to practices, constituencies, and judgments in wide circulation. It amplifies them and endows them with cosmic urgency. The film closes with young women singing the rock song with which it began: "The Revelation is comin' . . . I know that I will not be Left Behind." In the trailer attached to the film, the women weave back and forth in jumpsuits as they sing.

What about the fact that a time-line for these events has been set numerous times in the past, starting with Joachim of Fiore in the twelfth century and culminating with prophecies by American evangelists in the 1980s? Many contemporary devotees may not know this history, and those who do may treat the previous time-lines as mere mistakes in dating. Besides, timing is almost beside the point. The most dangerous thing about this prophecy of Rapture, Christo-terrorism, seven years of violent tribulation, the Day of Judgment, and hellfire for millions is the effect its cultural ethos has on the conduct and judgments of millions inducted into it. Yes, the vision and ethos are embraced to various degrees by different devotees. Thank God for that. But to embrace it enthusiastically is to place a series of constituencies, institutions, and doctrines under divine suspicion; it is to foment a collective will to revenge against the UN, nonbelievers, and dupes whose conduct is controlled by the Antichrist. Since followers of the Devil regularly present themselves as agents of beneficence, an aura of suspicion, resentment, and revenge slips into the daily perceptions of the faithful, encouraging the worst interpretations of those outside the fold and endorsing any scandalous story against them contrived by right-wing talk shows, the Republican advertising machine, internet blogs, and right-wing preachers.

The combination of a terrible fate reserved for most and the radiant promise for a few doubtless triggers feelings of anxiety among the faithful—who may worry whether they are faithful enough to end up on the right side. One way to ward off that anxiety is to externalize it, by defining one's adversaries as wanton sinners. The pressures to do so will escalate during a period of enhanced global awareness, as more and more believers discover that Christianity is very much a minority religion in the world as a whole. Hence the placement of the United States at the center of a worldwide movement on behalf of Christ in the "Left Behind" series. Self-doubt and uncertainty are transfigured into an implacable drive to revenge against those who deny that Christ is the son of God, has been resurrected, opposes the UN, enforces a narrow moral code, and will soon return to pass eternal judgment.

To be born again is to be protected; it is also to adopt unquestioning obedience to those ordained to interpret the will of Christ before the Rapture. As we come to grips with this existential element in the evangelical movement we can also discern affinities of sensibility between it and the right edge of the corporate machine. One line of connection, reviewed in chapter 1, is the conviction by many evangelists that entrepreneurial activity is the one worldly activity endowed with divine providence. That connection allows proponents on both sides to disparage welfare programs and collective efforts to curtail global warming. As you explore the avenues of connection between these constituencies it also becomes more clear why correlations between on the one hand economic interest, class position, formal religious doctrine, education level, and age, and on the other participation in the resonance machine of the right, are incomplete, uncertain, and shifting. The elements of sensibility and ethos intervene here, drawing some in congenial subject positions toward the machine, touching others in the same positions less intensely, rendering still others indifferent, and impelling others yet to run away as fast and far as possible. The social factors deployed to explain participation in a political assemblage are always relevant; but they are also compromised and complicated by the shape and intensity of the spiritualities that also help to compose it. That is why it is a mistake to equate belief in the main points of evangelical *doctrine* with automatic commitment to this resonance machine. Some believers incorporate into their sensibilities a degree of agonistic respect for those of other faiths, others demand revenge against those outside the fold, and others yet hover in uncertainty between these proclivities. The "Left Behind" series is designed to induct more believers into an ethos of resentment and revenge, and to silence believers who resist that ethos.

Why, though, assert that the economic leg of the assemblage is joined at the hip to the religious leg? Don't some cowboy marketeers hold their noses when they hear promises of divine revenge? Don't others identify with creeds and cultures, such as Judaism, atheism, and secularism, that would place them at mortal risk on the last day? Yes, yes, yes . . . But, still, why *merely* hold your nose while participating in such an ugly alliance, rather than break publicly with constituencies who press such vengeful stories and promises? Or, at the very least, work publicly to curtail their intensities? What, that is, is the attraction to the *spirit* of the "Left Behind" story for many amid dissent from the letter of its *doctrine*?

An abstract will to dismiss other constituencies and to disdain collective responsibility to the future helps to differentiate cowboys who align themselves with the right edge of the evangelical movement from those marketeers who break with it. The cowboy and evangelical spiritualities are not the same. Rather they resonate together. The bellicosity and corresponding sense of extreme entitlement of those consumed by economic greed *reverberates* with the transcendental resentment of those visualizing the righteous violence of Christ. Across these modest differentiations, the two parties are

bound by similar orientations to the future. One party discounts its responsibilities to the future of the earth to vindicate extreme economic entitlement
now, while the other does so to prepare for the day of judgment against
nonbelievers. These electrical charges resonate back and forth, generating a
political machine much more potent than the aggregation of its parts. It finds
variable expression in the promise to plunge millions into a fiery hell; the
legitimation and displacement of corporate crime; support for a preemptive
war in the name of anti-terrorism when you could know that Al Qaeda was
not based in Iraq; casual acceptance or disregard of Abu Ghraib, Haditha, and
the Guantánamo gulag; the production, purchase, use, and state deregulation
of the suv even when its supporters know the multiple threats to others and
the future posed by the vehicle;[7] the demand for new tax breaks for the rich
which impose sacrifices on the poor now and new generations in the future;
the decision by members of the "gang of five" on the Supreme Court to cast
aside their own myth of "strict constructionism" to put their man in office;
the endless scandal campaigns pushed by Fox News against the Clintons and
any actor, activist, or academic on the left; the sense of urgency in the voice of
Wolf Blitzer as he charts new dangers to the country and deflects critical
voices; the incessant celebration of tax cuts and an unfettered market on
investment news shows; and a general readiness to table any economic evidence or theological uncertainty that might temper drives against economic
egalitarianism, pluralism, and nontheism.

The spiritualities of the economic and theological wings of this machine
are linked through their demands for entitlement and revenge, with each
party affected to some degree by the demands given priority by the other. The
rest of us face movements to redistribute wealth and income toward the top,
impoverish more people, neglect racial inequality in the cities, reduce wom-
en's rights, escalate global warming, increase pollution, sacrifice wetlands,
wage reckless wars, increase domestic surveillance, and knock down social
supports for the old, the poor, the mentally ill, and the sick. The ethos informing this assemblage helps to insulate its participants against evidence that
contravenes its claims.[8]

You could call this machine "The O'Reilly Factor," because of how the
poster boy of the right expresses its temper in his facial expressions, vocal
timbre, insistent interruptions, demand for unquestioned authority, and accusatory style. You could also call it the Bush syndrome, in recognition of how
George W. pulled several of its elements together in one persona, through his
cadence of voice, rhetoric drawn from Revelation, definitive phrasing, shady

governmental accounting, economic cronyism, disregard for the Geneva Conventions, unwillingness to accept the strong evidence in support of global warming, and readiness to impose new economic burdens on low-income citizens and future retirees. Recall the argument that George W. had with his mother, widely reported in the media, about whether those who do not believe in Christ are doomed to hell. She denied that they were, according to the reports, and called upon Billy Graham to support her. George W.'s apparent belief to the contrary resonates with the practices of the Guantánamo gulag, Abu Ghraib, and Haditha. Many humans are disposable after death, others while still alive. With such a persona in mind, it is useful to recall that fraternity boy rebellion is typically mounted against a tradition grasped in a simple, crude way. When the rebellion peels away a few years later, its crude rendering is now embraced. Hence George Bush on Christianity.[9]

It is pertinent to see how figures such as Bush and O'Reilly dramatize the resonance machine. But while doing so, it is critical to remember that they would merely be oddball characters unless they triggered, expressed, and amplified a resonance machine larger than they. They are catalyzing agents and shimmering points in this machine; their departure will weaken it only if it does not acquire new personas to replace them. The machine requires these personas, but once it has achieved a certain level of salience it can generate new ones.

Is it possible to deepen our understanding of the ethos that this machine both triggers and amplifies? One might draw upon Baruch Spinoza or Max Weber. Spinoza draws attention to how the results of the struggle between the positive and negative passions that always circulate in a society flow into the state, the economy, and religious practices. Weber, whom we discussed in chapter 1, charts how the paradoxically structured spirituality of one wing of Protestantism helped to set the historical table for the pursuit of profit without pleasure, accumulation without excessive consumption, and disciplinary labor without love. Valuable as his analysis of early capitalism in northern Europe is, the spirituality that he charts differs notably from that discerned here. For while the Calvinists he attends to were often prepared to blame poverty on the dispositions of the poor, they were also oriented to a work ethic, to saving, and to investing for the future. Moreover, as we also saw in chapter 1, Weber believed that once the appropriate institutional structures became installed, spirituality would no longer play a prominent role in the capitalist system.[10] I suggest, however, that the porous structures of capitalism move along a relatively open temporal trajectory, one less closed than either Weberian, neo-liberal, or Marxist theories sometimes suggest. The quality of the ethos inhabiting it is always pertinent to its operation.

A little closer to the bone are the insights of Nietzsche's Zarathustra. He speaks to a cultural spirituality of *ressentiment* growing all too easily out of a will to revenge against mortality, time, and the modes of suffering that stalk embodied, frail mortals in this world.

> Behold, this is the hole of the tarantula . . . Welcome tarantula! And I also know what sits in your soul. Revenge sits in your soul. Wherever you bite, black scabs grow; your poison makes the soul whirl with revenge . . . and where there was suffering, one always wanted punishment too.
>
> But now learn this too: the will itself is still a prisoner. Willing liberates; but what is that puts even the liberator himself in fetters? It was—that is the name of the will's gnashing of teeth and most secret melancholy. Powerless against what has been done, he is angry spectator of all that is past. The will cannot will backwards; and that he cannot break time and time's covetousness . . . That time does not run backwards, that is his wrath.[11]

Zarathustra says that the spirit of existential revenge *whirls* in those who, for whatever reasons, resent most bitterly "the obdurate fact" of mortality, misfortune, existential suffering, and a world in which you cannot will the past again. Some may be responding to horrible misfortunes, others to failure to achieve the extreme sense of entitlement into which they were inducted, others yet to theological messages hammered at them daily, and many to several of these things as they inhabit and nudge each other. The key is not whether you strive for eternal salvation or accept death as oblivion, for either pursuit is compatible with joining others who value the future of this earth to forge a positive assemblage. It is the initial disposition toward alternative faiths in a world replete with numerous faiths that is most revealing. In one type of case, striving for salvation becomes hooked to implacable opposition to faiths that by the very fact of their coexistence call the self-certainty of your own faith into question. In another case, an underlying resentment against the weight of this generation's responsibility to the future makes you eager to silence voices of responsibility. Resentment against the future and persistent creedal diversity now surface as a will to take revenge against these who support responsibility to the future and appreciate diversity; it redefines your relation to God and the economy until one, the other, or both are said to *command* you to do what you already insist upon doing. Once that equation is secured, you now represent yourself to be only a servant who carries out commands issuing from the autonomy of the market or the will of God. Again, these conversion processes do not occur only in individuals: they also whirl in a larger cultural complex, as Nietzsche understood so well, producing a hurricane out of heretofore loosely associated elements.

I have already suggested that the parties to this machine participate in its ethos to varying degrees. And it is seldom articulated explicitly: it typically finds expression in the intensities with which entitlements are invoked, the future of the earth is discounted, enemies are defined, and secular or divine threats are hurled against these enemies. Occasionally the ethos of revenge finds more direct expression, as it did when Pat Robertson, the evangelical leader, president of Regent University, and host of the TV show "The 700 Club," responded in 2005 to the citizens of Dover, Pennsylvania, soon after they had turned out of office several school board members who had voted in favor of teaching "intelligent design" in the classroom: "I'd like to say to the good citizens of Dover: if there is disaster in your area don't turn to God, you just rejected him from your city. And don't wonder why he hasn't helped you when problems begin, if they begin. I'm not saying they will, but if they do, just remember, you just voted God out of your city. And if that's the case, don't ask for his help because he might not be there."[12] Robertson's voice is soft, but it resounds with the revenge themes of the Book of Revelation as refracted through the "Left Behind" series. Many who watch and listen to him are already attuned to his reading of that book and infected by the ethos that he promotes: the biblical text and his threats in its name reverberate back and forth, amplifying each other.

As will become clear, I do not suggest that faith in a transcendent Being automatically expresses an ethos of ressentiment and revenge, nor that this ethos is intrinsic to Christianity per se, nor that it is intrinsic to every version of evangelism. Far from it. Jimmy Carter is an evangelist and the vengeful sensibility is alien to him. In a recent talk Harvey Cox identified a host of thinkers who share the doctrine of evangelism while identifying with progressive politics.[13] And we will encounter others in later chapters who break sharply with the ethos charted here. The link between doctrine and ethos is real but attenuated, and there are also important variations of doctrine within evangelism. It is important, for both political and ethical reasons, to distinguish those who fill a doctrine with extreme entitlement and revenge from those who do not do so. One distinguishing sign is the extreme contempt that some carriers of evangelism carry for "liberal" versions of Islam and Christianity. Ted Haggarty, Robertson's associate, adopts this tack when he compares peace-loving Muslims to carriers of "liberal Christianity": "No doubt, a few Muslim scholars have tried to negate the 'annihilate the infidel' passages [from *Al Qu'ran*], but their arguments are weak, convoluted, unconvincing and considered nonmainstream to the most vocal and influential fundamentalist Muslim scholars throughout the world . . . These scholars are the equivalent of those in liberal Christianity who try to manipulate the Bible to make the case for homosexual marriage or 'save the whales' . . . These liberal interpretations are, to most of us, easily identifiable distortions of the biblical text. Likewise, many Muslims view the peace-loving Muslim clerics the way we would view our own liberal theologians."[14]

This line between moderate proponents of Islam, liberal Christians, defenders of homosexual marriage, and those concerned with species diversity attacks each dimension by associating it with the others. The line is not crafted from doctrinal commitments alone; rather, a bellicose spirituality is insinuated into it. That's why TV programs that mix a bellicose tone of voice, implacable facial expressions, sharp bodily demeanor, exclusionary doctrinal concepts, and scandal mongering can be so potent. Cultural induction into the idea of a vengeful God; intensification of the human fear of death; secret resentment against a world that requires it; unstated resentments against the imperious demands of your God; compensatory drives for special economic entitlement in this world; ugly campaigns to vilify those whose difference throws the self-certainty of your faith into doubt; a general disposition to punish those who diverge from you; a tendency to disparage human responsibility for the future of the earth—a powerful political assemblage weaves these dispositions into habitual patterns of perception, identity, interest, and judgments of earthly entitlement.[15] This effect, moreover, is not well covered by terms such as "manipulation" and "group-think"; for the messages in question already speak to the bellicose temper of those who receive them. The hope is that many who participate in the assemblage do not feel these sentiments so bitterly, and that they will respond to the formation of a counter-resonance machine.

Between the Second World War and the late 1970s the vengeful side of evangelism was less connected to a political movement.[16] The dominant tendency was to warn followers to prepare for an event that politics could not promote or prevent. Even Jerry Falwell counseled against the dangers and temptations of politics. But today, partly because of the left's neglect of the white working class in the late 1960s and 1970s, partly because of invitations from the Republican party and corporate right in the early 1980s, partly because of Karl Rove's campaigns to highlight public issues such as abortion, stem cell research, and gay marriage, partly because the multidimensional diversity of the United States has become both more visible and active, and partly because of 9/11 and the intensified antagonism between Christianity and Islam that it has fomented on the right, the right edge of evangelism is highly politicized. The important thing, under these conditions, is to come to terms with the spiritual element that draws two major constituencies into a theo-political assemblage.

We have seen how the parties to this machine seldom declare directly the ugliest existential investments that inspire them. This silence itself can be politically potent, providing a veneer of deniability over the campaign of mobilization. The spirituality does its most effective political and theological work when it finds indirect expression in the tonalities and intensities of its leaders and their selection of enemies. Consider in this regard the structure of Robert Schumann's *Humoreske* (1838), as reported by Frank Ankersmit. There are three staves. The upper staff is played with the right hand, the lower with the left. But the melody in the middle is not played. Rather, it is heard by the listener because of its location between the upper and lower hands. Here is what Ankersmit and Charles Rosen, the historian of music whom he draws upon, say: "Put differently, the melody . . . will be *listened to* by the listener, without actually being *heard* by him. Hence what one listens to . . . is the echo of an unperformed melody . . . ; it is both interior and inward, a double sense calculated by the composer . . . It has . . . its existence only through the echo."[17]

The ethos of existential revenge that helps to energize the evangelical-corporate machine generally subsists as an unsung melody. It reverberates back and forth between leaders and followers, until it becomes uncertain who directs and who sings the chorus.[18] Thus early in the presidential campaign of 2004 George W. Bush's entourage sped around a NASCAR track in front of 100,000 fans. Bush emerged from the only SUV in the entourage to an incredible roar of approval. The crowd responded to the SUV as a symbol of disdain for womanly ecologists, safety advocates, supporters of fuel economy, worrywarts about global warming, weak-willed pluralists, and supporters of international accords such as the Kyoto Treaty. Bush played upon the symbol and drew energy from the crowd's acclamation of it. But his handlers could say if asked that "he just happened" to ride in that vehicle, sending a surge of joy through followers who both love the message and the way it flummoxes critical commentators. Resentment against those who exude a feminine ethos of care for the future of the earth is not named by the leader or crowd: the message is expressed without being articulated.

Today resentment against cultural diversity, economic egalitarianism, and responsibility to the future whirl together in the same resonance machine. That is why its participants identify overlapping targets of demonization and marginalization, such as gay marriage; women who seek equal status in work, family, and business; secularists, those of Islamic faith, and atheists; and African American residents of the inner city who do not appreciate the abstract beauty of cowboy capitalism.

Take, for instance, Bush's and Rove's campaign to feminize John Kerry in the same election. Its logic was first to consign women implicitly to a subordi-nate status as flighty beings—an image already circulating between cowboy marketeers and hard-line evangelists—and then to define the Democratic candidate as womanly during a time when the unwavering hand of an aggres-sive leader was required. A TV image of Kerry tacking back and forth while wind-surfing amplified resentment against the effete branch of the upper class even as it symbolized the style of a flip-flop artist. The image contrasted with that of Bush in blue jeans cutting underbrush with a no-nonsense look on his face. Karl Rove's campaign of 2004 replicated one that Richard Nixon had run against George McGovern in 1972, in the middle of the Vietnam War. And it will return again, in some guise. To be "a flip-flop artist" is to be womanly, to lack unwavering commitment to a jealous God ("the Almighty"), to be wary of neoliberal economic policy, and to be averse to bellicose na-tionalism. The conviction that Kerry is a flip-flop artist was first peddled in ads early in the campaign, when most people were not paying attention. That strategy, according to advertising specialists familiar with the findings of neuroscience, is an effective way to plant an affect-imbued idea.[19] It enters the thought-imbued feelings of viewers before being subjected to critical scrutiny. The plant is then harvested months later, when much of the electorate con-cludes that it is being reminded of a disposition that it already had—the politics of perception. Iterations by Fox News, ads by Bush, endless repetition by the Cheneys, and statements by some Catholic bishops that Kerry should not receive communion because he was a soft supporter of his own faith coalesced to consolidate the perception. Kerry himself did not help to disperse these charges; he thought for too long that responding actively and forcefully to them would publicize them too much. Here too he replicated the hesitancy that McGovern in 1972 and Dukakis in 1988 displayed during their campaigns, with similar effects. The security frenzy gripping the country did make it difficult for Kerry to respond effectively. But the campaign of feminization launched against him—and implicitly against all women who do not embrace a subordinate status—took a major toll.

The point is to discern how media presentations both do much of their work below the level of explicit attention and encourage the coding of those experiences into the culture. Part of the reason, perhaps, is that the TV and film viewer is immobilized before a moving image and soundtrack, while the everyday perceiver is either mobile or one step removed from mobility. The viewer's immobility amplifies the affective intensities received, just as a basketball coach *feels* the intensities of the contest more than the players on the floor who *absorb* them into action.[20] This difference indeed dramatizes the wisdom of Nietzsche's commendation to act upon specific resentments before they ossify into ressentiment. And of course, it underlines the importance of coming to terms with the role that the mobilization of spiritual dispositions plays in religious life, political campaigns, corporate actions, consumer priorities, and state policies.

Alongside the feminization campaign against Kerry was another that deflected public attention from the general melding together of politics and show business. Talking heads on Fox News repeatedly "debated" the question, "Should actors take public positions on political issues?," focusing as they did so on actors who criticized neoliberal economics and the war in Iraq. The question was not posed about business celebrities, or retired generals, or Republican candidates who had been actors, or publicists employed by right-wing think tanks. The form of the question encourages people to identify show business with unpatriotic criticism, instead of discerning how critical films, rock music, selective TV dramas, and jazz are often associated with the democratic left, while country music, radio "talk shows," and evangelical-corporate celebrities are often associated with the right. Reiteration of the question in this form delinks the resonance machine of the right from show business while binding its opponents to it. The result is to divert attention from how politics, religion, and advertising all participate in show business today.[21] Those who incorporate these messages are not simply manipulated by the media; many are predisposed to them through the spirit of their preliminary orientations to being. The messages intensify dispositions already there, opening new circuits of contagion as they do so.

To expose and counter the politics of existential revenge and extreme entitlement does not mean that you demean specific economic grievances, resentments, and critical energies that propel positive democratic energies forward. To do so would be to embrace a spurious intellectualism that ignores the incorrigible role of passion in religious practice, economic activity, political struggle, and individual thinking. The target is the congealed disposition of ressentiment, not every mode of resentment. It is the spirit of ressentiment that vilifies a social ethos of agonistic respect across creeds and inures its bearers against care for the future of the earth.

Nonetheless, there is a danger that other constituencies too can become contaminated by such a spirituality as they counter this very machine. The drive to existential revenge, while perhaps more amenable to some economic creeds and religious doctrines than others, can in fact come to inhabit any faith, constituency, doctrine, institution, or machine. This possibility is magnified when one implacable machine seeks to divide the world into the forces of good and evil. Everyone faces the issues of mortality and time, and—if to varying degrees—we all run the risk of terrible misfortune. How to respond to such contingencies while quelling the voice of ressentiment? That is the question, and the rub. Zarathustra eventually appreciates this danger after "his ape" repeats parts of his own creed back to him in frothy tones of revenge. I suspect that no major existential tradition anywhere, including Christianity, Islam, Hinduism, Buddhism, and Judaism, and no minor or minute tradition such as Epicureanism, Kantianism, Nietzscheanism, and Levinasianism has succeeded in forging a fully satisfactory response to the obdurate fact of mortality, the irreversibility of time, and the risk of intense, undeserved suffering that comes with human life. The possibility of existential resentment thus resides in any and every mortal, in every existential faith, in every ideological doctrine, and in every political movement.

As a corollary, many advocates of any creed can attenuate or overcome the drive to revenge that often becomes attached to it, particularly if a countermachine is available to them. This is even true of some who adopt the reading of the Book of Revelation promoted by the "Left Behind" series. The temper that they bring to receipt of the doctrine may encourage them to pour a strong potion of self-modesty into their experience of it and to resist militant calls for attacks upon those outside the fold. It is faith in this potential tear or rent between a mode of *sensibility* and a *creed or doctrine* to which it is commonly attached that makes it possible for Nietzsche to call for a "spiritualization of enmity" between noble partisans of different existential doctrines, a spiritualization in which partisans imbue their relations with elements of reciprocal prudence, forbearance, and presumptive generosity. Nietzsche doubted that a majority within any creed would answer that call. Perhaps his pessimism was warranted, perhaps not, though the record of history is not too reassuring on this score. But even if a significant *minority* within a wide range of creeds responds favorably to a positive resonance machine that seeks to forge affirmative connections across significant differences of faith, an important step will have been taken in the right direction. Other pertinent steps will be reviewed in chapters 4 and 5.

But let's turn to a legitimate question posed to people like me: "How do *you and those who agree with you* forestall the all-too-human slide from specific political resentments to ressentiment?" For the risk grows as disaffection from the electronic news media, cowboy capitalism, the virulence of the evangelical right, and a large minority of the American electorate deepens. Accumulated resentments can, in this way, congeal into a disposition of fixed resentment against the actually existing world. And these dispositions can be reinforced by others who identify with your creed and share a similar disaffection. Intransigence breeds intransigence.

How to respond to the risk without sacrificing the militancy that is indispensable today? The most noble *collective* response would be to transduct the mutual inability of diverse existential faiths to resolve definitively some of the very issues and needs that call them into being into positive connections across lines of doctrinal difference. These points of insufficiency, mystery, or uncertainty—operative at different points in each creed—could be collected and transmuted into a general ethos of positive connection across notable differences in creed. This agenda requires the active coding of an ethos of presumptive generosity into the institutional practice of each creed. But the agenda of deep pluralism is not in the cards right now, to say the least. So today, the most viable critical response combines doing critical work on ourselves, diagnosing the resonance machine of the right, working to forge a counter resonance machine, and pursuing selective lines of connection with constituencies on the edge of the evangelical-capitalist machine. The goal is to make each strategy speak to the others. I focus in the following pages on a potential connection to one wing of evangelism and toward the end of this chapter on what evangelism in contemporary life can teach the rest of us about the pressures that contemporary life places on us. For evangelism is both a danger and a symptom of our time. Other components of a positive machine are engaged in later chapters.

There are multiple voices within Christianity. Besides the disparate figures discussed above, we could consult commitments to social democracy within Catholicism, the Mennonite vision of John Howard Yoder, and several other traditions as well.[22] Here I note a minority report within evangelism itself that may open a line of connection between a section of evangelists and the democratic left. This engagement is informed by two ideas. First, media claims that the evangelical-capitalist resonance machine was broken by the midterm election of 2006 are exaggerated. It will take the formation of a positive resonance machine to translate that (perhaps) temporary wound into a positive result. Second, it is important for those who criticize the right edge of evangelism to identify lines of contact and selective alliance with voices in the evangelical movement itself.

Proponents of "open theism" contend that the dominant view of God as omnipotent and omniscient runs the severe risk of making God complicit in evil. Open theists thus pray to a limited, loving god who *learns* as the world turns. The idea of a providential god whose way of proceeding is open to new experience touches the image of time-as-becoming that inspires in one way the nontheist Nietzsche, in another William James, the American philosopher of a limited god in a world of becoming, and in still another the Christian theology of becoming advanced by Catherine Keller. There are differences, which will receive further attention in chapter 5. Nietzsche keeps the universe open in principle, with no final purpose guiding its end. James embraces a "meliorism" of possibility that enables humanity to learn, if it will listen to the most sensitive mystics of the day, from the growing wisdom of a limited god, without providing a guarantee of a beneficent result.[23] There is a loosening of traditional images of time in all three of these thinkers. Even more pertinent to the issues before us, to read these thinkers in relation to the proponents of open theism is soon to feel the positive spirituality infusing the work of all of them. It is this ethos that creates potential lines of connection across creedal differences.

John Sanders, author of *The God Who Risks: A Theology of Providence*, came to open theism a few years after his young brother died. Fellow parishioners had told him how the death was part of God's inscrutable, providential plan.

He resisted that story, concerned that it could make God complicit in evil as undeserved suffering. Later he read scripture with this issue in mind, dissecting numerous sections in the Old and New Testaments, as he calls them, where God listens and reconsiders his previous plan. The Bible, he says, is full of such instances, including the successful attempt by Moses to convince Yahweh not to kill the Jews who had sacrificed the calf and moments when Jesus implores his god to listen. Prayer itself may suggest a god who listens, thinks anew, and periodically changes his mind. One moment that Sanders addresses is the accounts of the crucifixion in the Gospels. In his view, which he articulates after considering various ambiguities and emendations in these texts, while God appears to have known all along that the Son would be incarnate, he may well not have known in advance that Christ would be crucified. Texts such as Psalm 22:16, Ephesians 1:4, and Peter 1:20 seem to support prior divine knowledge of the crucifixion. But several of these can also be read to testify against it, as Psalm 22:16 seemed to do until subtle changes were made in the translation. Sanders's reading of scripture suggests that the crucifixion was probably not known by God in advance, and that He made adjustments after that defining event of Christianity occurred.[24] At one point Sanders summarizes his rendering of Scripture: "In wisdom God decided to fulfill his promises through the particular path Jesus took. In wisdom God decides how he continues to fulfill his promises, and the divine wisdom takes the changing circumstances of the world into account . . . God is free to do new things and so identify himself in new ways."[25]

Sanders does not insist that his scriptural interpretations are the only credible ones to be drawn from these diverse and protean texts; he presents them as reasonable possibilities among others. A bit like Arius centuries before him—though he is not an Arian in doctrine—he seeks to pluralize evangelical orthodoxy rather than replace one orthodoxy with another definitive statement.[26] Some advocates of open theism have been convicted of heresy in their schools and churches, but others are standing tall to date.[27] And the debate has moved into the pews of evangelical churches.

This counter-movement carries potential to pluralize evangelical Christianity from within, as it challenges the exclusive hold of the theology of omnipotence, time, knowledge, morality, and responsibility. Given the understanding that many Christians have of the ability of prayer to move God, there are already dispositions to support this reading of scripture. Most profoundly, the leaders of this minority movement convey an interpretive modesty with respect to scripture and a spirituality of care for the fragility of the world. Those confessing this faith thus make contact, across creedal differences, with the worldly quest of Zarathustra when he says: "For that man be delivered from revenge, that is for me the bridge to the highest hope and a rainbow after long storms."[28] They also touch others who confess divine omnipotence and refuse to fold the spirit of earthly revenge into their faith. Thus here are affinities of sensibility stretching across significant doctrinal differences, affinities that might be worked upon to draw proponents of several creeds into a larger assemblage of resonance. To undertake the effort, however, radicals, liberals, and secularists need to appreciate the role that a spiritual ethos plays in politics and economic life, overturning the self-defeating drive to pretend that religious creeds and modes of spirituality can be quarantined in the private realm.

This connection in sensibility across lines of doctrinal difference is doubly important. First, it opens a window to the formation of a new political assemblage. Second, it sets a living standard against which to *measure* the extent to which an ethos of existential revenge is now installed in several sectors of economic life. Consider the political promise. A risking, learning, and loving god might learn to expand its care for the diversity of being. It might decide someday that homosexuality is not a sin, that the world's resources are not infinite, that existing patterns of consumption impose too significant a burden upon future generations, that women are not ordained to be subordinate, that morality demands listening sensitively to new events as they arise, and that neoliberalism is no more necessary to economic life as such than an omnipotent God is to religion as such. If an earlier Christian hesitancy about libidinal adventurism within the confines of the nuclear family has already been breached by evangelists, as we saw in chapter 1, is it too wild to think that some of these latter orientations could be altered in the future? Of course, such issues and questions would be subjected to a series of painful debates, within and between churches, for any of these shifts to occur. And those of us outside the evangelical movement who appreciate the role of spirituality inside a cultural economy and a culture of economic life would also have to place some of our favorite orientations under critical review.

I do not say that the outcomes projected above are highly *probable*. I merely point to the urgent *need* for them and try to identify minority expressions within the tradition under scrutiny that could make them more *possible*. To secure this outcome the intercoded domains of scripture, philosophy, literature, church, labor organization, investment portfolios, economic inequality, media, and family turmoil must all be put into play. To remain outside those debates and domains today is to withdraw from the arenas in which the ethos of life is shaped. It is to withdraw from the passion of politics.

Those who resist the drives to existential revenge and extreme entitlement whirling within the evangelical-capitalist machine need to make connections with voices of relational modesty and concern for the future of the earth on the edge of it. Not because our creeds necessarily coincide with theirs, though they may in some cases. But because, first, they seek to insinuate an active pluralization of faith into evangelical Christianity, second, they often convey a protean care for being that must grow if democratic and pluralist energies are to expand, third, they diminish the element of dogmatism in the ethos of faith, and fourth, they drive a wedge into that ungodly alliance between cowboy capitalism and extremist Christianity that smothers the prospects for egalitarianism, pluralist democracy, and ecological responsibility.

We have noted a spiritual connection between cowboy capitalism and evangelism across creedal distance. Are there generic features of contemporary life that press toward cultural generalization of this spirituality? I think there are. Some of those features include the acceleration of several domains of life, including military deployment, global communication systems, air travel, tourism, population migrations, fashion, economic transactions, and cultural exchanges, disrupting older rhythms of life; a flood of films and other media that expose the complexity of visual experience and call punctual images of time into question; a yawning gap between the vaunted role that America is supposed to play in the world and its limited ability to do so; a haunting discrepancy between the American dream of abundance expressed in films, product advertisements, and TV dramas and the difficulty that many have in making ends meet as they participate in the available infrastructure of consumption; the cultural shock that the populace experiences at being treated by much of the world as an aggressive, self-serving empire when much of the populace imagines itself to set the moral center around which the world revolves; popular uneasiness over research in several domains of science that translate the Newtonian model of linear cause into the ontological uncertainty of emergent causality; scientific speculations that extend the theory of biological evolution—already troubling to many—to the unfolding of the universe itself; intense media attention to devastating earthquakes, hurricanes, floods, tornadoes, volcanic eruptions, and tsunamis that disturb both a providential view of the world *and* the image of natural regularities at ready human disposal; and a gnawing sense that the world's fragile ecology is careening into radical imbalance through practices that most Americans see as part of their birthright. The cumulative weight of these experiences exacerbates generic anger in many, a floating anger seeking vulnerable targets of release and attack.

The signs that these disruptive experiences have already taken a toll are multiple too. They include, on the aggressive/defensive side of the equation, the intensification in some circles of punitive orientations to diversity; escalating levels of violence and superhuman heroism in "action" films that seek to protect the model of human mastery under unfavorable conditions; the amplification of accusatory voices on the media even as these same voices profess to be operating in "no-spin zones"; the virulence of electoral campaigns; implacable assertions of American sovereignty in an increasingly interdependent world, expressed through hostility to diplomacy and the UN; and the translation of floating impulses to revenge into support or easy tolerance of preemptive wars, suppression of civil liberties, state practices of torture, and a disregard of the consequences of war exemplified by the suppression of Iraqi body counts. It may be that traditional modes of trust in God and attachment to the world have been rattled, while the underlying sources of anxiety and anger have yet to be addressed. The capitalist and Christian right respond to both symptomatically, as they foment a cultural ethos of existential resentment. The rest of us too often restrict ourselves to policy questions and rational persuasion, ignoring the need to engage the spiritual dimension of life under altered conditions of being. If the quality of the spirituality that underlies political and economic life is critical to civilizational health, then the question of how to recompose positive attachment to the earth has become timely. The exploration must find both theistic and nontheistic expression.

There is also a spiritual counter-movement to the evangelical-capitalist resonance machine almost at the tipping point. A large constituency, located in diverse social positions, is crafting new modes of attachment to a world marked by interdependent minorities, altered experiences of time, the disturbance of old traditions, and the weight of the future upon the present. A number of very popular films, to consider just one venue, both presuppose these proclivities among their audience and seek to extend them. Take films such as *Far from Heaven, I Love Huckabees, Time Code, Blow-Up, The Eternal Sunshine of the Spotless Mind, Memento, Waking Life, Hustle and Flow, Deconstructing Harry, Run Lola Run,* and *Mullholland Drive.* These films crack the molds governing many action films and TV dramas; scramble old habits of attachment in this way or that; highlight the role of sensory interinvolvement in organizing perception; render palpable the role of affect in memory and the layering of memory into perception; challenge the realism of simple objectivism; and call into question the self-certainty of both linear and providential images of time.

Several take another turn as well. They trigger or augment—as the case may be—an awakening that must amplified significantly in the next twenty years. To take one example, *I Love Huckabees* turns out to embrace the things that it first subjects to humor and mockery, including "existential detectives," ecological movements, environmental advertisements, and particularly the application of tactics by ourselves on ourselves to amplify attachment to the future of this world. The humor becomes part of the tactics of attachment. It is practiced on behalf of human self-modesty in a world in which temporality may be open, human efficacy is fragile, perception is complex, and the twin stories of providence and human mastery show signs of wear and tear.[29] *I Love Huckabees* and the other films pursue attachment to a new world, during a time when traditional modes of belonging have been stretched and strained. They can assume either a theistic or nontheistic coloration. They speak to "secular" and religious constituencies who have begun to see how cultivation of positive attachment to the future of the earth is important, and how new circumstances require adjustments in the way this attachment is fostered.

The quickest way to put the point is therefore to say that the evangelical-capitalist resonance machine both poses *dangers* to resist and expresses one *symptom* of a larger condition to be addressed. Those alert to its dangers must also become alert to how we participate in the larger condition of which it provides the most dangerous expression.

This is the juncture at which the experimental engagements with film enacted by Gilles Deleuze in *Cinema II* may speak to the task of fomenting a more positive ethos of contemporary life. I do not suggest, of course, that such films or his analysis of them is sufficient. But both provide positive resources in themselves and clues as to how to proceed in other domains. Deleuze concentrates on how shifts in the everyday experience of time speak to a subset of films and how the films amplify the experience. The stage is set for the crucial theme of chapter 7 in *Cinema II* by preceding explorations of *flashbacks* exposing uncertain moments of bifurcation in the past that could have taken more than one direction; *irrational cuts* that scramble the old action sequences; *aberrant modes of behavior* in comedies that express exquisite sensitivity to movements of the world otherwise overwhelmed by the dictates of singular action; musicals that slide us into *dreamy moments of transition*, drawing attention to the complexity of our mode of attachment to the world as we slide through these transitions; *crystals of time* that enact the complexity of duration, as images from past and present spiral back and forth to forge the very terms of experience; and *depth-of-field shots* that expose non-linear time in its "pure state." The idea is that most of us are already infected by the interplay between these films and the daily experiences to which they speak, even if many also devise intricate defenses against pursuing this interplay. The amplification of relays can be disturbing, because it conjures salient experiences outside the movie house as well as within it; it can magnetize drives to reassert in a bellicose way the existential understandings disrupted by the interplay. It can encourage others to retreat from the ugliness of public life. But Deleuze challenges both responses. He reads the films as one set of techniques among others to recode our subliminal lives, helping to integrate affirmative attachments to the world more actively into cultural activity. He seeks to deepen attachment to the fragility and complexity of this world as he challenges the dispositions of bellicose attack, passive skepticism, and authoritarian cynicism at the very nodal points of their emergence. By "this world" he certainly does not mean the established distribution of power and political priorities. He means the larger compass of being in which we are set.

Deleuze realizes that people harbor different interpretations of "the larger compass of being." The idea is to instill affirmative dispositions into more of them under altered conditions of being. Today, as he puts it, "whether we are Christians or atheists, in our universal schizophrenia, we need reasons to believe in this world."[30] For automatic modes of belonging do not suffice today, as the ethos of existential resentment in the evangelical-capitalist resonance machine reveals so well. By "belief" Deleuze does not merely mean a judgment about whether x or y is true, supported by an epistemic procedure of judgment. The word includes that, and cuts deeper: into spiritual dispositions to action that both flow below epistemic beliefs and well up into them, reaching a zone that prophets tap when they solicit trust in the world. Films, unlike the written word, mix image, music, rhythm, plot, words, and background sounds, mimicking the processes by which our initial orientations to being were formed. "Belief" now touches, for instance, the tightening of the gut, coldness of the skin, contraction of the pupils, and hunching of the back that arise when an epistemic belief in which you are invested has been challenged. It also touches that tacit feeling of vitality which flows through life when you are attached to the world.

If attachment to this world requires supplementary work today, a two-level process may be pertinent. First, you allow affinities between human embodiment and other dimensions of nature that normally slide into the background to come to the fore. Some films help here. Other possibilities arise too. Thus, to take an example from another venue, you may now note more sensitively than heretofore how the rhythm of waves during a gentle day at the beach communicates with your mood and thoughts at the end of the day. Or profit from the positive effect, recently confirmed in neuroscience, of inaudible vibrations in organ music upon your mood and disposition. Experiments indicate that powerful emotions are invoked when rhythmic vibrations emanating from the organ below the threshold of audibility are received. Those same emotions are quelled when those inaudible vibrations are stifled. Indeed, "different parts of the body resonate at different frequencies," with lower areas responsive to frequencies below the level of audibility, and the hands and arms responsive to higher frequencies.[31] These examples support a general view adopted here: patterns of rhythm, resonance, dissonance, and reverberation not only play a role within cultural life, but as we can see with respect to the evangelical-capitalist resonance machine, they also forge subdiscursive modes of communication between us and other parts of nature.[32] It is pertinent to amplify these subdiscursive resonances under new conditions of being. In chapter 3 I explore how resonance and amplification function in nonhuman systems.

Second, as you absorb the effects of these affirmative resonances you also allow them to find expression in the things you speak, write, and do. You allow subliminal shifts to find active expression in the higher intellectual registers and cultural exchanges. You thus recode the tonalities of belief at both levels, allowing each to loop into the other as you proceed. Such strategies of augmentation may be linked to a sense of divine grace, or find expression in a deeper sense of our implication in nature. Either or both. In each case awareness of the human body as a medium through which resonances pass is enhanced. In each case we work on the spirituality through which to engage a world moving faster than heretofore. Several religious traditions, including Buddhism, Christianity, Judaism, and Hinduism, adopt specific rituals at these points of intersection. My point is not to address those rituals specifically; it is to show how comparable exercises are also important to those who do not participate in one of those congregations. The rest of us must come to appreciate how spiritual work is demanded by the contours of contemporary life, partly because of the critical role that spirituality plays in the defining institutions of contemporary life.

So it may be important to join Deleuze in exploring anew how to deepen belief in this world as we come to terms affirmatively with altered experiences of time that cannot be easily erased from the human sensorium. The above examples—of imbrications between film and the everyday and of nature-culture resonances—merely scratch the surface. The point is that it is important to continue down this trail to challenge the ethos of revenge and its points of inception.

Amplification of care for the future of this world under new conditions of being could not, of course, *suffice* to bring about the positive politics needed today—though some may project that assumption into these comments. Rather, positive modes of attachment must be lifted into larger circuits of resonance, linking the micropolitics of everyday life to positive social movements and both of these to the macropolitics of the state. These linkages will be explored in later chapters. But those explorations find one of their anchors in the activities by which we amplify attachment to this world.

The evangelical-capitalist resonance machine is paradoxical. First, it threatens the world, as its very emergence teaches us about the ubiquitous role that spirituality of some sort or other always plays in state-capital institutions. Second, its leading members are often resistant to thinking about new conditions of being; but they are engrossed in turning them back through the micropolitics of everyday life. That combination generates a powerful political formula, even as it jeopardizes the democratic future. Secular divisions between the spiritual and the political and between the private and the public, still haunting many on the democratic left, weaken efforts to infuse care for the world, future generations, and the diversity of being into a positive resonance machine.

CHAPTER THREE

Contending Problematics

A method of research is apt to express a set of metaphysical commitments to which the methodists embracing it are attached. I do not mean anything technical by "metaphysical" here. The word means merely your most profound image of being and world. Differences in world image between Sophocles, Epicurus, Augustine, Spinoza, Kant, Charles Taylor, and Gilles Deleuze can be taken to be metaphysical in this sense. Sophocles and Augustine diverge not only on the method that each deploys. They diverge also in their conceptions of time, divinity, providence, and contingency. The same thing could be said of the relation of both to Spinoza, and his deductive approach, embrace of an ethic of cultivation, denial of a personal god, and opposition to theocracy. Similarly the differences between Charles Taylor and Gilles Deleuze find expression in their respective methods, with Taylor pursuing a hermeneutic account of politics meshing with a pursuit of transcendence and Deleuze adopting an ethological mode expressing faith in a nonpurposeful world composed of multiple systems periodically colliding, colluding, and commingling.

If you flinch at the term "metaphysical," I can drop it in favor of another.[1] The phrase "existential faith" highlights something that the cold term "metaphysic" downplays. An existential faith is a committed view of the world layered into affective dispositions, habits, methods, loyalties, and institutional injunctions. The intensity of commitment to it typically exceeds the power of the arguments and evidence advanced on its behalf. Each figure listed above is a carrier of a distinctive existential faith. The faith in which each is invested has not been definitively established in a way that rules out of court every alternative to it. It is a contestable faith. To say that it is contestable is not to deny that impressive, comparative considerations might be offered on its behalf, or that it might be subjected to critical interrogations that press its advocates to adjust aspects of it. An existential faith is not immune to argument and evidence; commitment to it, rather, is not exhausted by them. Better, the presentations of argument and evidence are themselves invested with an element of faith.

Existential faith is ubiquitous. To be human is to be invested by faith before you reach the age of critical reflection, even if these investments are laden with ambivalence, periodically marked by crisis, and occasionally susceptible to reconfiguration. An existential faith is lodged on the visceral register of being as well as the more refined intellectual register to which the visceral is linked by multiple circuits. It infiltrates habits of desire, conscience, and perception as well as the presumptions of reflective judgment.

The secular division between private faith and public life is compromised by these considerations. The private-public division is not nearly as sharp as some pretend, even in the face of counter evidence provided by devotees of evangelism, Judaism, Islam, Unitarianism, and neoliberalism today. You could strive more than some advocates of each faith do to forge a degree of separability between private faith and public profession, but even then the line would be more like a porous membrane than an iron curtain.[2]

Some existential faiths are theistic, others nontheistic. Some discern providence in being, others a nonprovidential world covered by rigorous laws, and still others protean forces in an undesigned world not entirely covered by laws. Yet other faiths—such as those of tantric Buddhists and Jamesians—are lodged in that fugitive space between "theism" and "nontheism," as each is commonly understood. Some faiths may appear at one time to be defeated by new evidence, powerful arguments, or new modes of witnessing, as some (but not most) devotees of the Enlightenment thought Christian monotheism was by the Newtonian revolution. But a new response to that apparent defeat might emerge, as when Kant sought to make Newtonianism and Christianity safe for one another again. Or consider how the Epicurean faith in a swerve in nature was rejected by early modern natural science because of the discrepancy between its unruliness and the lawlike image that modern science endorsed, only to return in revised form later. Or how the Vatican finally rendered its doctrine roughly compatible with the theory of Galileo after condemning him for centuries, and then accepted a version of evolutionary theory after resisting it for over a century.

An existential faith, again, is not immune to the effects of argument, new technologies of perception, the pressure of new events, and theoretical revolutions. Its reflective proponents are often plagued or inspired by them. And some faiths do bite the dust. But an affectively imbued faith that speaks to urgent existential needs can marshal impressive resources to protect or amend itself in the face of such challenges. It might protect core elements through new "clarifications," or convene inspired witnesses to explain the necessity of paradoxes and mysteries that now cling to it. The repackaging of creationism as a theory of "intelligent design"—presented as an alternative to the model of evolution through natural selection—represents one recent example of rescue through creative reconstitution. It will not be surprising to see that theory become more sophisticated in the years ahead. Another example, already cited, was the heroic effort by Kant to save Christianity and Newton together in one philosophical system, anchored by a set of "necessary postulates" about God, grace, salvation, and freedom. Newton himself had already taken a turn in that direction through his secret defense of Arianism.[3]

What, more closely, are the relations between an existential faith, method, and theo-political conclusions? My sense is that these dimensions are loosely connected, but that you cannot simply read off the links by describing a position globally as "Aristotelian," "Trinitarian," "neo-Kantian" or "empiricist." The devil resides in the details. It is thus necessary to work with specific cases. One complication, as we saw in chapter 2, is that an operational faith is itself composed of at least two elements, a creedal dimension and the lived sensibility infusing it. Things become even more complicated when you keep in mind that each creed invokes a set of rituals or disciplines that devotees follow to incorporate the creed into their conduct: creed, method, sensibility, discipline. This is true of "secular" creeds as well as "religious" creeds. The way secularists dress, express themselves, fold hesitations into their speech, and practice methods of inquiry both expresses and helps to incorporate their creeds.

A few formulations about method and faith from another time might illuminate the issue. *On Christian Doctrine*, by Augustine, was a problem-driven book, set in the fraught political context of the church and the Roman Empire in the fifth century CE. I pursue Augustine on this front to become more thoughtful about the relations between faith and method. The comparisons that I make to contemporary traditions are suggestive; more details would be required to test them. Augustine sought to resolve uncertainties that arise when holy Scripture, taken to reveal the truth of divine incarnation, the resurrection, the Trinity, omnipotence, benevolence, and salvation, contains formulations that appear to transgress these very articles of faith. He was concerned both to honor the God confessed by his church in relation to "pagan" faiths and to show how Scripture proved the putative Christian doctrines of Manicheanism, Arianism, and Pelagianism to be heresies. So he devised an authoritative method for reading the sacred text. The first methodological dictate is a "rule of faith": "This faith maintains, and it must be believed: neither the soul nor the human body may suffer complete annihilation, but the impious shall rise again into everlasting punishment, and the just into life everlasting."[4]

When you consult Scripture you must follow this fundamental rule of faith. Otherwise you cannot participate in the spirituality that permeates the text; and your interpretations will be weak, sinful, or incoherent. This rule might be compared to an operational rule of faith (or "regulative ideal") in rational-choice theory in economics and political science: the rule that preferences are individual, orderable, and transitive.[5] To *say* that this premise is merely a convenient assumption of inquiry may underestimate its power. The question is whether it plays a fundamental role in the thinking of the researchers governed by it, and whether elaborate strategems are deployed to protect it as an assumption of inquiry. Augustine's rule of faith might be compared as well to two other rules attractive to conventional empiricism and rational-choice theory: that the dichotomy of the analytic and the synthetic is an elemental distinction that everyone must adopt, and that the world is susceptible in principle to rigorous explanation through general laws. When social scientists ask one another, "Is that claim analytical or empirical?" they invoke the primacy of the first methodological injunction. Its importance can be shown by noting that if you support the analytic-synthetic dichotomy you are under pressure to define causality as a "synthetic" relation in which factor A, separate from factor B, can induce changes in B only because the two are separate. To articulate a more complex model of causality is to call this dichotomy itself into question. If these two dogmas—the dichotomy and the conviction that the world is composed of laws—are fundamental elements of faith, adherents of the method will treat them as sacrosanct conditions of inquiry rather than as assumptions readily open to critical revision.

Let's turn to Augustine's second rule. It operates in tandem with the first. This rule calls upon the devout reader to place each part of the text in the larger context in which it operates, with the most fundamental context being the rule of faith itself. This second rule comes into play whenever a "locution" in Scripture seems to contradict the basic faith: "When investigation reveals an uncertainty as to how a locution should be pointed or construed, the rule of faith should be consulted . . . But if both meanings, or all of them, in the event that there are several, remain ambiguous after the faith has been consulted, then it is necessary to examine the context of the preceding and following parts of the ambiguous places, so that we may determine which of the meanings which suggest themselves it would allow to be consistent."[6]

This methodological stricture bears a family resemblance to that articulated today in hermeneutical, interpretive, and phenomenological approaches to cultural inquiry. Both Augustine and they play up the interwoven character of life and language, as well as the role of context in setting meaning and enabling interpretation. They also converge in saying that contemporary empiricist and rationalist images of culture, in adopting the analytical-synthetic dichotomy and a designative philosophy of language, underplay both the open texture and complex web of connections constituting the intersubjective life of embodied, linguistic beings. Many practitioners in the hermeneutical tradition also seek contact with a *trace* or *whisper* of transcendence in the world. They thus share something with Augustine, though he invests transcendence with more definitive presence and authority than contemporary practitioners such as, say, Charles Taylor, Paul Ricoeur, and Karl Jaspers. Other contemporary interpretationists, however, while sharing these Augustinian and hermeneutic critiques of the analytic-synthetic dichotomy and the primacy of the designative dimension of language, do not hear the whisper of God. This too affects the way we proceed. We are apt to adopt a double-entry orientation to interpretation, oscillating as a matter of principle between critiques of consolidated interpretations and the production of positive accounts that connect cultural life robustly to the domains of biology, neuroscience, climatology, and evolution. Our philosophy of time as becoming also secretes a more volatile image of being. We contend, for instance, that because there are differential capacities of self-organization in a variety of interacting human and nonhuman systems, agency is not reserved to human beings and human culture alone. Given these considerations, we tend to resist the attractions of "deep" interpretation, seeking to *intervene* creatively in processes that are not under the full control of any agency or set of determinable laws.

Back to Augustine. He concedes that the commands of the church can sometimes appear to be countermanded by Scripture, even after a reader, already schooled in devotion, has adhered to the first two rules of method. In these instances a supplemental guideline is needed. That which "appears in the divine Word that does not literally pertain to virtuous behavior or to the true faith you must take to be figurative."[7] Now, some sort of distinction—tacit or explicit—between the literal and the figurative seems unavoidable. When I say that you are raining on my parade, I carry the meaning from a street parade to that of theoretical critique. But you know what I mean. The intriguing thing is that once Augustine forges this distinction, he also risks reopening debates between the true Christian faith and the dangerous heresies that he discerns whirling around it. If he does not regulate the use of the distinction closely, scriptural interpretations of Jesus as a Jew, Jesus as a human prophet who became divine through resurrection (one version of Arianism), the capacity to earn salvation by human effort alone (Pelagianism), or a tragic reading of the Book of Genesis might become feasible.[8] So he insists that the serpent in Genesis *must* be a figure standing for Lucifer; it cannot embody the wisdom that the Caananites had symbolically invested in reptiles. Augustine thus insists that everything in Scripture corresponding to the first rule of faith is literal, that only Biblical formulations appearing to be at odds with that rule are figurative, and that these figures must be read in an authoritative way to separate true faith from the deviations and heresies plaguing it. Now you have the makings of a single, rigorous reading of the holy text.

Augustine's division between the literal and the figurative might be compared to the division in contemporary empiricism between the designative dimension of language and its expressive, normative, and performative features. The two sets of distinctions do not correspond perfectly, but they do function in similar ways. In the empirical tradition the designative dimension is given priority over the normative, performative, and expressive dimensions, and valiant efforts are made to demarcate it from them. To concur that these dimensions are interlocked would be to take a giant step toward an interpretive approach in the human sciences. It would also chip away at the wall between empirical inquiry and normative judgment that has been so important to the self-identity (and political protection) of many social scientists. Both rational-choice theorists and empiricists thus keep their eyes focused anxiously on language, to ensure that the network of terms that they extract from ordinary language do not transport them too close to the territory of interpretation or hermeneutics. As with Augustine in his relation to pagans and heretics, empiricists and rational-choice theorists seek to maintain a wall between themselves and interpretive theory. But that wall is erected less through the production of positive examples of linguistic purity than by repetition of the *accusation* that advocates of other methods use language in imprecise, vague, normative, impressionistic, or ideological ways. The perpetual task of language cleansing is as critical to the method of rational-choice theory and empiricism as Augustine's management of literal and figurative meanings is to the stability of his faith.

Still, Augustine realizes that uncertainties persist even after a devotee has applied the rule of faith, attended to context, and managed the literal-figurative distinction carefully. So he introduces yet another rule: "But just as it is a servile infirmity to follow the letter and to take signs for the things that signify, in the same way it is an evil of wandering error to interpret signs in a useless way. However, he who does not know what a sign means but does know that it is a sign, is not in servitude. Thus it is better to be burdened by unknown but useful signs than to interpret signs in a useless way so that one is led from the yoke of servitude only to thrust his neck in the snares of error."[9]

Let us set aside the horrendous toll in Europe and the New World paid by those "idolatrous pagans" accused of confusing signs with the things they signify, even as we note that Augustine himself hesitated to condone war against the pagans. Let us even set aside the tendency among adherents of each world religion to accuse others of the sin of idolatry, even when they themselves use statues, icons, and symbols. We focus instead on the importance of the "unknown" in the Augustinian problematic. The introduction of what might be called *a rule of mystery* does considerable work for Augustine. He invokes it when pagans ask him what his omnipotent God was doing "before" It invented time and when he is asked to explain how the three elements of the Trinity are both united and distinct. This rule, however, is invoked *after* Augustine has revealed his God to be omnipotent, omniscient, benevolent, and salvational. The timing of the invocation of the rule of mystery is important. If it is introduced too soon, there will be no solid doctrine or creed within which it circulates. My suspicion is that every faith and doctrine so far invented runs into zones of paradox, mystery, and enigma that could be drawn upon to reject it as "incoherent" *or* invoked to deepen faith in it. So I am not critical of Augustine for invoking either mystery or paradox; my critique begins only when he is unwilling to extend similar charity to other theistic and nontheistic creeds.

Muted invocations of selective mystery emerge today in the hermeneutic and interpretative traditions. Is there a functional equivalent in rational-choice theory and classical empiricism? Not exactly. But many practitioners do invoke *an opposing rule* at the same strategic point. The disdain that advocates of both sometimes display toward old and "new mysterians" expresses a faith that the world *must* be fully explicable in the last instance, if not in fact then in principle. This faith is articulated as a "regulative ideal" that everyone "must" adopt if rational inquiry is to proceed. Otherwise madness sets in and "anything goes." To the extent that such a regulative ideal is affirmed as susceptible to being qualified by other considerations, it is not advanced as a profound article of faith. To the extent that it is advanced as necessary, practices of inquiry which encounter and even appreciate a modicum of mystery are demeaned from the start. Such an injunction could well rule out, for instance, a conception of *emergent* causality in which the interplay between disparate factors in producing a new formation is said to exceed our capacities for detailed knowledge and prediction. If this regulative ideal is *really* treated as a problematic assumption (rather than a set of assumptions guiding one school) such a temper will find expression in a hesitancy to reject another theory merely because it does not conform to this stricture. It will find expression in a willingness to appreciate a large plurality of methods, even theistic *and* nontheistic faiths that project an element of mystery, enigma, or paradox into the nexus between inquiry and world.

What, then, are the relations between an existential faith and a methodological discipline? The review of Augustine suggests that these dimensions are loosely interwoven. Sometimes, as with Augustine, a basic faith secretes a method that helps to separate it from other faiths in circulation. At other times induction into a method and the successes that it occasions recoil back upon the initial faith, encouraging adjustments in it. These two dimensions now loop back and forth until a new equilibrium emerges. The loops become more complicated yet when you reintroduce the triadic relation between creed, method, and sensibility, each element circulating into the others without being entirely reducible to it.

Therefore I want to suggest that faith and method are interconnected without devising a general formula to cover that connection. You can't, for instance, say that those who seek a place for transcendence must, for that reason alone, adopt one method over another. The generic idea of "transcendence" is too vague for that. There is a world of difference between, say, William James—the hesitant protestant who expresses faith in a limited god in a pluralistic universe—and Augustine—who prays to an omnipotent god of mysterious grace and finds several Christian heresies to condemn—even though both invoke transcendence. Nonetheless, the existential faith of James *is* relevant to the method of "radical empiricism" that he embraces. His critiques of Augustinianism, "intellectualism," "rationalism," and "logical empiricism" are designed in part to open the self to a mode of mystical experience which expresses his particular version of transcendence.

If method is inflected by existential faith, and each faith—once its elements are specified appropriately—is more consonant with some methods than others, what can be done to adjudicate disputes between method/faith/sensibility complexes, or—as I call them—problematics? This is the triumphant question that methodists pose to people like me, with the implication that unless we accept the autonomy of method we will forever find ourselves poking around in the dark. My view, however, is that numerous possible considerations might move you in one way or another on the questions of method and faith. But there is, so far, no super-problematic or quasi-Kantian transcendental field so cleansed of contestable faith that it provides a neutral touchstone to resolve all inter-method disputes. That is why such disputes are persistent, with advocates of each advancing considerations that press upon the others, but no single one simply emerging triumphant. The demand for a definitive resolution is haunted by what Hegel called the "dilemma of epistemology."[10] The problem is not that there are two few considerations available to resolve the issue. The problem is that there are so many, and that they often point in different directions. Or to put the point another way, the problem is that the existential faith with which you start plays a role in sorting out and weighing disparate considerations. Welcome to the real world of politics and politico-economic inquiry.

A "problematic" consists of a method, an existential creed congenial to it, and the sensibilities attached to both. Most problematics come equipped with characteristic paradoxes and problems, treated by devotees as either intrinsic or to be deferred to the future, or both of these at different points. We also develop loyalties to the problematics to which we are habituated and to those who share them with us. In an extreme case it is an act of disloyalty to your allies to change your mind. A significant turn from one problematic to another therefore involves a corollary shift in thought-imbued sentiments layered into the visceral register of identity as well as the refined intellectual register. A significant shift is more akin to a *conversion* than to a change of opinion. A rational-choice theorist who converted to hermeneutics would go through a trial more severe than if she adopted empiricism and less severe than if she gave up publicly a belief in God while living in a community of believers. When such conversions are up for consideration, then argument, evidence, identity issues, status considerations, constituency loyalties, and existential hopes will jostle and move each other, sometimes activating a shift and sometimes fomenting a reactive attitude of militant protection. It is hard to predict how the decision will go unless, as Augustine did, you invoke your God after the fact to show how necessary the change was before the fact. That amounts to invoking the point at issue to resolve the issue. Methodological disputes in the human sciences are intense, first because our visceral identities, faiths, and loyalties are touched by these disputes, and second because of the dubious expectation, installed in much of the human sciences and secular culture today, that the question of method can be divorced from issues of faith about the world. Wherever there is dogmatism there is faith, but, as the noble example of James shows, tactical work on ourselves can promote relations of agonistic respect between carriers of alternative problematics.

It would be a travesty to reduce this account to saying that theists accept one method and atheists another. There are too many varieties of each disposition to make that possible and too many elements involved, as the division between Augustine and James on "one side" suggests and that between Bertrand Russell and Friedrich Nietzsche on "the other" does too. What is involved, again, is neither autonomy nor reducibility but an interplay between several sometimes unruly elements.

One consideration in favor of this reading is that it helps us to understand the intensity accompanying methodological disputes in the human sciences. Another is that it points toward reworking the global distinctions in secular culture between "religion" on one side and "science" and secular doctrines on the other. That sort of rethinking has been going on for some time in several sectors of popular culture, anthropology, and religious studies. It is timely to pursue it more generally in the human sciences.[11] An additional point is that by paying attention again to the ugly history of religious conflict we might pick up leads to help us cope with methodological disputes in the human sciences, which are often permeated with a tone of religiosity.

I realize that all this is dangerous, and that an underlying consideration against ventilating these connections in the way proposed is the possibility that the human sciences might become subject to more stringent control by churches and states, two of the four hundred pound gorillas of our day. It is a worry. But that worry itself suggests that the connections noted here are actually in play. My sense is that the political cover provided to the human sciences through the separation of faith from method has now become too unconvincing to do the work it once did. It has also helped to protect a couple of problematics that would otherwise be subject to more critical contestation within the human sciences. It is time to confront the issue squarely, and to run the risks that the engagement requires. If we don't do so ourselves, the carriers of dogmatism will resolve the issue on their terms. As they already seek to do.

Immanent Naturalism and Existential Faith

So far I have almost acted as if I float above the issues discussed. Yet it is, for God's sake, unlikely that I embrace either Augustinianism, rational-choice theory, or logical empiricism in its classic form. And I have become critical of the sufficiency of interpretive theory in recent years too. Partly to overturn the impression that I regard the loosely textured relations between method and faith as not applying to me, I will say something about the problematic that inspires me.

A preliminary way to distinguish my perspective from that of Augustine is to say that it is naturalistic and nontheistic. By naturalism I mean the faith that nature and human culture survive without the aid (or obstruction) of a divine force. The specific form of the naturalism that I embrace represents a minority confession within it. It questions the *sufficiency* of the lawlike model of nature endorsed in classical natural science. I concur with Charles Peirce when he writes that "conformity to law exists only in a limited range of events and even there it is not perfect, for an element of pure spontaneity or lawless originality mingles, or at least must be supposed to mingle, with law everywhere."[12] My view also emphasizes how human culture and the rest of nature are differentially mixed into each other, through multiple transactions between economic life and the forces of nature, and subliminal connections between the pulsions of nature and the rhythms of human being. The human body is the site of complex relays between nonhuman nature and human life. No aspect of nature can definitively be defined as "external" to cultural life. A force that appears external at one moment—because it provides a stable background to the activity in question—may become a volatile internality at the next, as hurricanes, climate change, drought, asteroid showers, floods, plagues, state regime changes, and soil depletion periodically disclose. Augustine and I would agree that the modern social scientist's attempt to isolate internalities from externalities, while having limited experimental value, too easily devolves into operational denial of the volatility and complexity of the world. We just disagree about what animates that complexity.

My dissent from Augustine is not based in dogma alone. I dissent even

more from the dogmatic way he conveys his dogma. Let's compare him to a
modern Augustinian, Stanley Hauerwas. Hauerwas confesses the dogmas of
resurrection, the Trinity, and the indispensability of witnesses to spread and
deepen Christian faith. In doing so he confesses how numerous forces infiltrate the very logic of argument and evidentiary considerations; he also implies that non-Christian and nontheistic doctrines embody elements of faith
that help to set them in motion. Yet he then emphasizes how Christian faith,
to be true to itself, must be supported through a combination of witnessing,
argument, and textual exegesis that attracts converts. Its essence is abrogated
if induction attempts take the form of profound institutional pressure, forced
conversion, or state violence. Hauerwas is not a relativist; he confesses a
dogma appropriate to all times and places. But he is a pluralist at a second
level, in that he evinces (what I call) agonistic respect for alternative faiths,
theistic and nontheistic.[13] Such a combination of strong faith, confession of
its contestability in the eyes of others, and limits to acceptable modes of
contestation is noble. It expresses the maturation of Augustinianism. Thus I
join Hauerwas in opposing capital punishment; I am touched—though pre-
sumptively rather than categorically—by his commitment to nonviolence;
and I press hard against his opposition to doctor-assisted suicide. In each case
I draw sustenance from a different faith. Do the connections between us
express a complementarity of sensibility that leaps across creedal differences?
I would like to say so. One thing is certain: it is urgent today to negotiate
positive connections across significant creedal differences.

But what relation does the naturalism embraced here bear to other varieties of naturalism? Let us define eliminative naturalism as a view that re-
duces the experience of consciousness to nonconscious processes and lawlike
naturalism as denying any role to transcendence, while finding both nonhuman nature and human culture amenable in principle to explanation by
precise laws. *Immanent naturalism,* by comparison, claims that the lawlike
image of science lives off the remains of a providential theology that it purports to have left behind. According to immanent naturalism, if the world is
not designed by a god it is apt to be more unruly in its mode of becoming or
evolution than can be captured entirely by any set of lawlike statements.
Stephen Jay Gould and Ilya Prigogine qualify as immanent naturalists in the
fields of biological evolution and chemistry. Gould doubts that if we had been
in a position to discern the volatile conditions from which biological evolution
started we could fit the resulting process into a lawlike pattern or predict the
outcome to this point. Prigogine studies systems in "disequilibrium" that

periodically issue in new patterns of partial equilibrium incapable of having been predicted in advance of their emergence. This is partly because latent capacities for self-organization within the system can become activated in new ways when it encounters novel factors.[14] Kenneth Boulding is a distinguished economist who has also taken this route. In *The Future* he argues that economies, because of their complexity, shifting connections to other systems, and internal capacities for mutation, radically exceed human powers of predictive explanation.[15]

Perhaps the most basic projection—or existential faith—of immanent naturalism is vague essentialism. This projection, briefly noted in chapter 2, finds differential presence in the work of Nietzsche, Prigogine, and Gould. Here is an expression of it by Gilles Deleuze and Félix Guattari. They speak of immanent forces intensive enough to make a difference in an undesigned world of becoming. These volatile forces flow through and around historically established entities, and they are not fixed enough to be identified as stable theoretical objects: "So how are we to define this matter-movement, this matter-energy, this matter-flow, this matter in variation that enters assemblages and leaves them? It is a destratified, deterritorialized matter. It seems to us that Husserl has brought thought a decisive step forward when he discovered the region of *vague and material essences* (in other words, essences that are vagabond, anexact and yet rigorous), distinguishing them from fixed, metric and formal essences . . . they constitute fuzzy aggregates. They relate to a *corporeality* (materiality) that is not to be confused either with an intelligible formal essentiality or a sensible, formed thinghood."[16]

In this perspective uncertainty exceeds the assumption of limited information adopted in conventional empiricist and rational-choice methods. Uncertainty includes that. But it also resides in the difference between human capacities of observation and conceptualization and volatile elements inherent in matter-energy flows themselves. An example of such a field of matter-energy is the human body-brain system before it is finely wired through intensive exchanges with a particular culture. Even after being wired it is traversed by surplus energies, unstable mixtures, and static that might, given an unexpected shift in the environment, trigger new developments in it. Another example is the intensive energy mobilized when a faith constituency is subjected to repeated acts of humiliation, sometimes fomenting responses that exceed established concepts of conventional warfare, revolution, and criminality.

Emergent Causality

One distinctive move an immanent naturalist makes in cultural theory is to reconfigure established concepts of causality. The idea is to challenge the sufficiency of the model of causality in social science *and* acausal images of mutual constitution in interpretive theory. Efficient causality sometimes operates. But we need a concept of *emergent causality*, applicable when previously stabilized systems enter a period of heightened disequilibrium. Emergence, when it occurs, is *causal* (rather than merely a web of definitional relations) in that a movement at one level (or system) induces effects on another. But it is *emergent* in four respects: first, the volatile elements are not knowable in detail before the effects that emerge; second, some of them become *infused* into the very organization of the emergent phenomenon, so that the causal factor is not fully separate from the new formation; third, the new infusions tap into heretofore dormant capacities of self-organization within the affected system; and fourth, a series of loops and feedback loops flow back and forth between these forces—sometimes generating a new stabilization and sometimes intensifying disequilibrium.[17] The emergent condition is altered by external forces that become imparted into it, by forces that impinge upon it, and by activation of its own previously undertapped capacities for self-organization. The emergent is the effect of spiraling movements back and forth between these elements.

If you now introduce looping entrant and re-entrant combinations across several relatively open systems, emergent causality becomes yet more complex.[18] The complexity is endemic to a world composed of multiple systems, moving at different speeds, with differential degrees of openness, periodically impinging upon and flowing into one another. The review in chapter 1 of Deleuze's and Guattari's survey of multiple elements in the formation of capitalism provides one instance of a new equilibrium. The discussion in chapter 2 of patterns of resonance between the evangelical movement, members of the white working class, and strategic capitalist élites provides another. "Resonance" here is not only a metaphor: it speaks to rhythmic patterns of inter-fusion that exceed mechanical modes of causality.

Emergent causation produces real effects without being susceptible to full explanation in a classic sense, partly because what has been produced was not adequately *conceptualized* before its production and partly because of the element of real uncertainty in these movements back and forth. It is true that some domains now taken to exemplify emergent causation may be reduced to patterns of efficient causation in the future. But the wager-faith of immanent naturalism is that this is not apt to happen in many zones. Concepts such as volatility, rhythm, reverberation, resonance, amplification, and emergence now become pertinent to some domains of nature, several domains of culture, and the intricate patterns of imbrication between them. Indeed, it is important to blur widely accepted boundaries between "nature" and "culture" by coming to terms with innumerable resonances across these lines, as when the cacophony of sounds and rhythms in the Amazon jungle finds expression in Brazilian music, the quiet rhythm of waves at the seashore communicates a benign quality to your thinking at the end of the day, the roaring dissonances of a tornado send terror into your soul, a herd of cantering horses becomes insinuated into your breathing and heartbeat, troughs and swells in bodily hormonal secretions find expression in shifting moods, and the waxing and waning of cicada sounds on a summer's day carry you toward a meditative state. The dependence of capitalist economies upon natural resources and the periodic mutations of diseases from animals to human populations show how that list merely points to the tip of an iceberg. When we further recall how tactics of the self and micropolitics affect human bodily processes, we identify a yet larger series of loops and feedback loops linking nonhuman nature, human bodies, and cultural dispositions.[19]

But perhaps you are most dubious about the role of resonance and amplification in nonhuman nature. Consider "rogue waves." Destructive waves a hundred feet tall or more—sometimes as wide as a street block—have been reported by mariners for centuries. Until recently most scientists treated these stories as superstitions, despite numerous shipwrecks that remained inexplicable. Today thousands of rogue waves have been detected, even though the statistical laws previously applied to wave patterns had predicted a wave rogue only once every ten thousand years. Rogue waves often arise, as if from nowhere, when two ocean currents collide or when one current meets a storm going in the other direction. In rather unpredictable ways, a confluence can "focus wave energy," sometimes setting off another stage. At the tipping point the growth of the wave "cannot be explained by linear theory." Rather, it " 'breathes' itself up at the expense of the neighborhood waves." As another author puts it, "some small perturbation in local conditions can have a huge effect, out of proportion to the triggering cause."[20] The rogue wave is an emergent formation, involving initial volatility and self-amplification through positive feedback procesess. These waves, once established concepts of causality are altered to encompass them, help us to understand how and why the

Bermuda triangle is so dangerous, though mysteries still attend the repeated punctuation of ocean regularity by these rogues.

Or take the confluence of John Calvin, the city of Geneva as a magnet for artisans, and attempts by the Vatican and secular state powers to rein in both during the sixteenth century. There may have been considerable volatility and auto-catalytic power involved in these relations. Perhaps the city's drive to independence, the theology of Calvin, the attraction of artisans to the city, and the desire to resist Vatican control interacted until each element became incorporated to some degree into the shape of the others. When the complex reached a tipping point, new energies of self-amplification were fomented. By the time Calvin's theology was complete, proto-capitalism was established in one city, and a new artisan class was consolidated. After a point it may make little sense to separate out these "factors." Each becomes intertwined with the others to some degree, and the emergent assemblage is irreducible to the elements that entered into resonance. Welcome to Geneva.[21] Meet Calvin, the rogue theologian. I suspect that Weber was reaching for the idea of emergent causality in his exploration of imbrications between capitalism and Christianity in northern Europe, though there was perhaps not yet sufficient ferment in allied fields to enable its elaboration.

An immanent naturalist locates an element of volatility in nature, in culture, and in the imbrications between them. One thus neither places a principle of full explicability where Augustine locates mystery nor denies a place to mystery altogether, as many naturalists do. Rather, we *naturalize a place for mystery*, incorporating a modicum of intrinsic uncertainty into patterns of emergent causality. Economies of political life and cultures of political economy provide sites par excellence of emergent causality. The evangelical-capitalist resonance machine discloses one such instance in motion. That machine was not implicit in the parts from which it was forged, and the shape of each part has been altered through resonances back and forth between them. Immanent naturalism and emergent causality are two sides of the same coin, although of course it is possible for those proceeding from another problematic to forge a concept with family resemblances to this one. William James, whom we consult more closely in chapter 5, did so.

In the sphere of ethics, immanent naturalism secretes an ethic of cultivation anchored in care for this world rather than a morality of command authorized by a god, a transcendental subject, or a fictive contract between fixed agents. It is at the points of conjunction between the cultivation of care and the emergence of circumstances unanticipated by the established interpretation of formal principles that this orientation does its most noble work. We do appreciate obligation, responsibility, and judgment as secondary formations, acquiring specific shapes depending upon the extent to which, say, the constituencies involved cultivate gratitude for existence or resent existence as such. It is our refusal to confess a juridical *basis* for morality that disturbs many in the theo-juridical traditions. They would like to convict us of committing a "naturalistic fallacy," asking "How can those who place their highest faith in an abundance of life over identity *be* ethical?" We commend a bit more self-modesty to our critics at this point, calling upon them to experiment with this perspective themselves before issuing blanket critiques of it. There may be more here than they have fathomed.[22] It is well to recall that both Leibniz and Kant were shocked by how "virtuous" Epicurus and Spinoza were, even though from the perspective of each critic it would be impossible or "incoherent" to be so. Wouldn't it be noble—more ethical—to honor such commitments while exuding wonder about how they arise among those who do not confess your juridical faith? A commitment to pluralism is shallow until its participants honor a plurality of fundamental sources from which positive connections to others can be forged.

Immanent naturalism challenges the hubris of total explicability "in principle" often pursued by empiricists and rational-choice theorists; it qualifies the propensity to deep, authoritative interpretation advanced by some practitioners of interpretive theory; and it contests the power of transcendental reason pushed by descendants of the Kantian revolution. Indeed, it replaces the transcendental field of Kant with an immanent field that like it is inscrutable in detail but unlike it generates neither the "necessary postulate" of a designing, legislative, moral God nor faith in life after death.

Does immanent naturalism contradict or subvert itself by subtracting the probability of full explicability from the world that it seeks to explain (or adding an element of uncertainty to its model of explication)? Doubtless, some will say so. I propose rather that it sanctions a double-entry orientation to the paradox of political interpretation. When an inquiry is launched, investigators may act *as if* complete explanation is possible. But in a second gesture made as the inquiry proceeds, we contest the hubris invested in that regulative ideal. We do so for onto-political reasons—ontological in that the world presents an element of opacity to us, political in that such an assumption encourages noble engagements with the politics of becoming. It is in moving back and forth between the quest to explain and a confession of volatile elements exceeding this capacity that inquiry proceeds. This bifocal orientation exceeds the "fallibilism" sometimes adopted by scientists, unless that fallibilism includes within it the possibility of significant revision in established concepts of explanation, nature, and causality.

One task of students of political economy drawn to immanent naturalism is to occupy strategic junctures at which new dangers and possibilities appear, *intervening* in ways that might help to move the complex in this way rather than that, accepting some conditions to ward off others. Explanation as intervention; intervention as engaged involvement; engaged involvement as ethico-political activity, ethico-political activity informed by love of this world. Intervention, that is, involves explanation, participation, evaluation, and attachment to the world mixed into a compound not reducible to any of these concepts in its putatively pure form. We are particularly interested in exploring contexts of emergent causality, where new faiths, identities, rights, and economic practices hover on the edge of actualization, without yet being solid, real, or formed enough to be stable "objects" of inquiry.

One advantage of this orientation is that it encourages investigators to range broadly when examining the sources of an established equilibrium or an accentuation of instability. You might, in addressing threats and possibilities facing a political economy, focus on a newly activated religious movement, a new technology, climate change, a new financial instrument, a changing ethos of labor, resource depletion, a novel economic doctrine, a shift in orientations to the future by corporate or political leaders, a reckless war policy, acts of terrorism, a plague, an economic deficit, civilizational trauma, a rising state power, or any subset of these working back and forth on each other. A political economy *is* an assemblage of heterogeneous elements that have become interlocked, with some remaining relatively quiescent as others destabilize. Defenders of seventeenth-century capitalism did not need to be concerned with its contribution to a changing climate that threatened to turn against it. They were concerned about attempts by princes, churches, lords, and peasants to rein in the contract form and the profit motive.

One challenge is to engage change without reducing it to an aggregation of elements that precede it. This challenge draws some biologists, evolutionary theorists, neuroscientists, climatologists, cultural theorists, and cosmologists to the idea of emergence. But a philosophy of immanent naturalism faces another challenge too. If we participate in a universe of becomings, what makes things become consolidated into relatively stable things, selves, systems, and civilizations? How does deceleration occur to make a thing persist, a species consolidate, a regime survive, a faith perdure?[23] One point to note is that a world of becoming consists of multiple processes set on different tiers of chrono-time, with each tier periodically conjoining, colliding, or meshing with others. An atom in nuclear fission is faster than the body-brain network, which is faster than the emergence of a civilization, which is faster than species evolution, which in turn is faster than the evolution of the universe. The periodic conjoining and disjoining of relatively open systems set on different speeds and trajectories helps to explain the stabilization of particular things and systems. Moreover, we do not seek to explain *why* things persist. That question enjoins the sort of theology that we resist. We seek rather to increase knowledge of *how* things stabilize in a world of becoming.

That being said, the issue still constitutes an enigma of sorts within imma-nent naturalism. In providing a counterpoint to other modes of inquiry, we run into quandaries too. Nonetheless, in an age of acceleration in several zones of life this mode of inquiry carries an advantage. Rather than act as if the norm is equilibrium, it addresses constitutive variations in rates of accel-eration and deceleration, being and becoming, flux and stabilization, relative equilibrium and radical disequilibrium. In the contemporary world, in which speed has increased in several domains, in which therefore the gap between the slowest and fastest zones of cultural life is greater than heretofore, and in which many constituencies resent these characteristics of life as well as their positions in the scheme of inequality, it may be wise to engage a philosophy in which interconnected things and systems participate in varying degrees of disequilibrium. The challenge now becomes how to negotiate life-sustaining balances and, as we saw in chapter 2, to deepen attachments to this world, rather than to demand that the world "return" to a market, national, or civili-zational equilibrium that was never there.

Immanent naturalism reminds us that the introduction of radical disequi-librium into too many zones at once would defeat the very possibility of human life. Attention to speed and system interconnections heightens our awareness of the fragility of the earth as a rare planet hospitable to human life. A problematic that draws attention to the complex interactions between systems in various degrees of disequilibrium may be well designed to come to terms with significant challenges of the future, such as the sources and ef-fects of climate change, the volatile potentialities of capitalism, the activation of intense religious movements, and the exchanges between all three zones. Nothing in this problematic encourages us to pretend that climate simply takes care of itself. To put the same point another way, we suspect that a providential image of God and self-equilibrating theories of the market provide dangerous compensations in late modernity. What the market metaphor gives up in otherworldly compensation it takes back in a dangerously benign image of unfettered capitalism.

It would be false to this faith/philosophy to deny another consideration on its behalf: it *feels* plausible to those who adopt it, given our experience of the world, the inability of faith in divinity to move us, the sense that a providential image continues to haunt secular theories, concern about the hubris often attached to the human sciences, and worries about a spirit of dogmatism that readily becomes attached to the desire to overcome human mortality. An immanent naturalist invites more people and churches to struggle to respond without resentment to death as oblivion. We then recoil back on our faith enough to acknowledge the power of other ways of dealing with mortality and the world, soliciting alliances across distance with those who embrace lawlike or providential visions and drain those visions of a spirit of ressentiment. For a variety of sensibilities can be integrated into each vision, and the wonder of being contains the possibility of positive connections across these differences, particularly when partisans cultivate reciprocal modesty about the ability to convince others of their own creed. And when they overcome pressure to resent life itself if the others are not converted.

I hope I have said enough about this existential *creed*, comparative *considerations* on its behalf, the open-ended *method* linked to it, the *problems* to which its practitioners are drawn, the concept of *emergent causality* that it entertains, the characteristic orientation to *ethics* and *mortality* that it adopts, some *enigmas* that it confronts, and its *contestable* character to suggest lines of difference and potential connection with other problematics. Perhaps its delineation can help to loosen fixed lines of debate in the human sciences between "explanatory" and "interpretive" theory.

An Ethos of Academic Engagement

It is pertinent to see how the philosophy of immanent naturalism sketched above resonates with some Christian theologies of becoming. The orientations differ at a critical point, but they also touch across this line of difference. For instance, in *Face of the Deep: A Theology of Becoming*, Catherine Keller argues that the second verse of Genesis secretes a God who created the world by acting upon chaotic materials from "the deep" already there. She delineates, in league with a significant minority in the history of Christianity and Judaism, a theology of becoming from this base. We are "created not from nothing but from this ambiguous pattern of preconditions," and this experience can be transformed into distinctive patterns of self, sin, guilt, and responsibility.[24] Moreover, Keller recognizes that her transcendent faith touches a post-Newtoniam tradition in science close to the one I have delineated above. She agrees with complexity theorists that the universe is not in full equilibrium, that numerous entities have capacities for self-organization periodically defying human capacities for prediction, that these systems periodically interact in surprising ways, and that several nontheistic philosophers and scientists, including both Gilles Deleuze and Ilya Prigogine, speak to the theology she embraces.

I note the work of Keller in part to draw attention to its brilliance and pertinence to the human sciences, in part to open communication across that jagged line of separation between faith in transcendence and in immanence, and in part to suggest that the secular academy could learn something from the relations of agonistic respect often established between different theologies in schools of divinity and religious studies. Today some schools of religious studies appear more effective in negotiating differences across faiths within their discipline than many departments in the human sciences are in negotiating differences of method. There may be several reasons for this. But one seems particularly important. Many faculty members in religious studies now conclude that differences of religious faith are apt to persist as long as human life survives on earth. The question therefore becomes how to cultivate your own faith while responding with nobility to that diversity. Many now conclude that the methods favored by Augustine to control the play of diversity within his church are too restrictive and arbitrary, even though they were mild by comparison to those introduced by later theocracies, the Inquisition, the conquest of America, fascism, and totalitarianism.

The condition of the human sciences is rather different. Many social scientists, feeding off the hubris of secularism and the Enlightenment, feel in their bones that if their method were to triumph they would be secure in their faith and the world would become more transparent. The alternative sense is that as long as social scientists participate in the politics they interpret, a significant diversity of problematics is apt to persist. I don't mean to say that the future shape of the human sciences will correspond to the options now before us. I doubt that this will be so. Immanent naturalism, for instance, did not have an active presence on the American scene fifteen years ago. Its activation waited upon creative work in chemistry, evolutionary theory, and neuroscience, where new problems of causality, explanation, prediction, and method were encountered. And its transduction into the human sciences has required engagements with culturally oriented philosophers such as Nietzsche, Charles Peirce, Henri Bergson, William James, and Gilles Deleuze. As this option is added to the field of competitors, new contrasts, comparisons, and contests emerge.

It is true that one problematic could come to command the field for a time. But I suspect that methodological pluralism will persist in some form, unless one faction successfully grabs the reins of institutional power. To do so, it would have to align itself with other forces outside and inside the academy. Were that to occur, new factions and schisms would soon arise out of the resentments and debris that triumph promoted.

So the question arises: If method, faith, and sensibility are loosely intertwined, and no single problematic has yet inspired all reasonable parties, what is the most admirable ethos to negotiate between contending problematics in the academy? And how is that ethos to be fostered among those who are *also* partisans to these very disputes? The problem of pluralism in the academy, in short, mirrors the problem of pluralism in the larger world.

The first thing is to articulate comparatively the problematic that you support with as much energy and skill as you can marshal, pressing others to take it seriously as a possibility, while attending to the relations between faith, method, and substance in it. Here the devil is in the details, more than in glosses of global relations between generic types. The second thing is to come to terms publicly with the *contestability* in the eyes of others (and perhaps even part of yourself) of your own problematic. William James, who as a "radical empiricist" anticipates some themes adumbrated here under the heading of "immanent naturalism," is exemplary on these counts. After presenting a strong case in favor of treating the universe as "unfinished" and "pluralistic," after making it clear that the image he embraces challenges the sufficiency of both rationalism and logical empiricism, James keeps a window open to these competitors even as he insists that his own doctrine may be true. "On that possibility," he says, "I do insist."[25]

I agree with James. I would love to convert more Christians and secular humanists to immanent naturalism. But I accept the probability that many will continue to resist conversion. Besides, the elements involved in conversion or steadfastness are too multiple and interwoven to be under the full control of any individual or group. Next, it is pertinent to work on my regret that you do not convert, so that this disappointment does not become transfigured into resentment against you for being obstinate or against the world for being filled with so much diversity. Through all this, I insist with James that unless you do a hell of a lot better job than you and others have done so far, immanent naturalism remains a possibility to which it is reasonable for many to be attached. I invite you to forge a relation of agonistic respect with us, even while each of us tries, within reasonable constraints, to convert the other. Who knows, one of us may blink, as Augustine did when he converted from a flirtation with Epicureanism to Manicheanism, and later from Manicheanism to the Trinity. Had he engaged the Greek tragic tradition, he might have blinked again.

If contending partisans admit that faith, method, problem, sensibility, and findings are loosely bound together, if we reciprocally concede that any single problematic is unlikely to marshal conclusive evidence in its favor in the near future, if we acknowledge that a currently unknown problematic may emerge to scramble the terms of debate again, and if we work upon ourselves to subdue resentment of the world for harboring these uncertainties, the human sciences may forge a new ethos of generosity and forbearance. This would be an important achievement. For just as Christian witness helps to inspire new converts, the institutionalization of an ethos of pluralism in the academy could help to inspire its expansion into other zones. Change proceeds by attraction, exemplification, and inspiration as well as by argument, coercion, power, and intransigence, which never subsist alone.

What kind of practitioner is equipped to come to terms affirmatively with the persistent plurality of the human sciences? I admit to being biased on that question. My hunch is that those who cultivate modesty about our place in the universe and our capacity to control natural-cultural processes are well placed to do so, particularly those who recognize an element of fecundity in forces of nature such as stem cells, species evolution, hurricanes, wetlands, and various animal species. These two orientations help to deflate the hubris of the human animal and to enhance our appreciation of being densely implicated in multiple systems that range beyond our sphere of control.

The quest for secular compensation may reside in the insistence that to the extent the world is not designed for us by a loving god it *must* be susceptible to the ardent human desire for control. The world *must* be for us in *this* or *that* way. Do these two demands disclose a link between traditions that often take themselves to be at odds? Again, whence comes *either* "must"?

It is timely for more of us to contest both existential demands together. Nietzsche—an immanent naturalist who diagnosed the "advent of nihilism" accompanying the crisis in Christendom *and* the nineteenth-century image of science—has something to say about the kind of practitioner needed today: "Who will prove to be the strongest in the course of this? The most moderate; those who do not require any extreme article of faith; those who not only concede but love a fair amount of accidents and nonsense; those who can think of man with a considerable reduction of his value without becoming small and weak on that account."[26]

To love a fair amount of accidents and nonsense, while struggling for a global equilibrium that supports human life with decency. That's a noble combination.

CHAPTER FOUR

IS ECO-EGALITARIAN CAPITALISM POSSIBLE?

The Paradox of Consumption

In thinking about an egalitarian economy I do not focus strictly on income distribution. That is because changes in the general infrastructure of consumption could both improve the welfare of people at the lower end of the income hierarchy and encourage middle-income citizens to oppose politically steep income differentials. So a broader definition is needed: an egalitarian economy is one in which those at lower income levels participate in the good life rendered possible by the established infrastructure of consumption, including (within "the infrastructure") state and social supports for modes of housing, education, health care, travel, cultural experience, waste disposal, and retirement. Thus an infrastructure of consumption in which public provision of roads, road maintenance, traffic lights, and traffic policing is costly, while it is also difficult for low-income citizens to buy, maintain, and insure cars, contributes to inequality. One built around a more even mix of cars, mass transit, bicycles, trains, trolleys, and buses improves general access. By an ecologically sound economy I mean one in which climate change is reversed; soil, air, and water pollution are curtailed; the food system promotes health; waste disposal systems are organized around recycling; and nonrenewable sources of energy are increasingly replaced by renewable modes.

Marxists often contend that a capitalist system can be neither egalitarian nor ecological.[1] This is surely correct in the most radical sense. But that does not detract from the need to pursue an interim future in which considerable progress is made on both fronts. Neoliberal economists, on the other hand, seldom give priority to the eco-egalitarian objective, with the most radical claiming that its pursuit is counterproductive and grounded in irrational envy. Those on the right edge of neoliberalism contend that free-market growth will enable those in the bottom tier tomorrow to enjoy amenities exceeding those enjoyed by the middle tier today.[2] They see the role of the state in the same limited way that Milton Friedman did in 1993: "to defend the nation against foreign enemies, to prevent coercion of some individuals by others, to provide a means of deciding upon our rules, and to adjudicate disputes."[3] They then interpret these strictures in narrow terms because they find the market to contain incredible powers of self-equilibration in support of the general interest. At least by comparison to the image of capitalist volatility endorsed here, they incorporate a providential assumption into their reading of the market. Friedman thought that the problems of crime, homelessness, family values, medical care and travel congestion could be solved by taking the government out of those arenas and letting the market handle them. Keynesians care more about equality within capitalism; but they approach it through a combination of state management of growth, progressive taxation, a high minimum wage, and welfare for those displaced by market competition.

The approach supported here starts a bit differently. You first try to *imagine* an interim future in which substantial progress has been made on both fronts within capitalism, broadly defined. The importance of projecting an *interim* future is in part tied to our inability in a world of becoming to imagine constructively beyond an interim horizon, in part to the urgent need to relieve the suffering of several constituencies soon, and in part to the short time left to come to terms with the devastating potential of global warming. You then work back from that point to specific reforms that could actualize the image. But why participate in *visualization* at all? You do so because imaging is ubiquitous and unavoidable in thought, and if negative images are not countered by positive visualizations the creative potential of thought and action is stifled.

Others may not see things this way. They may think that imaging is unimportant or goofy; only rigorous critique is needed. Elise Boulding, however, takes visualization seriously. She challenges implicit images already extant with alternatives that are productive, explicit, and vivid. She has organized workshops in which participants imagine a positive future no more than twenty years away. With such a time horizon, she says, interim visualizations can be linked, through discussion and analysis, to strategies to move from here to there, even if surprising events and unexpected coalitions may well pull you back to the drawing board before the period in question passes. It is important to achieve high visual intensity, so that the images we form both activate creative thinking and filter into affective dispositions to action. In some of Boulding's workshops participants found themselves imagining a green world with clear, blue oceans. I am drawn to the power of that image too. I also visualize walking in Copenhagen during a drizzly morning, on a street sprawling with pedestrians, riders traveling on wide bike lanes, considerable bus traffic, and small cars moving through a city where poverty and crime are present but not rampant. Copenhagen sets an interim image for me; it is important to an American living in a city where poverty is widespread, many African Americans are blocked from the good life generally available, and ecological concerns are far down the list of public priorities.

Recent work in neuroscience supports the importance of positive imaging. The discovery of "mirror neurons" distributed unevenly throughout the brain already defeats the assumption of the isolated agent of self-interest assumed by many economists. This research shows how the conduct of others is incorporated into the development of our skills, habits, emotions, interests, identifications, and aspirations from the very start. Mirror neurons are activated when you observe others doing something and when you yourself visualize accomplishing something while not yet engaged in the activity.[4] As when a basketball coach has his players lie on the floor before a big game and visualize making free throws. Phil Jackson did that before a NBA championship game with a team of notoriously bad free-throw shooters, with salutary effect.

The single most important effect of positive visualization is the effect it has on our energy to act militantly in support of the interim future visualized. Positive imaging about the economy is indispensable during a time when electoral campaigns, economic practices, media reports, church sermons, and governmental decisions foster national insecurity and consumption practices that are self-defeating for the economy as a whole.[5]

Fred Hirsch may have been a practitioner of imaging. He seems to have imagined an alternative organization of consumption; such an imaginary allowed him to better understand the logic of "positional goods" in capitalism today. His book *The Social Limits to Growth* made a minor splash when it appeared in 1977. The splash was short-lived, however. Hirsch's focus on the paradox of consumption in a capitalist economy lacked the revolutionary punch of Marxism; it did not speak immediately to low- and middle-income constituencies eager to increase their income within the existing scheme of consumption; and its focus on irrationalities of consumption was anathema to neoliberal economists, corporate advertisers, and business élites, as well to as many young adults tantalized by the prospect of accumulating vast wealth.

It also held little interest for the evangelical right, though they were politically quiescent at the time.

Hirsch goes some distance in explaining why eco-egalitarianism is so hard to promote today. His analysis, joined to a positive imagination, could also help to sow the seed of a counter-movement, a movement that pursues an eco-egalitarian agenda *initially* by reconstructing the social infrastructure of consumption. I will address salient themes in Hirsch's book. I will also draw selectively upon a complementary account advanced by Michael Best and me in *The Politicized Economy*, adjusting and revising both accounts to fit the circumstances of today.[6]

The paradox of consumption can be stated briefly. When a market economy works without the appropriate ethos and public regulation, it focuses purchases around goods and services that provide the most value to consumers if they are not also attained by a majority in the same system. As such goods and services proliferate, however, they intensify the isolation of consumers' desires from long-term collective effects, amplify the *need* of those at the lower and middle rungs of the income scale to attain the very goods whose relative value has started to decline through proliferation, and decrease the willingness of all classes to address poverty or protect the collective future. How does this work? Here are a couple of formulations by Hirsch:

> Social scarcity is a central concept in this analysis. It expresses the idea that the good things of life are restricted not only by physical limitations of producing them but also by absorptive limits on their use. Where the social environment has a restricted capacity for extending use without quality deterioration, it imposes social limits to consumption. More specifically, the limit is imposed on satisfactions that depend not on the product or facility in isolation but on the surrounding conditions of use.
>
> Strictly speaking, our existing concept of economic output is appropriate only for truly private goods, having no element of interdependence between consumption by different individuals.
>
> The choice facing the individual in a market or market type transaction, in the positional sector . . . always appears more attractive than it turns out to be after others have exercised their choice.[7]

The key phrase in Hirsch's lexicon is "positional goods." A positional good is one that satisfies the consumer at the initial stage but declines in value as its use is extended. The social effect of extending a positional good to the larger populace is comparable to what happens when people stand on their toes to see a speaker at a rally. It works at first. But when some people do it, the view of others is blocked unless they do it too. Once everyone does it, no one's view is that good anymore; and now all grow tired of standing on their toes. The whole crowd is worse off than before. The parallel to positional goods is close but not perfect; it gets closer when you factor in initial differences in height.

A micro-example of a positional good is orthodontic braces. When the first generation of upper-income children receive them they benefit from the relative improvement in their appearance. Soon those at the next income level make the same purchase, to increase their relative standing. Once a tipping point is reached, those with braces see the relative value of braces decline, while those who cannot afford braces find that with their teeth unstraightened their smiles are even less attractive than before. Low-income parents now face considerable pressure to buy braces, even if they cannot afford them. When this pressure is joined to the pressure to acquire numerous other positional goods, the political and economic pressure to increase the absolute income level of each constituency grows, and public willingness to produce more widely available goods and services declines.

Another example of a positional good is coaching for SATS and GREs. The generalization of this good increases the expense to everyone without leaving anyone in the superior position envisaged when the first group enrolled. The relative disadvantage to students unable to afford the program increases. Other examples at a comparably minor level of importance include cosmetic surgery for the eyes, nose, and face, liposuction, high-end clothing, Viagra, exotic facial creams, air purification systems, cell phones, portable computers, professional lawn maintenance, central air conditioning, first-class air travel, private gyms, exercise trainers, technologically advanced medical care, and nannies. Many of these goods and services were either absent or much less prevalent when Hirsch's book appeared in 1977.

These, again, are relatively mundane examples, even though their effects can pile up. Unfortunately, however, more fundamental goods such as private education, vehicle design, suburban living, air travel, vacation retreats, health care, private health insurance, and home security systems participate in the same logic, if to varying degrees. Take the SUV, a vehicle whose widespread use Hirsch could hardly have imagined in the 1970s. It was introduced for passenger use by corporations in the United States under the category of a "light truck" to evade the emission, safety, and fuel standards that had recently been set for cars. The romance with it included the fantasy, reinforced by TV advertising, of driving off road once or twice a year to isolated places where cars with low axles could not go.[8] The proliferation of suvs increased fuel consumption, emissions, the average cost of family vehicles, and the risk of rollovers, as well as obstructing the visibility of those who drove cars. Because of the weight and high bumpers of suvs, car drivers were also placed at greater risk of injury and increasingly pressured to buy suvs or large cars as a defensive measure.

The spread of positional goods creates new pressures for public expenditure. In the case of suvs these public expenditures included energy subsidies, increased military expenditures to maintain the supply of foreign oil, and collective health costs caused by more accidents and higher pollution levels. Positional goods also increase the need to purchase what Hirsch calls "defensive goods": "private expenditures that are induced as an offset to some deterioration in the individual's position."[9] Defensive goods include, in this instance, more expensive auto insurance, gasoline, and cars (because of their greater size and need for door reinforcements). In a related area of defensive expenditures, the rapidly escalating cost of house insurance on the East Coast is traceable, according to the insurance companies themselves, to new levels of damage created by more intense storms and floods, which in turn are entangled in the collective refusal to address global warming.

The introduction of a new defensive good, interestingly, adds to the domestic national product, even though it does not add to net consumer satisfaction. Other examples of defensive goods include increasingly elaborate security measures (from simple locks, to complex locks, to security systems, to private security forces and neighborhood watch groups); organic produce (as conventional produce becomes less safe); health clubs (in place of unusable public parks); bottled water (as urban water systems are contaminated); greater use of day care (necessary at a time when most families need to have two breadwinners, and therefore two cars); more expensive insurance policies in several domains of life (to adjust to an increasingly litigious society); and greater amounts of time and money invested in pursuing pristine suburban homes of the sort that draw affluent families further and further from city centers.

An array of positional and defensive goods forms an interdependent complex, as when suburban life binds families to two vehicles, makes it imperative to drive the kids everywhere, promotes pressure for state freeway construction, and generates higher insurance costs. So positional goods, once widely extended, become institutionally entrenched and politically protected. After the supporting legislation, public exemptions, and use of suvs was generalized, pressure on the state to protect low gasoline prices intensified. And public commitment to improving vehicle mileage, exploring alternative fuels, subsidizing hybrids, and strengthening emissions standards dissipated. Until 2006, an excellent way to lose an election in a suburban area would have been to call for new regulations in the production and use of suvs. The suv even became a symbol of American patriotism. Several of these themes can be heard in a statement by the founder of the International Hummer Owners Group (IHOG): "The H2 is an American icon . . . It's a symbol of what we all hold so dearly above all else, the fact we have the freedom of choice, the freedom of happiness, the freedom of adventure and discovery, and the ultimate freedom of expression. Those who deface a Hummer in words or deeds . . . deface the American flag and what it stands for."[10] While writing this chapter (June 2006), I watched a tv ad in which a mother is upset with another mother who lets a child jump in front of hers to ride the playground slide. The next scene shows the upset mother at a car dealer, driving off with a look of smug entitlement in a Hummer with a mile-high bumper. A corollary ad aimed at men ends with the statement, "Take back your manhood." Hummer sells aggression and bellicose resistance toward efforts to incorporate care for the collective future into private consumption decisions and state consumption policies. It is not that the state stays out of consumption in the case of suvs and intervenes in the case of hybrids. It is involved up to its neck in both, just in different ways.

Unlike Hirsch, I do not suggest that the implicit coalition between producers, state officials, and consumers to extend positional goods is driven simply by innocent individual desire, unmindful of its collective and distributive effects. Nor do the inducements of advertising and the entrenchment of new economic interests explain it entirely, though each plays a role. Another cause is the role that tv dramas, films, and situation comedies now play in helping to set reference groups. These shows expand the gap between the income position of many and the consumption reference groups selected for emulation. Juliet Schor has shown how the choice of reference groups has shifted upward; this shift, we can add, contributes to the proliferation of positional goods, the growth of credit card debt, an increase in bankruptcies. and the concomitant need for more defensive goods.[11] These effects are exacerbated in turn, as more and more people bind their consumption habits to the display of their personal identities to others. All these elements together create a spiral, one difficult to escape by individual, local, and associational actions alone.

These pressures are amplified by a political ethos of militant opposition to reform, one that emerges as middle-income people trying to make ends meet resist taxes to support low-income people trying even harder. This ethos of aggressive resistance grows in part out of the large gap between the high-end reference groups that the media encourage and the actual consumption possibilities available to numerous constituencies. This attitude can harden into an inflated sense of natural entitlement by some members of the upper and upper middle classes. That effect is discernible in the equation between SUVs and patriotism stated by the president of IHOG, and in the ads reviewed above. The couriers of the ethos become hostile to those outside their class, suburb, town, or ethnic group and unconcerned about the cumulative effects of their own practices upon the collective future. Does it go further? Do SUV producers and consumers sometimes bind themselves to a vision of unfettered, self-equilibrating markets *in order* to foster a sense of entitlement and evade engagement with the future, collective effects of current patterns of consumption? It would not be surprising. The innocence that Hirsch discerned in the 1970s has given ground today to a more aggressive stance, in which market ideology becomes a commodity purchased to ignore the adverse, aggregative effects of consumer selections, narrow corporate decisions, proliferating positional and defensive goods, and state support for all of them. To put the point more politely, there is resonance between public commitment to the established infrastructure of consumption, the economic ideology embraced by many, and the intensity with which financial media reporters brush off concerns about inequality and the future.

That is why I cannot entirely embrace Hirsch's resolution. Writing in the 1970s, he thought that individual product desires had lost contact with traditional religious (meaning Christian) moorings and restraints that previously tied them to collective concerns. A renewal of "the religious tradition" was crucial, in his view, even as Hirsch doubted that this renewal would actually occur in places such as the United States. In this respect his thinking inverts that of many secular economists. While they separate "the economy" from the spiritual ethos that inhabits it, Hirsch thinks that the old system had a positive ethos and that the new one operates autonomously. He wants to reinstate what has been lost. To me, however, there is no economy without an ethos—or several contending orientations—inhabiting it. And Christianity, as we have seen, is a many-splendored thing.

A shift is definitely needed in the spiritual ethos that inhabits investment practices, the work ethic, personal identities, consumption priorities, the infrastructure of consumption, political ideology, military policy, police codes, church regimes, local movements, voluntary associations, scientific research, media programming, and state mandates. But not a generic "return" to the Christian tradition, some aspects of which are at odds with contemporary needs and others of which speak to them.[12] What is required is a significant reconfiguration of the ethos of economic life, involving a new pattern of interplay between church sermons, state actions, electoral shifts, workers' movements, consumption activism, media exposés, and private investment decisions.

I will contend in chapter 5 that it is dangerous to hitch a capitalist economy to the providential image of history manifest in some versions of Christianity. Market apologists often do that implicitly; publicists of a divine injunction in favor of unfettered markets do so explicitly. Such a link between markets and providence initially assumes that things will take care of themselves as long as the system is not interrupted much by state regulation and receives large state subsidies. But when things turn sour, supporters of the equation can easily turn ugly. The equation between markets and providence fosters denial and can easily devolve into aggressive fatalism. This tendency is reflected in stories on Fox News that previously denied global warming and now assert that it is too late to do anything about it.

Back to Hirsch. He says that in a society organized around the generalization of positional goods those with low incomes face a double disadvantage. They are excluded from the type of good around which the infrastructure of consumption is organized, and the consumers above them now push for tax reductions so as to afford the positional-defensive goods complex that has been adopted. Few are ready to pay for public education after they have been pressed to place their own kids in private schools. The opportunities of low-income people are thus squeezed while the willingness of middle- and high-income people to support public programs oriented to the collective future is blunted. And as we have already suggested, those with high incomes find it easiest to square their economic priorities in these circumstances with their social conscience if they embrace a market vision of economic life. They receive an updated version of this message every day from Lawrence Kudlow's financial report on CNBC.

What are the ecological implications of generalized positional and defensive goods? The same. In a political economy organized around positional and defensive goods there is considerable pressure to ignore ecological damage. One way to legitimize that imbalance is to deny that current modes of consumption pose risks to the future, by claiming that climate change is a wild theory advanced by only a few wacky scientists or that market solutions will emerge automatically before the issue becomes intractable.

The collective cost is high. According to James Gustave Speth, environmental activist and dean of the School of Forestry and Environmental Studies at Yale, the minimal probable rise in sea level in the twenty-first century will be about three meters if current world production and emission projections are maintained, while the maximum risk is much higher. Even at the lower level, "the rise could be extremely serious, undermining coastal ecosystems, communities and livelihoods. In the United States, Florida and Louisiana are especially vulnerable. In Bangladesh, seventeen million people live fewer than three feet above sea level. Small island nations in the Pacific and Indian Oceans are threatened, as is the Netherlands, where half the population lives below sea level."[13] And the probable effects on the world supply of water for drinking and crops are also severe.

Climate change research is going through a rapid series of adjustments, and the points summarized above may well be out of date by the time this book appears. For example, recent research into stratospheric feedback to atmospheric conditions indicates that the shifts may be more radical and arrive sooner than earlier anticipated. According to Fred Pearce, "As greenhouse gases cool the stratosphere, this cooling alters energy distribution within so as to strengthen stratospheric winds. In particular . . . the stratospheric jet, which swirls around the arctic each winter, picks up speed . . . In this way, a stratospheric feedback is amplifying global warming . . . It is a . . . startling, and, until recently, entirely unexpected feedback."[14] Speth reports that conflicts between North and South and between poor and rich nations seriously obstruct efforts to forestall these global effects. He adds, however, that "if there is one country that bears the most responsibility for the lack of progress on international environmental issues, it is the United States."[15]

Speth links foot dragging to American arrogance and "exceptionalism"; he ties both to wasteful modes of production and consumption. But by explaining American consumption patterns primarily through the power of TV advertising—as his hero John Kenneth Galbraith had done before him—he ignores the paradox of consumption that grips a rich, capitalist country once positional goods have become entrenched in several zones. The paradox of consumption creates multiple barriers to the pursuit of ecological and egalitarian objectives. Its effects become more dangerous yet when the analysis of consumption is tied to a providential image of a self-equilibrating market. The sunny side of this image is blind optimism; its dark side is fatalism after optimism has been dashed; its black side is an ethos of revenge seeking vulnerable targets upon whom to focus responsibility for the lack of fit between a market system assumed to be providential and the experience of history.

Exclusive and Inclusive Goods

Hirsch discerns part of the dynamism between a pattern of consumption, inequality, and a dismissive orientation to the future. But his theory needs another amendment. To proceed down this trail, let's establish a schema that sorts out positional goods with less profound effects upon inequality and planetary ecology from those that have the most serious effects. We will build into the equation the dependence of each mode of consumption upon a dense social infrastructure to maintain and extend itself. An economic culture organized around the primacy of private auto use, for instance, requires massive programs to build and maintain roads and expressways, staff police departments, and pay the hospital costs of uninsured victims of accidents; it also sets up political resistance to expanding rail, bus, and subway systems, as well as bike lanes that would allow low- and middle-income people to ride to school, work, and leisure activities while reducing collective fuel and health costs. A health care system built around private fee payments and medical insurance linked to relatively high-income jobs shifts to public hospitals a lot of costs incurred by poor people and the temporarily unemployed. Similar points could be made about public subsidies to private schools and colleges, the skewed priorities of private philanthropy, the power of right-wing think tanks funded by tax-deductible gifts from the rich, the formation of suburbs, the burgeoning criminal justice, pollution, safety, and welfare costs created by national neglect of the inner city, and the suffering that this last mode of neglect imposes upon inner-city residents.

With this background we can define the differences between *exclusive* and *inclusive* product types. An exclusive mode of consumption in any product domain has the following features. Its generalization from the upper to lower middle class (1) decreases the private value of the good or service to those who initially received it; (2) increases the private costs of its use as it is extended to new constituencies; (3) accentuates adverse future costs in terms of sustainability and egalitarian objectives; and (4) imposes heavy costs upon the state to create and maintain its supporting infrastructure. As exclusive goods are generalized, they increase pressure on the household budgets of lower- and middle-income families; they discount costs to future generations; and they increase resistance to collective action to produce, support, and maintain inclusive modes of consumption. An inclusive good in any product or service domain reverses these pressures. Its private value is retained or increased as it is generalized; its unit costs of public maintenance are stabilized or reduced as it is extended; its generalization supports ecological and egalitarian objectives; and its generalization decreases the collective burden that the present imposes upon future generations.

It is not that every product alternative in each domain fares equally well or poorly on all four criteria. But the eco-egalitarian goal is to promote product forms in the basic sectors of life that perform well on several criteria. To introduce the schema outlined above is not to suggest that all positional goods should be eliminated now or in the future. In an economy where consumption practices also mark differences in age, culture, class identification, religious affiliation, and life style, positional goods that do not impinge severely upon eco-egalitarian objectives should be maintained. These are light on the register of exclusive goods because they do not weigh so heavily upon the burdens of the future and the comparative ability of people to participate in the common life available. Religious modes of attire and jewelry, housing choices (up to a point), styles and colors of cars, beauty products, entertainment choices, and so on must manifest considerable variety if the values of a pluralist culture are to find ample expression. Again, the key to an egalitarian practice of consumption is to make it possible for low- and middle-income individuals, couples, and families to make ends meet while participating in practices of education, travel, housing, medical care, job security, and retirement supported by the public infrastructure of consumption.

Another proviso is needed. Reform of the infrastructure of essential consumption must start from the system now in operation, revising and reforming it to render it more inclusive and sustainable. The reforms needed in Japan differ from those needed in the United States, and each of these differs from those needed in Denmark or China. That MacDonald's in Denmark is legally mandated to restrict trans fats in its hamburgers while the trans-fat level from the same company remains very high in the United States means that MacDonald's poses less severe health and medical costs there than here, so the starting point in this product-company domain differs in each place. The idea is to modify the existing infrastructure of consumption to *launch* an eco-egalitarian trajectory in each domain.

We reserve for later the following questions: What else besides a shift in the structure of consumption is needed to foster eco-egalitarianism? At what point does an eco-egalitarian economy stop being capitalist because it is eco-egalitarian? To what extent does successful reform of a state territorial economy require reform in the global system to which it is tied by a thousand forces, threads, and pulleys? For now, we merely assert that the initial changes to be supported here are consistent with a state organized primarily around production for profit, a growth agenda, the commodity form, a fair degree of market competition, and the contractual system of work. With these provisos, consider changes in the established infrastructure of consumption that could incline the economy of the United States in a more eco-egalitarian direction.

1. COMMUTING AND TRAVEL. Auto makers in the United States are in steep decline, partly because of health insurance costs and the large number of retired employees, but also because of the companies' refusal for decades to produce cost-effective, ecologically sound vehicles. The state could stem the decline by subsidizing low-emission, high-mileage hybrid cars and electric vehicles, while setting high rates on gas-guzzling, unsafe, and high-emission vehicles.[16] Turning to a single-payer health care system would help the dying American auto industry to compete in the world market too, creating more decent jobs for high school graduates. Following the model of cooperation between federal and state governments during construction of the national expressway system, the state could subsidize the construction of rapid transit systems between large cities that are, say, no more than 350 miles apart. This system of subsidies would include not only New York to Washington but Detroit to Chicago, Cleveland to Pittsburgh, Kansas City to St. Louis, and Dallas to Houston and would take pressure off crowded auto and air systems currently subsidized so highly. It could provide federal grants to help finance rapid transit systems within large cities and to assist in constructing bike trails and lanes in cities, towns, and suburbs, linking them so that bike commuting could become more common and urban adventurers could take cycling vacations. In each of these instances the immediate benefit to the environment and lower-income consumers would be doubled by the provision of good jobs to high school graduates currently compelled to take low-income jobs with minimal benefits in the service sector. The state could also introduce and publicize low-cost auto insurance to compete with private insurers, who would be pressured to increase coverage and reduce charges. Additionally, a cross-state movement could be launched to encourage other

countries to tax imports from the United States whose production promotes global warming. This tax would offset the implicit subsidy that the American state now gives to those products by allowing the collective costs to be distributed to the world and the future.[17]

2. HEALTH CARE. The United States could move to a single-payer health care system in which care is guaranteed for every resident. If the experience in other countries is a sound test, general health care would improve, unit care costs would be reduced, the indirect public costs created by emergency room treatment of uninsured patients would be curtailed, and preventive health care would be emphasized to reduce obesity, diabetes, cancer, and heart disease. Private payments to participate in the plan could be adjusted to income levels. High-income citizens who failed to participate in the collective plan could be assessed a compensatory fee to cover the cost of their free ride upon a system that improves the health of the country and curtails the collective costs currently imposed by the epidemics listed above.

3. FOOD SUPPLY AND DIET. The production, sale, and purchase of unhealthy food could be taxed more highly, to make those who produce and buy it contribute to defraying the horrendous public health effects generated and to encourage the production and purchase of healthy food. Public education programs and product labeling could be improved greatly. The United States could follow the lead of other countries in banning fast food advertisements from children's programming, and it could also dramatize the health effects upon adults of numerous food products on the market today. On the other side of the equation, producers of organic produce, which promotes dietary health while taxing the soil and environment less intensively, could receive positive tax incentives. The long term effect of these programs would be to improve the health of low-income citizens, relieve medical costs now borne by them and the state, and reduce strains on the local and planetary ecology.

4. THE POWER GRID AND WASTE DISPOSAL. Public subsidies could be provided for the production of wind, water, solar, and geothermal power, ecologically sound production of ethanol, and other systems. Countries such as Germany, Denmark, and Brazil have made impressive strides in these directions. The effect of such an effort on the military budget would also be real, since dependence on foreign oil in unstable regions would be reduced. These subsidies, in conjunction with the other changes listed above, would reduce the

costs to consumers of defensive goods such as homeowners insurance, air conditioning, air filtration, and medical costs for pulmonary diseases. Some of these savings could be poured into other state subsidy efforts. Companies that produce products with high disposal costs currently absorbed by cities and states could be required either to change the composition of the product, arrange for ecologically sound disposal when the product life is over, or pay a disposal fee to the city or state. The current system of energy production, consumption, and waste disposal is already subsidized by the state in numerous ways; the point is to shift the direction of those subsidies.

5. HOME MORTGAGES AND GREEN EFFICIENCY. Home and apartment construction that meets high standards of environmental safety, low energy use, water conservation, and safe lawn care could be rewarded by direct tax incentives and expanded mortgage interest deductions. The costs to the state treasury created by these subsidies could be compensated by imposing a limit on the deductibility of mortgage interest for older houses, owned by people above a reasonable income threshold, unless green expenditures are made and by eliminating interest deductions outright on all second homes, a law that would also have a salutary effect on existing income differentials. The United States could also adopt a program like the one in Japan, where the government identifies the company in each product domain that achieves the greatest energy efficiency, and then sets this company's efficiency level as the standard that all companies in the domain must achieve within a short time.[18]

Consumers and home builders can contribute directly. The U.S. Green Building Council has a checklist of products and designs to build green houses.[19] They include recommendations for site selection, landscaping, grey waters, irrigation, high-efficiency toilets, faucets, furnaces, and refrigerators, heat recovery, building materials, insulation, and lighting. The production and sale of green homes reduce energy use and greenhouse gases, and encourage the news media to publicize and the state to subsidize eco-wise construction.

6. EDUCATION. Public education forms the backbone of thoughtful citizenship, inclusive cultural participation, and effective economic performance. To the extent that the scope and quality of public education are enhanced, low-income families participate more actively in the larger culture and the differential advantages created by private education are reduced, as are the high costs imposed upon the budgets of middle-class families to escape weak

public schools. Significantly increased federal support for city schools is imperative. The long-term economic effect will be to draw diverse groups back to the city, lift the life prospects of inner-city youth, reduce urban crime and its spread to the suburbs, and slow the rising costs of policing, prison construction, and inmate control. It would spur the economy, because the city is the place where many creative and productive economic experiments occur.

When you remember that every form of capitalism in history has included a large state component, the preliminary reforms listed above retain the basic capitalist axiomatic. They also begin to reconstitute modes of consumption critical to the welfare of low-income citizens, to enhance connections across classes and races, and to reduce the collective burdens that today's economy imposes upon the future. These reforms, taken together, launch eco-egalitarianism within capitalism. But they merely provide a start.

Institutional Reform and Microeconomic Experiments

Such initiatives could inspire a productive political spiral, enabling the introduction of additional actions. What could these be? They certainly include the traditional social democratic agenda of a high minimum wage, a more steeply progressive income tax, and a stiff inheritance tax on high-end estates. But another reform is needed, one which may require a preliminary shift in the infrastructure of consumption to make political consideration of it feasible. It is concerted social pressure and effective state policies to establish ceilings at the high end of the income scale. To the extent the income hierarchy remains steep, the wealthy retain the motivation and means to exacerbate collective problems while devising private escapes from them, setting off new spirals of competition for positional goods and creating the need for expensive defensive goods that strain the budgets of ordinary consumers.

How to pursue this goal? Experimentation is needed. One strategy could be to set a target range between the highest and lowest income levels for each sector of the economy, linking that range initially to those operative in each domain in capitalist countries such as Canada, Denmark, or Japan. Or, more radically, bringing it closer to flatter income curves in one of the microeconomic experiments to be discussed below. Once a target differential is set, corporations could be given incentives and penalties to meet it. Thus American auto companies—currently struggling in the global market because of a history of irrational priorities and unwise state subsidies—could be given research grants and tax breaks to produce energy-efficient vehicles and reduce the gap between the highest-paid and lowest-paid employees. Public and private universities could be pressed, through pressure from students, faculty, parents, and legislators, to reduce the salaries of presidents and coaches while lifting maintenance staffs to a living wage. One upshot of the preceding account of exclusive and inclusive goods, by the way, is that admirable struggles to promote a "living wage" for those at the bottom of the income hierarchy place the beneficiaries on a squirrel wheel unless the infrastructure of consumption is reformed and effective income ceilings are promoted.

Reducing the differential between the lowest- and highest-paid employees is as important strategically as it is difficult to accomplish. Success, for instance, could spur new patterns of investment, political pressure to reform the infrastructure of consumption, the proliferation of cooperatives, and other creative experiments with the property form. But resistance to this sort of change is intense, in part because of the widespread view that market competition is solely responsible for the size of high-end salaries. To counter that idea it is critical to show, through comparisons with successful micro-experiments, how unnecessary and counterproductive to everyone except the superrich the existing distribution of wealth is in the United States. It is also necessary to disrupt a popular chain of associations between the creative power of God, His mundane expression in entrepreneurial life, and the automatic justice of the unregulated market. Another way of putting this is to say that the evangelical-capitalist resonance machine must be contested on every front if reforms are to lift off.

In some respects, Denmark sets a decent, interim standard, though its limits are also real. It is a capitalist country with "one of the most rapidly growing economies . . . and one of the most equal societies in the world in terms of income distribution," providing a positive contrast to the American model.[20] Its policies of "flexicurity" are worth noting. It adopts neither the sticky labor markets typical of many countries in Europe nor the policy of periodic dismissals followed by unemployment and lower-paying jobs in the United States. It combines market responsiveness with a strong social safety net and employer-funded state programs of worker retraining to keep pace with innovation.[21] Denmark also shows signs of chauvinism, however, during a time when a Muslim minority, including many low-income families, seeks active participation in its way of life.[22] This example reminds us that consumption reform, the reduction of inequality, and a decent safety net do not suffice to overcome a bellicose ethos. But they help to do so, if they are complemented by micropolitical work in churches, schools, families, workplaces, localities, and electoral campaigns to integrate care for the future and the diversity of being into the mores of cultural life.

Some neoliberals may say that specific features of Danish culture make its work and incomes programs possible. Yes, precisely. But it is not that "culture" plays a role in Denmark while American capitalism is pure and untainted by culture. As I have been arguing, there is no such thing as pure capitalism: its financial, investment, profit, work, educational, distributive, consumption, ecological, and state practices are always infused with an ethos, organized through the understandings of the populace, propelled by the relative power of multiple constituencies, refracted through state laws, and embodied in the habits and presumptions of its participants. The United States desperately needs to refashion its governing ethos of capitalism again, as it has at other times in its past. It will take changes on multiple levels and sites to turn things around.

Income ceiling targets with real bite would support the consumption reforms presented earlier. They do so by making more people feel squeezed by the growth of defensive expenditures and more amenable to collective responses to these collective issues. But is it "structurally" possible to reduce the range between the lowest and highest incomes? Or to reorganize the infrastructure of consumption? Yes, it is. Demonstration projects already in operation reveal these possibilities, as they also provide valuable testing grounds for perfecting them. They remain, however, below the radar of financial news reports on TV, neoliberal economic theory, and—to some extent—Marxist theory.

Take the Mondragon experiment, started in the Basque country of Spain in the 1950s and still going strong. It was inspired by a Catholic priest before the Vatican slid closer to a neoliberal vision of economic life.[23] Father Arizmendi sought a mode of economic life that could compete in the market while promoting product innovation, modest pay differentials, workers' investment in enterprises, sustainable products, and investment of a portion of profits into retirement and local communities. As J. K. Gibson-Graham show in their admirable study, this experiment was deemed unworkable before it started by many socialists and neoliberals alike, but it has in fact fared rather well. Today it employs over 68,000 people, maintains an income differential of between 6-1 and 9-1 (depending on how it is measured), competes in the global capitalist economy, trains workers for new assignments when they are displaced by innovation, produces sustainable goods, and generates a fair measure of consumer loyalty among workers and others knowledgeable about it.[24] Its pay differential of 9-1 is a little better than the 435-1 ratio—according to the AFL-CIO—prevailing in large American corporations in 2004.[25] This microeconomic experiment challenges the claim that the existing distribution of income and product priorities expresses the inherent rationality of capitalism per se. These firms participate in global capitalism, but the ethos underlying production, work, investment, and consumption challenges that currently underlying American culture.

Other micro-experiments are in motion. The Mararikulam experiment in Kerala, India, creating cooperatives to use the local resource of coconut oil and to secure purchase pledges from residents, builds upon its own resource base and seeks to expand into other areas. The E2M business model in western Massachusetts may show some promise. And a "third Italy," consisting of a band of small firms experimenting with unorthodox patterns of industrial organization, represents another attempt with a measure of success.[26] According to Michael Best, the "third Italy" experiment remains strong: "The region is still well off and maintains global leadership in many 'design led' and fashion oriented industrial sectors."[27]

A final micro-experiment to be noted is the Bruderhof communities in the United States, Canada, and England. Founded by a branch of Christian Anabaptists, they participate in capitalist markets. But they subject them to policies inspired by an Anabaptist ethos. Close telephone ties and exchanges are maintained between sister communities across territorial lines; a portion of profit is poured back into the community; and numerous strategies are deployed to reduce the proliferation of positional goods. The participants are inspired by Acts 2:44–45: "And all that believed were together, and had all things in common; And sold their possessions and goods, and parted them to all men, as every man had need." To quote Joel Kovel, who participated in one Bruderhof community for a time: "The Bruderhof have found a way to offset the capitalist market by inserting a spiritual moment into their worldly practice."[28] My way of putting this is to say that this Christian minority challenges the dominant spirituality of American capitalism with an ethos that turns and twists the capitalist assemblage in a distinctive direction. This microeconomic adventure discloses, through its contrast to the evangelical-capitalist resonance machine, the significant role that an embedded ethos plays in economic practice. It also renders vivid by contrast the destructive character of the ethos fomented by the evangelical-capitalist resonance machine.

Most of these experiments have gained a measure of success by cutting against the grain of the dominant corporate ethos, existing state priorities, and the demands of international financial institutions such as the World Trade Organization and the International Monetary Fund. These latter entities, you might say, have an interest in proving that the experiments must fail; they contribute to that effect by ignoring or obstructing them. Think what might happen if more states, consumer movements, religious congregations, and international agencies worked with rather than against such experiments. The experiments suggest that what is commonly taken to set the structural parameters of capitalist enterprise as such—especially in the United States—conforms more closely to the boundaries of cowboy capitalism. Those limits are maintained by the intransigence of a large section of the capitalist class, an entrenched managerial ethos, the paradox of positional goods, state support for the hierarchical corporate model, church sermons and academic legitimations, and media financial news reporting. These forces combine to focus the vaunted productivity of capitalist enterprise upon the production of exclusive goods, significant inequality, the proliferation of unsustainable products, and the veiling of massive state support for every aspect of the neoliberal economy except welfare and the military budget.

Before turning to possible strategies to promote these objectives, we need to face an objection posed by one segment of the left: "Don't you depend a lot upon the state, when it must be viewed as the enemy?" My response is threefold. First, there is no way to take on global warming without engaging the state in the effort as well as international agencies, and global warming is a key danger of this epoch. Second, it is less the state itself and more its existing subsidies and priorities that are at issue. If you were to oppose both the market and the state you might reduce the democratic left to pure critique, with no presentation of positive possibilities and strategies. But critique is always important and never enough, as the left has begun to rediscover and as the American right has known for forty years. Third, although one must acknowledge the issues of cumbersome state bureaucracy, corporate cronyism, and state corruption, all three increased radically when the evangelical-capitalist resonance machine achieved hegemony, and they will get worse unless eco-egalitarians enter the fray at the intercoded levels of micropolitics, microeconomic experiments, and the state. It is unwise to act as if the state must always be what it has become. Challenging the media is critical in this respect, making it become a watchdog of corporations, the state, religious movements, and the multiple imbrications between them. My view, as becomes clear in the next few pages, is that no interim agenda on the left can proceed far without finding expression in state policy, and state policy must draw inspiration from microeconomic experiments initially launched outside its canopy: microeconomic experiments and creative state policies must inform each other. We thus seek to include the state without becoming statist. Those who invest hope in revolutionary overthrow may oppose such a combination. I suspect that revolution, were it to occur, would undermine rather than vitalize democratic culture.[29]

A Political Formula

As this thought experiment has proceeded, it has glided effortlessly from the politically implausible toward the near utopian. All along it has focused on one question: whether it is *possible* to institute eco-egalitarian practices within the broad parameters of a capitalist axiomatic. The answer is that it is possible to launch significant steps in this direction, even if it is difficult to foment the political drive and economic muscle to do so. As we have proceeded, one threat, hovering between "the structural" and "the political," has been simmering off stage. What about a capital strike? What about the migration of capital to other countries if a reform movement acquires momentum? The risk is real. But there are considerations that may make this sort of migration more difficult than heretofore. Investment in American capitalism is more global in character today than in the past. And many capitalist states around the world find the United States to be the advanced state that has done the most to obstruct global ecological agreements and the reduction of inequality. If a movement emerged *here* to promote a positive agenda, corporations could attract more investment from abroad rather than less. Moreover, firms based abroad that currently hesitate to locate in the United States might be attracted to do so. Toyota, for instance, recently forsook the United States in favor of Canada, because of its national health plan and low crime levels. And calculations of this sort surely enter into the less visible judgments of numerous firms deciding between the United States and elsewhere. Energy costs and supplies, for instance, are less uncertain in countries that have eased their dependence upon foreign oil through collective investments in wind and solar power, ethanol, conservation, and public transit systems. Thus a capital strike is a danger, but the danger of a capital strike by foreign investors against key corporations in the American economy looms at least as large as a strike by domestic capital against American reforms.

But what are the prospects for a political movement to support these possibilities within a country as large as the United States? The barriers are impressive. They include the primacy of an economic ideology that deflects pursuit of eco-egalitarianism; the right edge of an evangelical movement that discounts the importance of the earthly, collective future while waiting for Armageddon; financial reporting oriented to the immediate interests of high-end investors, and TV news that ignores lower- and middle-class consumption binds and the proposals of poor people, labor leaders, left-leaning economic analysts, and moderate Christian, Muslim, and Jewish clergy. The combination of advertising oriented to positional goods and the steady flow of corporate leaders and retired generals into the news media also sets a high barrier. We saw in chapter 2 how such forces and constituencies reverberate back and forth to create a reactionary resonance machine more powerful than its separate parts.

But there are counter forces at work too. There is, first and foremost, a new awakening among several constituencies about how climate change, violent storms in the Bible Belt, increased energy dependence, soil and water depletion, air pollution, and irrational patterns of consumption make the American capitalist adventure today at least as fragile as it was during the Great Depression. That earlier crisis was caused by irrationalities in state regulation of investment; the crisis awaiting us now flows from the proliferation of positional goods, the expansion of defensive goods, the militarization of welfare, strains on the earth's absorptive capacities and resource bases, the refusal of many to acknowledge these pressures, and resentment by most of the world over the obstructionism and interventionism of the American regime. Even as the expansion of positional goods and services proceeds apace in the civilization of productivity, there is a gnawing sense that the keg from which it draws is running low. The flow could reach a tipping point, when new pressures upon use and declining supply meet. This has already occurred in the fishing industry, where a steady flow of cod for decades was suddenly reduced to a dribble by the cumulative effects of competitive, technologically advanced fishing and the reduced ability of cod to reproduce.[30] There is also increasing public wariness of the utopian claims of neoliberal theory, as the promises it has made over the last thirty years are measured against performance. This skepticism is joined to growing public awareness of how the right edge of evangelism links the promise of Armageddon to neglect of the future of the earth. Neoliberals and the evangelical right have had at least three decades to propagate their visions, and a large fund of experience makes them less appealing. There are, moreover, signs of a reawakening among young people, as they ponder the future and encounter legions abroad appalled by recent

American policies of environmental degradation, poverty, torture, urban decay, preemptive wars, and domestic surveillance. There is also the political emergence of low-income immigrants—legal and illegal—who contest the demand that they remain silent if they are to stay here. And finally, there are signs of political resurgence among Christian, Jewish, and Muslim congregants who are at odds with the bellicose voices that have pretended to represent them in public for three decades. This resurgence joins a growing sense among nontheists and secularists that we must forge alliances with moderate religious constituencies intensely concerned about the future of the country and the earth.

The gnawing sense that the collective future is bleak if remedial action is not taken recoils back upon the spending habits, investment priorities, religious affections, and political judgments of large segments of the populace. To the extent that this recoil becomes attached to an energetic political movement to reconfigure the infrastructure of consumption, positive potentialities become discernible. To the extent that inspirational leaders in churches, labor unions, localities, corporations, and public office do not emerge, the growing sense of the fragility of things could intensify a negative dynamic already in motion, increasing the prospect for a fascistic version of capitalism in America.

At this point it may seem that I have avoided a critical topic: the global dimension of capital flows, environmental issues, and economic inequality. I concur that capitalism is global in character. Any political movement that proceeds far must engage global corporations and international agencies. Cross-state citizen movements are equally essential, to press the United States and other states from the inside and outside simultaneously.[31] But it is also true that a concerted movement must find one of its key anchors in the United States if it is to proceed far. That is not because capitalism in the United States is self-contained—far from it. It is because among advanced capitalist states the United States has dragged its feet the most, imposes the greatest burdens on the future, exerts significant power over international agencies, and retains considerable power inside and outside government to stymie the initiation of viable global practices from elsewhere. The United States is a key place to engage, partly because many other regimes have already started; that start must be linked to regional and global pressures on the United States to alter its priorities.

Every new political movement looks unrealistic and inchoate before it lifts off, like a swan grunting and groaning before it flies. That is what makes it new. This is true of some ugly movements, such as Nazism in the early days, and of noble movements such as the American labor movement in the 1930s, the civil rights movement, the feminist movement, and India's drive for independence after the Second World War. Certainly, as Hirsch's prescient analysis in 1977 discloses, urgently needed movements can fail. Nonetheless, the situation that Hirsch addressed then is more acute today, and the prospect to engage it politically may be somewhat more promising. One spur can be provided by intellectuals and academics who join critiques of cowboy capitalism to the imagination of positive interim agendas. These interim agendas form indispensable bridges, enabling resigned and depressed constituencies to identify new public possibilities and to participate in individual, local, associational, state, and global initiatives to support them.

So while the probabilities are stacked against eco-egalitarian capitalism, the *need* is urgent and movement in the right direction is *possible*. The most plausible possibility is to form an eco-egalitarian resonance machine that generates more collective power than the sum of its parts. It would be energized by micropolitical efforts to visualize a better future; intensive consumer movements that point to the adverse collective effects of exclusive goods while using direct action and electoral politics to change the mix; pressure from small investors and large pension funds to change existing production priorities; campaigns by rich athletes and business leaders to return a larger portion of capital and energy to the communities from which they have sometimes emerged; aggressive publication of promising microeconomic experiments here and elsewhere; extensive publicity about global warming, resource depletion, and strains on the earth's absorptive capacities; inventions that provide needed technologies and democratize communication; local and state initiatives that draw inspiration from these experiments and inventions; positive experiments that become incorporated into labor negotiations, church sermons, and interfaith publicity campaigns; consumer organizations to change the habits and state subsidies of consumption in key product areas; candidates for office and cross-state citizens' movements that draw sustenance from the foregoing groups, actions, and pressures; international pressure for new treaties; events that dramatize fuel shortages and the effects of global warming upon the common future; efforts by young people and grandparents from a variety of creeds to shame corporate élites and public leaders into taking action; and new attention by the news media to the intercoded issues of consumption, storms, global warming, resource depletion, the steep curve of inequality, and the increasingly vulnerable condition of America. These images, forces, campaigns, witnesses, candidates, worries, inspirations, shaming, laws, and events must loop into each other, with each loop amplifying those that preceded it, generating a positive resonance machine more powerful than the elements from which it was formed.

Is eco-egalitarian capitalism possible? Given the history of shifting imbrications between the capitalist axiomatic, spiritual energies infused into its modes of investment, saving, work, and consumption, priorities of the state, the infrastructure of consumption, the practices of science and technology, the fund of usable resources, the susceptibility of the population to chauvinist appeals, the changing dynamism of natural events, and limits to the earth's absorptive capacity, we can surmise that progress on this front is possible though not highly probable. But what if significant progress were made with each initiative supported here, including significant shifts in consumption, a more progressive tax, a high minimum wage, revitalization of the state safety net, and an effective ceiling on incomes? Would the capitalist axiomatic then tip toward an assemblage not well described through the extant categories of neoliberal capitalism, social democracy, neofascist capitalism, or state socialism? Could yet further changes in the distribution of wealth and corporate control be triggered by the accumulating effects of these changes? Perhaps. But I will leave this thought experiment at the interim point visualized so far. I find it as difficult to think with specificity beyond that point, as others found it to visualize capitalism itself before the elements from which it was composed were bound together in a series of knots.[32]

CHAPTER FIVE

CHRISTIANITY, CAPITALISM,

AND THE TRAGIC

The Untimeliness of the Tragic

In *Antigone* several figures try to correct an apparent wrong done by others, only to find themselves drawn into a vortex that deepens the suffering of all. Antigone seeks to obey the unwritten laws that require the burial of her brother; Creon, the ruler, orders obedience to the law to leave unburied anyone who attacks his own state; Ismene seeks to temper the singular passion of her sister; Haemon, son of Creon and betrothed to Antigone, urges his father to relent while honoring his authority as he does so; and Tiresias, the blind seer, seeks to warn Creon that this series of actions is about to swirl out of anyone's and everyone's control.

Consider what Tiresias says after Antigone has been condemned to death and Haemon has rejected his father. He has been greeted by Creon who confirms his wisdom and invites him to speak: "Then mark me now; for you stand on a razor's edge."[1] But Creon cannot, or will not, mark his words. The more he hears from Tiresias, the more the virile Creon is moved to condemn him as a partisan and a feeble old man. Indeed, many in this drama seek to rise above the fray while identifying others as partisans, only to find themselves pushed into partisanship by events, their own actions, and the responses of others. The seer, who is reputed to be part male and part female, is made a partisan by the timing of his arrival, the intensity of passions already aroused, and his insistence that the sovereign reverse himself.[2] His plight might remind you of the millions who warned George W. Bush, just before he launched that ill-begotten invasion of Iraq. In Thebes too, Tiresias is labeled unpatriotic. Tiresias responds, as scorned seers do: "Then hear this. Ere the chariot of the sun has rounded once or twice his wheeling way, You shall have given a son of your own loins to death, in payment for death—two debts to pay; One for the life that you have sent to death, the life you have abominably entombed; One for the dead still lying above ground, Unburied, unhonored, unblest by the gods below. You cannot alter this. The gods themselves cannot undo it. It follows of necessity from what you have done. Even now the avenging Furies, the hunters of hell that follow and destroy, are lying in wait for you, and will have their prey, When the evil you have worked for others falls on you."[3]

The vengefulness that underlies this prophecy reflects both the desperate nature of the situation and Creon's refusal to listen as he sits on that razor's edge of time. There is no good time for a seer to deliver such a message. And there is no guarantee that the recommended action would succeed even if followed. It might be too late already. Either Haemon, Antigone, or both might refuse the withdrawal of Creon's ultimatum. Or another event might enter the picture from the outside. But if Creon waits, even "the gods themselves cannot undo it." They are powerful forces, but even they cannot undo a tragic course once its terms are locked in place.

What about those furies and gods? Are they to be understood as *beings* in whom the participants believed, or as *figures* whose names condense a variety of forces that impinge upon human life? Time could be one such force, if the gods are figures. The unruly play of passion upon passion in an incendiary situation would be another. While it is reasonable to treat the Greeks' gods as beings, and while many did receive them that way, I receive them as figures, as some of Sophocles contemporaries are reputed to have done.[4] Treated as figures, they point to an uncanny resemblance between a classic tragic vision and a modern image of time as becoming that harbors the seeds of tragic possibility within it. On this image, the larger-than-life qualities of the heroes are pertinent to tragedy, and the chancy conjunction of disparate forces at untimely moments is too.

As figures, the gods suggest a world composed of diverse forces that do not always harmonize. The world is unbalanced. These forces periodically enter into conjunctions and collisions. The array of forces can include a variety of human doctrines, the volatility of individual and group passions under stress, the dearth of wise judgment or readiness to hear it at key moments, the breakout of a plague, an invasion, a triumph that encourages overstepping, an earthquake, a radical change in climate, a swarm of locusts, an asteroid shower, and other forces yet. Forces of different types set on different temporal trajectories, periodically forming chancy conjunctions, for better or worse. Indeed, the themes of the gods as beings and as figures are rather close, at least from the twin perspectives of a world governed by providence or susceptible to human mastery. For if the gods are either figures for contending forces—many of which are indifferent to our fate—or real beings often hostile to us, the themes of providence and consummate mastery bite the dust together.

Evil, as extreme, undeserved human suffering, can occur anytime, but it is very apt to do so when the collisions between disparate forces are sharp, noble or defensible ends collide, and each party insists that its role, faith, or demand must receive full priority in these fraught circumstances. According to such a vision, to act as if the world either follows a providential course or is your oyster is to tempt the wrath of the gods, whether they are conceived as beings or figures. A *tragic drama* by Sophocles concentrates a tragic result into one play. A *tragic vision* builds such a set of possibilities into its fundamental conception of being. You approach a tragic vision if you doubt the providential image of time, reject the compensatory idea that humans can master all the forces that impinge upon life, strive to cultivate wisdom about a world that is neither designed for our benefit nor plastic enough to be putty in our hands, and cultivate temporal sensitivity to how this or that concatenation of events could issue in the worst.[5] Again, a tragic vision could find expression in the idea that the gods are adamantly hostile to human welfare or that the volatility of a world without gods exceeds our ability to know or master it.[6] If you adopt the second stance, a tragic vision edges toward what William James calls "meliorism," that is, the possibility that reflective action taken in concert at the strategic moments might, given a measure of good luck, promote a better world or forestall the worst. If you conclude that the gods are hostile—or even that a single, omnipotent god archly ignores the needs, efforts, and hopes of human beings?—your view becomes both more tragic and more dismal. It would be difficult not to resent profoundly a world so ordered.

From the vantage point of a tragic vision, supreme confidence in providence can sometimes make things worse than they otherwise would be. Augustine supported a providential view. He invoked it not only to support hope for salvation, but to vindicate a series of human exclusions, injuries, and punishments against those who contest his version of it. John Sanders, whom we consulted in chapter 2, accepts a modulated image of providence. His vision is not tragic, because it expresses faith in the final victory of an outcome judged to be beneficent. But he attenuates the providential image by praying to a God who *learns* as the world turns. More radically, several late modern devotees of monotheism find it advisable to curtail self-confident knowledge about the divinity they worship and to incorporate something close to a tragic element into their faiths. I would include Paul Ricoeur, Theodor Adorno, Charles Taylor, Catherine Keller, Karl Jaspers, William James, and Jacques Derrida on that list. Catherine Keller, whose work we encountered in chapter 3, articulates a Christian theology of becoming, in which the recalcitrant materials that the Creator used to shape the world continue to vibrate with both positive and negative possibilities.[7] Paul Ricoeur is also notable, as a Catholic philosopher who struggles with the issue, placing the tragic, Jewish, and Christian "myths" into prolonged conversation. At one point he writes that "the preeminence of the Adamic myth gives rise to the thought that evil is not a category of being; but because that myth has a reverse or a residue, the other myths are invincible. Hence, an anthropology of evil can neither posit nor take away the right of an absolute genesis of being, to which evil would belong primordially."[8] Ricoeur hears and respects a tragic tradition that deviates from the providential faith he embraces. His attention to it ensures that he does not succumb to the "promise" of Armageddon. The latter tradition differs from a tragic vision in prophesying a fiery future, filling it with divine revenge, and treating it as providential for those who receive its eternal reward.

Finally, consider the stance of Karl Jaspers, a thinker who lived through the Holocaust and integrated elements of a tragic vision into a protestant mode of Christian faith. In *Tragedy Is Not Enough*, he sees how an engagement with tragic binds opens the door to religious experience. He finds that "the substance" of tragic knowledge "must escape the Christian. Nevertheless, this tragic knowledge, if it remains philosophic . . . is also a way for man to transcend his limitations." The tragic conviction that "Being has a crack running through it" becomes "perverted if it sets free the turmoil of dark impulses." But it is noble when it responds "through trust . . . and an open mind" to the opacity of Being itself. Jaspers and Nietzsche, as I will show later, express similar sensibilities while diverging on the issue of transcendence. Nietzsche would call this positive connection across a chasm of difference "the spiritualization of enmity." Jaspers puts the point in a way that touches Nietzsche's idea but does not coincide with it: "Far from being an illusion, such solidarity is the existential task of human life."[9]

The Arian-Trinitarian Controversy

Greek tragedy is set in a particular way of life. But can a tragic vision illuminate life beyond ancient Greek culture? Let's note a fateful period during the fourth century CE, when Catholicism and the Roman Empire were forging a new unity, ending the persecution of Christians and setting up a religious orthodoxy. I do not interpret these events as most Arians, Trinitarians, Emperors, Jews, Goths, and Huns did, for each placed the blame on their competitors for the immense suffering that resulted. There is ample blame to be parsed, but it might be wise to do so within a vision that attends to a concatenation of actions, surprising events, and creeds that manufacture a destructive outcome foreseen by no figure at the outset, a concatenation that attenuates blame without eliminating it. The result does not fit the exact contours of a Greek tragedy, but it can be illuminated through recourse to a tragic vision of being.

In the early part of the fourth century Arius, a lowly, charismatic priest living in Alexandria, where the church was then popular and active, supported the omnipotence of God by endowing Jesus with a subordinate role in the scheme of things. He contended that this view was to be found both in the Gospels and in any understanding of *mono*theism that makes God omnipotent. This "subordinantism," as it was called by many, ranged over time between construing Jesus as a divine being subordinate to God and treating him as a noble man who became divine upon the resurrection. The opponents of Arius, led by a young bishop named Athanasius, insisted that Christ is co-eternal with God, and that the Trinity of Father, Son, and Holy Ghost forms an intrinsic unity. The salvational stakes were high, since all parties to this struggle sought to obey a divine imperative higher than themselves. The Arians accused the Trinitarians of jeopardizing faith in God's omnipotence. The Athanasians accused the Arians of befouling Christ, by making him all too human. And each accused the other of sinking into paganism, the first by putting too much confidence in the ability of human beings to earn salvation through their own merit—as they said Jesus had done until the moment of resurrection—the second by drawing perilously close to the idea of multiple gods. The parties to this struggle were not distributed uniformly across the Empire. Many in the West were less concerned about theological issues but inclined toward the Trinity when they addressed them; the East was more inclined to the subordinationist view; and the Mediterranean city of Alexandria was sharply divided.

Although popular accounts suggest that the issue was more or less resolved in favor of the Trinity at the Council of Nicene, called by the Emperor
Constantine in 325 CE, the struggle really lifted off at that point. During this
period theological debate often spilled into street riots, particularly in Alexandria, where Greek philosophy, Jewish tradition, and Christian sects col-
lided. Here are a few moments in the "controversy," following the Nicene
Council. Arius goes to Rome to plead his case anew, turning Constantine in
his direction. Athanasius and his followers refuse to reinstate Arius, inspiring
a round of riots in Alexandria. The Council of Rimini-Seleucia, convened by
eastern bishops and supported by Constantine, overturns the Nicene Creed in
359 CE. But Arius is again driven away, as Athanasius and his supporters still
refuse to reinstate him. New charges are pressed by Constantine and key
bishops against Athanasius, accusing him of disobedience and of murdering
some opponents. He flees to the desert, as he will at other times and as those
on both sides of this struggle do periodically. Arius is admitted into the fold
again, through the intervention of Constantine after the fourth Council of
Bishops following the Nicene Council. But just as Arius and his group are
celebrating a bishop's order to receive him the next day into the Church of the
Apostles, Arius is suddenly stricken by a stomach ache. He is found dead in
the bathroom by his friends shortly after retiring to it. Rumors abound about
the cause of his death, in a world where poison is the murder weapon of
choice. Athanasius describes it as a "wonderful and extraordinary" event,
expressing the opposition of God himself to Arianism.[10] Upon the death of
Constantine, one of his sons, Constantius, now emperor of the East, migrates
toward Arianism; the other, Constans in the West, moves closer to Trinita-
rianism. Wars between the brothers are waged, with this issue as one of
the causes.

During these twists and turns, riots occur in several cities; priests and
bishops are accused by their brethren of terrible things and forced to flee; and
intense plotting to produce the next reversal takes place. Soon the events and
stakes become yet more intense. Julian, during his reign as emperor of the
West (355–61) and then sole emperor (361–63), seeks to reinstate the primacy
of the old gods, to mixed reviews. His goal seemed to be to inflame struggles
within Christianity so as to weaken its credibility. Struggles flare in the streets
again. But he is soon killed in a battle against the Persians that has also posed
questions.[11] After the death of Julian, Jovian, who eventually reveals himself
to be a Nicene Christian, is selected by the soldiers in the Persian theater to
replace Julian. He soon dies, again innocently enough, because a charcoal

brazier was left on in his tent all night. Valentinian now emerges to rule in the West, as does Valens, sympathetic to Arianism, in the East. After more twists and turns a new group of monks, the Cappadocians, compose a doctrine that preserves the Trinity while seeking to placate moderate Arians. And Valens is defeated in the worst and bloodiest defeat of Rome to that date by the Goths at Hadrianopolis, a city north of Constantinople. After this bloody battle Theodosius becomes the emperor.

The Cappodocians, who impress Theodosius, modify the doctrine of the Trinity to emphasize two components. First, the role of the Holy Ghost is now emphasized more than heretofore, and Father, Son, and Holy Ghost are defined to be three *hypostases* expressing the same *homoousios*, or essence of divinity. Second, the bishops no longer seek to forge a close, positive account of the Trinity—similar attempts had thrown their predecessors into a theological hornet's nest—insisting instead that exactly how this diversity within unity is attained must be received as an unfathomable mystery disclosing the limitations of human reason in a world under the governance of God. A key test of Christian faith, to them, is the readiness to embrace the Trinity as mystery.

By the middle of the 380s the Cappadocian version of the Trinity had triumphed. That triumph is accompanied by immense suffering for several constituencies. Theodosius now punishes dissenters with an iron hand: pagans are strictly forbidden to sacrifice to their gods or participate in other rites; Manicheans are hunted down and often killed; "bands of wandering monks attack synagogues, pagan temples, heretic's meeting places, and the homes of wealthy unbelievers in Mesopotamia, Syria, Egypt, Palestine and North Africa"; and trinitarian Christians riot against Jews and Arians in Alexandria.[12] Each side had regularly accused the other of heresy, but several heresies are now officially identified and banned by the regime and the church together—with Arianism and Manicheanism leading the list and Pelagianism soon to follow.

Doctrinal struggles did not shape these events alone; the carriers of each doctrine were often under the thumb of this or that ruler interested in other things. But the rulers cared about these issues too, and as the repetition of riots and councils suggests, they were limited in their power to control the streets. Moreover, the parties to this long struggle encountered one contingency after another, including Constantine's early surprise to find his troops to have been inspired by the Cross, a series of untimely deaths, a plague of insects forcing a troop withdrawal in Persia, periodic riots in several cities, rumblings in one army or another, the rise of a pagan emperor, a burning brazier, the activation of Visigoths, Ostrogoths, and Huns at pivotal moments, and conversions by rulers to various versions of paganism or Christianity.

The triumph of the Nicene doctrine carried consequences. More so than Arianism, it separates Christianity sharply from both Judaism and paganism, delaying for centuries the consolidation of real pluralism within the territory of Christendom. As Gregory of Nyssa, one of the Cappadocians, asserted, "It is as if the number of the Three were the remedy in the case of those who are in error as to the One [i.e. the Jews] and the assertion of the unity for those whose beliefs are dispersed among a number of divinities [i.e. the polytheists]."[13] While the triumph did not guarantee a later breakup of Christianity into two territorial churches, a history of pogroms against Jews, or the emergence of an Islamic faith challenging the Trinity with a singular monotheism, it may have made unwitting contributions to those future events. The seriousness of the issue is merely suggested by this statement in 1833 by the Catholic theologian J. H. Newman: "I will not say that Arian doctrine is the direct result of a Judaizing practice; but it deserves consideration whether a tendency to derogate from the honor due to Christ was not created by the observance of the Jewish rites, and much more, by that carnal, self indulgent religion, which seems at that time to have prevailed among the rejected nation."[14]

A providential image of history might suggest that all this suffering contributed to a beneficent result. This is the tendency of Augustine in *The City of God against the Pagans*, as when he writes, after noting some of these events, "We have shown sufficiently, as it seemed to me, what is the development in this mortal condition of the two cities, the earthly and the Heavenly, which are mingled together from the beginning to the end of their history. One of them, the earthly city, has created for herself such false gods as she wanted from any source she chose—even creating them out of men—in order to worship them with sacrifices. The other city, the Heavenly City, on pilgrimage in this world, does not create false gods, and she herself is to be his true sacrifice. Nevertheless, both cities alike enjoy the good things, or are afflicted with the adversities of this temporal state, but with a different faith, a different expectation, a different love, until they are separated by the final judgment, and each receives her own end."[15]

The phrase "even creating them out of men" reveals how Augustine accepts the divine origin of Christ as a noncontroversial belief of Christianity, now contrasting it sharply to pagan faiths that create divinities out of men. The phrase with which he begins the larger statement, "as it seemed to me," promises a presumptive generosity to other points of view that is not pursued. I have come to see how many draw an ethos of generosity from Augustinian themes about "the priority of grace, the pervasiveness of love, the obscurity of the will, the beauty and contingency of a world created out of nothing."[16] But this element, valuable for future believers to draw upon, was at the time trumped by Augustine's drive to define several minorities within his church as heretics, to sanction their exclusion, and to interpret bad things that happen to pagans and heretics as expressing the providential course of history. Another distressing thing, to me, is Augustine's definition of his church as an object of persecution even after it has become the official church. As when he writes, "It started with Abel, the first righteous man slain by an ungodly brother, and the pilgrimage goes on from that time right up to the end of history, with the persecutions of the world on one side, and on the other the consolations of God."[17] To say that devout Christians are *persecuted* until the end of history—even after Christianity has become the officially sanctioned creed in the Empire that Augustine inhabits—sets out notions of extreme Christian entitlement with destructive implications for the future. It seems to support the idea that "we" are *persecuted* unless our faith prevails entirely. Augustine's writings are too rich to be *reduced* to this tendency. But it is there.

A tragic vision reads the long, bloody controversy between Arians and Trinitarians differently. It detects an element of stubborn narcissism in the contending parties and a constitutive instability in scriptural presentations of God and Jesus that keeps returning. This instability helps to explain why pieces and fragments of Arianism reemerge periodically, in the nominalism of thirteenth-century Catholicism that reasserted the omnipotence of God over a providential view of history taken to limit it, in the Calvinist theme of predestination and its emphasis on God's unfettered omnipotence, in Spinoza's conception of divine substance as univocal, in the Arianism of Isaac Newton, in Thomas Jefferson's retranslation of the gospels to read Jesus as a noble human prophet, and in the long, shifting battle between "prophetic Christianity" and "Constantinian Christianity" that Cornel West reviews so eloquently. If I understand him correctly, West does not *equate* the prophetic tradition in black and white churches with Arianism and the Constantine tradition with the Trinity. Whispers of that debate can be heard in these struggles, however, for the prophetic tradition connects to an earthy Jesus who supports the poor and downtrodden, while the Constantine tradition is

often tempted to join the will of Christ to the dictates of empire. "Constantinian strains of American Christianity have been on the wrong side of so many
of our social troubles, such as the dogmatic justification of slavery and the
parochial defense of women's inequality. It has been the prophetic Christian
tradition, by contrast, that has so often pushed for social justice."[18] The most
renowned American proponent of the prophetic tradition is Martin Luther
King. This tradition sends out ripples to other traditions of Christianity, and
to currents outside it as well, issuing a call for a new political assemblage of
diverse creeds connected by a spirit of presumptive cultural generosity and
economic egalitarianism.

A related version of the prophetic tradition can be found in the work of
James W. Robinson, one of the "Q scholars" who seek to protect the early
sayings of Jesus from judgments inserted into the texts after his death. For
him Jesus sought to bring the "reign of God" to earth, by building up human
trust and a propensity to charity. The "Constantine" revision, consolidated
during the fourth century, transducts Jesus into a supporter of violence, empire, and authoritarianism.[19] Few participants in the fourth-century struggles
wished the worst for their opponents when the dispute began, except perhaps
Athanasius. But events careened out of control. No powerful force rose above
the quest for either partisan control or thin ecumenicism to sanction broad
diversity within the church and the regime so that both would forge generous
relations to numerous articles of faith.[20] The tragic effect is that for several
centuries the church turned into itself and toward Empire, consolidating
tendencies to institutional closure that still haunt it. The minor chord, however, is that the element of mystery in the Trinity, treated initially to justify the
authority of the priesthood, later became a spur for many to presumptive
generosity toward others. The upshot seems to be that when you encounter
unfathomable mystery in your faith in the right spirit, you may become
inspired to appreciate corollary elements of paradox, mystery, or uncertainty
at different points in other faiths; this very appreciation can encourage a
positive connection with them across difference. Here we find the same
general *creed*, compatible with infusion by either a generous or domineering
spirituality.

Tiresias, had he appeared at a strategic moment in these struggles, would
have been shuffled aside as a blind, old pagan. But if his voice had been heard
by some on the razor's edge of time, it might have left a vibrant legacy of
minor memories from which to draw, encouraging future generations to
incorporate it *somehow* into their spiritualities.[21] The struggle against ressen-

timent which stalks the human condition carries the most promise when the carriers of providence, world mastery, and a tragic vision become modest about the universal appeal of their doctrinal beliefs and alert to the need to become responsive to minor traditions. That is why Paul Ricoeur, Karl Jaspers, Cornel West, John Sanders, and Catherine Keller are so important as exemplars, and why William James—to be addressed below—is equally so.

Meliorism and the Tragic

The will to philosophy not only competes with the task of interpreting scripture; it also grows out of it. Different books of the Bible, written in different voices, languages, and times, conflict at key junctures, as we saw in chapter 3 in our review of Augustine's rules for reading the Bible. Speculation or inspiration is required to stitch them together, or to decide which formulations are literal and which figurative, or to give some statements priority over others. So Arius, Athanasius, Gregory of Nyssa, the other Cappadocians, Augustine, Calvin, Sanders, and others have found themselves moving back and forth between scripture and speculation. The Greek terms *homoousios* and *hypostases*, for instance, are found nowhere in the gospels. They were introduced later, to turn them one way or another.

The relation goes the other way too. Modern thinkers such as William James, Gilles Deleuze, and Friedrich Nietzsche, not inspired foremost by Biblical texts, nonetheless find themselves engaged with conceptions of God, time, will, freedom, morality, responsibility, punishment, and redemption growing out of biblical texts. Here I place these three thinkers into a conversation. Two embrace a tragic vision, while the third, James, adopts a form of meliorism that carries him to its edge.

James confesses a limited God who participates in the world without being in charge of it. James believes "that there is a God, but that he is finite, either in power or in knowledge or in both at once."[22] The world and this God coexist. This is not a god to engage primarily through scriptural interpretation or a spirit of primordial indebtedness. It participates with us, and we with it, particularly when circumstances take a dramatic turn. Between the lines, so to speak, James implies that this God too learns as the world turns. This links James to the theology of John Sanders, discussed in chapter 3, even though there is a difference of degree between the two. If I understand James correctly, he does not think that a final purpose is given at Creation, with merely the means and strategies adjusted as history proceeds. Time is more open to

James than to Sanders, more susceptible to radical alteration. His is not a providential image of the universe. It is a melioristic image, conveying faith in possible attunement between God and exceptional human beings at pivotal moments of historical change. You might worry about how progress is to be measured, given such a picture; but I will not tarry on that question now.[23]

James's meliorism is grounded in the faith (or experience) that those with sensitive ears can hear the soft voice of God as they encounter surprising twists and turns of time. Could such a voice inspire people to listen attentively to evidence about global warming, a process that was not on the horizon of perceived possibility when James wrote? And to respond affirmatively to its urgency? "Yes" and "yes," James, as I receive him, would say. Those with the ability to commune closely with God are unusual, about as rare as the saints identified by the Catholic church, the wisdom of a Tiresias, or the noble lovers of the earth whom Nietzsche celebrates. When a cosmic break occurs, "the threshold lowers or the valve opens, information ordinarily shut out leaks into the mind of exceptional individuals."[24] The key is whether others will listen to these seers.

James does not define morality in the first instance through concepts of command, obligation, or debt. Touching a chord in Gilles Deleuze—the modern critic of faith in transcendence—James defines ethics (in the first instance) through inspiration, attraction, and attachment to an abundance of being that courses through as well as around us. The idea is to cultivate such a disposition more fully. A morality with strictly defined principles and universals lacks the flexibility to respond sensitively to a "world in the making." It might even protect itself by ruling out of court from the start any philosophy of time that calls its credibility into question.

His god separates James from a tragic vision; but its limited power carries him to the edge of that vision. He cannot deny tragic possibility, since people may ignore transcendent warnings and promises, or God may not be wise or influential enough to foresee or to avoid the worst. James can only assert that the world is not predisposed profoundly to a tragic result because no set of contending gods is hostile to us and because his god is predisposed to us.

There are three links across difference between James and Gilles Deleuze. Two can be marshaled through the Jamesian ideas of "litter" and of time as "always in the making." While James complains that "philosophers have always aimed at cleaning up the litter with which the world apparently is filled"[25] in their pursuit of closed explanations, Deleuze speaks of "difference in itself." Difference in itself, as we saw in chapter 3, consists of chaotic, relatively unformed energies that inhabit stabilized things, beings, and processes, helping to compose a world of torsion between being and becoming. Deleuze moves closer yet to the Jamesian idea of "a pluralistic universe" when he asserts, "It is therefore true that God makes the world by calculating, but his calculations never work out exactly, and this inexactitude or injustice in the result, this irreducible inequality, forms the condition of the world."[26]

In a world of "inexactitude" or "irreducible inequality," some entities, species, and institutions may endure for millennia, but no thing, god, system, or mode of being survives forever. Deleuze and James are both indebted to Henri Bergson in this respect, as they attend to the "duration" through which past and present resonate together to foment variations that periodically accumulate to puncture established stabilizations.[27] The third connection between them is an affinity of sensibility that makes it possible for them to commune together across lines of creedal difference.

What are the differences? The two ideas of attunement to immanence and to mystical experience lean toward each other, in that each solicits the cultivation of sensitivity toward new possibilities in the making. But Deleuze does not pursue communication between a limited god and human beings. Deleuze, rather, experiments at those fugitive junctures during which tradition encounters the real uncertainty of twists and turns in the making.

The most telling difference between James and Deleuze may lie elsewhere: in the *status* that each bestows upon his philosophy. Daniel Smith presented a thoughtful essay on "Deleuze and Immanence" at a conference on Deleuze at Trent University in 2004. Deleuze, he says, constructs transcendental arguments to secure the superiority of a philosophy of immanence over that of transcendence.[28] There is something to be said for Smith's account.[29] At least, one does not find in Deleuze those focal points in James, at which he expresses his philosophy of transcendence and then acknowledges it to be profoundly contestable. James affirms faith in transcendence; he strives to give persuasive arguments in support of it and to open his readers to a wave of inspiration on its behalf. But he insists that after his best efforts are in, his faith remains legitimately contestable to many others. It is reasonable for others to dissent from this philosophy, or faith, because he has neither proven it, nor located a lucid, authoritative text that endows it with unquestioned authority for everyone, nor connected us all to a wave of irresistible authority. Late in the book we are reviewing, James characterizes the standing of his philosophy/faith in his own eyes: "The only thing I emphatically insist upon is that it [pluralism] is fully coordinate with monism. This world *may* in the last resort, be a block-universe; but on the other hand it *may* be a universe only strung-along, not rounded in or closed. Reality may exist distributively just as it sensibly seems to, after all. On that possibility I do insist."[30]

With Deleuze I am drawn like a magnet to the idea of radical immanence; and I regard representations of that philosophy given by many who do not participate in it as flawed. These defects cannot easily be avoided, perhaps, since the interpreters are not *inhabited* by the faith they represent. I thus find myself throwing off arguments that purport to show how it is self-contradictory to resist the idea of the Transcendent, or how you cannot be ethical unless you do so, or how the very experience of time requires you to do so. I find the charges of performative contradiction rather easy to turn away, especially by accusers who acknowledge points of uncertainty, mystery, or paradox in their own faiths. The ideas of litter, difference in itself, and energetic inexactitude resonate with the way of the world as I experience it. And I am impressed by the extent to which that experience finds support in some theories of thermodynamics, biological evolution, and neuroscience. Moreover, with Deleuze I connect ethics in the first instance not to a primordial debt, divine obligation, categorical imperative, responsibility to alterity, or mystical experience, but to gratitude for an abundance of being that exceeds the specific identity I cultivate as, say, male, nontheist, former athlete, and professor. Deleuze informs me in these ways.

With James I concur that a preliminary faith becomes instilled in you as you absorb the induction routines, rewards, punishments, theo-philosophical debates, public rituals, existential surprises, and earthy shocks of everyday life, that the emergent creed / philosophy is often susceptible to deepening through a mixture of argument and experimental tactics by constituencies on themselves, that conversion to another faith / creed involves agonizing changes on several registers of being, and above all, that no single existential faith to date, including radical immanence, has been demonstrated so convincingly that it would be foolish for any individual or congregation to deny it. Like James, I blur the lines of differentiation between faith, creed, doctrine, and philosophy that have stalked the academy at least since the field divisions sanctified by Kant in *The Conflict of the Faculties*.[31] I may well be surprised again, as a new competitor emerges. As Athanasius was, perhaps, the first time he encountered the idea of the Trinity. Or as I was the first time I ran into the idea of a limited god. But unlike Athanasius in one way and perhaps Deleuze in another, I doubt that any set of considerations is apt to make my philosophy / faith so airtight that it must be incorrect (or heretical) for others to affirm a different faith. Nor do I accept the idea that nontheists are "unbelievers"; for we support a distinctive set of beliefs about the fundamental contours of the cosmos. What is the outer limit to these lines of potential contestability? I don't know. I have not so far found a philosophy or theology that demarcates a line in advance with sufficient sharpness and necessity. So I simply take live issues as they arise.

James is also wise to focus on the *possibility* of meliorism. Even within a nontheistic creed a certain potential for meliorism can be located in the conjunction of chanciness with human capacities for reflective engagement. Tragic possibility with meliorist potential . . . or perhaps the other way around.

I indeed am a Jamesleuzian. I find this combination to both provide me with preliminary bearings and to support the commitment to cultural pluralism that each already evinces. In a world where the globalization of capital multiplies the number and type of minorities, the pursuit of deep pluralism would become more feasible if more advocates of each faith acknowledged without resentment the legitimacy of its contestability in the eyes of others. From my point of view, it would also help if more advocates of each vision were to incorporate a sense of tragic possibility into their conceptions of being or, where that is too much to ask, to come to terms reflectively with the power of a tragic vision that they themselves do not embrace.

A Tragic Vision and Gratitude for Being

James and Deleuze are both philosophers of abundance. One binds that experience to the soft voice of a limited god, the other to the fugitive experience of radical immanence. James is a more hesitant participant, because of the bouts of depression that he periodically struggled with and against. He wished he could be more like Spinoza, who maintained a love of the abundance of being amid the immense suffering that he experienced and observed. But James sometimes found it difficult to get up in the morning, even while leading an easier life than Spinoza. Go figure.

What is "abundance"? It is the experience of vitality and fecundity, of having more to draw upon in negotiating life than needed to cultivate your faith, secure your identity, make a living, rear your children, defend your creed, nourish your partner, develop your thinking, or advance your basic interests.[32] It takes work, energy, and concern to pursue these latter tasks. So the experience of abundance is marked by fragility and vulnerability. While it shows a certain resilience after a setback, it can be lost through ill-health, the death of loved ones, profoundly discouraging events, torture, political repression, aging, a devastating war, or other misfortunes. The vitality of life is haunted by contingency. It can drift into lethargy, slide into conceit, or twist into existential bitterness.

It is no coincidence that Friedrich Nietzsche, a nontheistic philosopher of gratitude for the vitality of life over identity, doubles as a modern prophet of the tragic. He is a modern descendant of Sophocles. He embraces both gratitude for the abundance of being and a tragic vision, belying those fools who equate a philosophy of abundance with "optimism" and calling into question those who automatically link a tragic vision to the temper of resignation. Let's allow Nietzsche to enunciate each side of this sublime equation. First, abundance and gratitude: "What is astonishing about the religiosity of the ancient Greeks is the lavish abundance of gratitude that radiates from it. Only a very distinguished type of human being stands in that relation to nature and to life."[33] This "lavish abundance of gratitude" finds expression in a presumptive disposition of generosity toward others. That is why ancient Greece, on Nietzsche's reading, could sometimes allow multiple theologies to contest each other on the same territorial space. Sophists, Platonists, Democriteans, and tragedians often contested each other, but they less often defined each other as heretics.

Nietzsche, at his best, calls for a "spiritualization of enmity" between partisans of different faiths, encouraging them to weave reciprocal forbearance, thoughtfulness, hesitation, and presumptive generosity into their differences. But the organized Christianity of his day was hard on those who sought to render life more diverse. This experience led Nietzsche to suspect that those transfixed by the hope of eternal salvation would seldom respond with agonistic respect to those who invest themselves entirely in this world. To do so might place their investments in eternal salvation too much at risk. The risk takes the form of a worm of doubt crawling into your soul as you encounter those who live well enough without confessing your faith. On Nietzsche's view, the worm of doubt and the confession of infinite debt to a transcendent power readily combine to foment a spirit of existential revenge. "Great indebtedness," Zarathustra asserts, "does not make men grateful, but vengeful, and if a little charity is not forgotten it turns into a gnawing worm ... But I am a giver of gifts. I like to give as a friend to friends."[34] The element of paradox for Nietzsche himself is that some of the very friends you seek are those who acknowledge infinite debt but, in ways opaque to him, translate that acknowledgement into presumptive generosity to others.

The "unjust" faith of Nietzsche—a faith he sometimes but not always expressed—is that a significant minority within each faction of monotheism might someday accept the invitation to spiritualize enmity. He was unconfident that a majority would ever do so. He also doubted that more than a minority of modern atheists were prepared to do so. That is the zone in which *his* pessimism resides.

Nietzsche did not accept affirmatively enough the positive possibilities of negotiating affirmative relations with carriers of a creed that he himself dropped after his youth as the devout son of a Lutheran minister. It is too bad that William James was not available as he addressed the Christian politics of his day. Or that he did not have recourse to the spirit of Paul Ricoeur, Catherine Keller, Stanley Hauerwas, Karl Jaspers, or Charles Taylor. Nietzsche and James might have negotiated a spiritualization of enmity across an abyss of creedal distance. That is the possibility that I invest in these two thinkers, the world, and the tragic vision. It is, though, only a possibility and not written in the stars.

Should Nietzsche have been more invitational, given his quest to spiritualize enmity? Yes. Nonetheless, this philosopher of immanence makes a case to cultivate gratitude for being and to pursue generous relations with others across significant lines of difference, if they allow it. Zarathustra, his alter-ego, contends that the affirmation of joy in life, amid the suffering and grief that life brings, opens the door to ethical nobility: "Verily, I may have done this or that for sufferers; but always I seemed to have done better when I learned to feel better joys. As long as there have been men, man has felt too little joy: that alone our brothers is our original sin. And learning better how to feel joy, we learn best how not to hurt others or to plan hurts for them."[35] Nietzsche solicits gratitude for the abundance of life in a world without providence or intrinsic meaning. I would adjust his thought to say that the experience of abundance is vibrant in those of whatever existential creed who subdue, by some strategy or other, the tremors of existential resentment coursing through their souls and culture.

Are some regimes better equipped than others to curtail the cultural fund of abstract revenge? Nietzsche thought so. At one point he invokes Zeus, who notes "how mortals complain so loudly of the gods" whose actions bring pain. They "make themselves wretched through folly, even counter to fate," says

Zeus. Nietzsche interprets the comment: "this Olympian spectator and judge is far from holding a grudge against them or thinking ill of them on that account: 'how foolish they are!,' he thinks . . . ; foolishness, not sin! Do you grasp that? . . . In this way the gods served in those days to justify man to a certain extent even in his wickedness, they served as the originators of evil— in those days they took upon themselves, not the punishment but, what is nobler, the guilt."[36]

As "the Greeks" showed, human beings are not doomed by an unbreak- able logic to act out of existential resentment. One way to proceed in a culture that encourages a logic of revenge is to ascertain whether you can live nobly without insisting that life comes pre-equipped with infinite debts, obliga- tions, and a providential design, or the compensatory assurance that the world is susceptible to human mastery. For some do *affirm* a tragic vision without becoming bleak about existence as such. But what if you continue to find a providential image compelling? Another test is to ascertain whether you can coexist with, and not resent, those who confess faith in a world without divine providence as publicly as you confess faith in the Trinity. To accomplish that is to take a large step—from your side—toward the spiritual- ization of enmity.

To simulate these tests let's listen to the case that Nietzsche presents on behalf of *his* theodicy, of a world of becoming replete with tragic possibility:

> This type of *artists' pessimism* is precisely the *opposite* of that religio-moral pessimism that suffers from the 'corruption' of man and the riddle of existence—and that by all means craves a solution, or at least a hope for a solution . . . The profundity of the tragic *artist* lies in this, that his aesthetic instinct surveys the more remote consequences . . ., that he affirms *the large scale economy* which justifies the terrible, the evil, the questionable—and more than merely justifies them.
>
> This pessimism of strength also ends in a *theodicy*, i.e., in an absolute affirmation of the world—but for the very reasons that formerly led one to deny it—and in this fashion to a conception of this world as the actually-achieved highest possible ideal.
>
> *I have been the first to discover the tragic* . . . Even resignation is not a lesson of the tragic, but a misunderstanding of it! Yearning for nothing- ness is a *denial* of tragic wisdom, its opposite.
>
> The faith that a good meaning lies in evil means to abandon the struggle against it.[37]

In these enunciations, composed after the youthful work on tragedy that he had come to reconsider, Nietzsche challenges theodicies that link suffering and evil to the eventual victory of divine providence *or* reduce it to disobedience of divinely imposed laws; he affirms "the large scale economy of the world as such," a vast economy without providence or susceptibility to consummate mastery which surges, bumps, and bounces into human culture; he construes tragic possibility to be wired into the chancy collisions and conjunctions between forces set on different tiers of time; he suggests that attempts to redeem existential suffering through faith in providence can weaken the struggle against fate when things go badly; he resists resignation in the face of tragic effects; he encourages the fight against tragic binds as they arise; and he suggests the need to cultivate strains and tremors in us that prize the abundance of being in a world without providential design, the promise of eternal salvation, or entitlement to human mastery of the world. All these components surge into Nietzsche's "theodicy." The near-paradox is that to affirm—that is, to acknowledge without existential resentment—"the large scale economy" of a world without purpose is also to mobilize energy to struggle against a tragic event on the razor's edge of time. This is a hard insight to grasp for those who resist the tragic vision or who entertain it only after losing confidence in providence or mastery. Nietzsche's orientation contests the theme of providence at two levels: it challenges human entitlements invested in it and the existential bitterness that can overwhelm people when those hopes are dashed. This bitterness can find expression in a desire to take revenge against the old faith, that is, in the belligerent assertion of pale theism, or, more often, in drives to cultural revenge against constituencies whose very mode of being calls self-confidence in your faith in divinity into question. The risk accompanying faith in providence is either resignation or an ethos of existential revenge. Nietzsche's vision or theodicy, again, resists both: it combines a tragic vision with positive energies of attachment to the abundance of being over identity and a willingness to struggle against binds on the edge of becoming. Its risk, as Karl Jaspers has seen, is a fall into despair or the rise of callousness toward the suffering of others.

But how can Nietzsche's theodicy be *tested* against alternative orientations? Is there an *argument*, *book*, or source of *inspiration* that settles the issue in his favor? Nietzsche joins James in both encouraging us to run tests and doubting that any of those available will be definitive for everyone. Though the nobility that James exudes is anchored in a different creed, both he and Nietzsche acknowledge that the issue we are now addressing is to be tested above all through existential experiments. By trying a tragic vision on for size, by experimenting with the thoughts, actions, and exercises that it commends, by tapping the existential gratitude that it solicits, *you run the most basic tests to which it is susceptible.* The most radical tests of gratitude for being amid tragic possibility are performative, experimental, and existential. Here Nietzsche's spirituality touches positive chords in the religions of the Book. The results of the experiments, if we are lucky, become embedded in the soft tissues of life, informing our dispositions to perception, judgment, and action.

To appreciate the ubiquity and cultural compass of these tests, recall the intense debates in Europe accompanying the death of Spinoza, the inveterate philosopher of immanence, joy, and an ethic of cultivation, who burst onto the scene in the seventeenth century to shock Christian philosophers, disturb Jews in Amsterdam, rattle the chains of Cartesians, and inspire a series of subterranean movements in several countries. The intense debate about his last days, which continued for decades, revolved around the question of whether life *can* be infused by gratitude for being without also being tied to the promise of eternal salvation. Did Spinoza die in serenity? Some, such as his opponent Pierre Bayle, confirmed the testimony of Spinoza's friends that he did. Many, however, insisted that Spinoza must have faced a wretched death, regretting his life. Hector Gottfried Masius, German court preacher, "poured scorn on Bayles' account of Spinoza's death, maintaining that there are no 'true theoretical atheists,' men who are categorically convinced there is no God. But . . . there are undoubtedly dangerous men, professed speculative doubters and mockers . . . at the head of whom stands Spinoza."[38] Spinoza, Masius insisted, died acknowledging the God he had "mocked," in abject misery that he had been so prideful.

The public debate is revelatory, as have been those over the deaths of Moses, Socrates, Jesus, Buddha, Nietzsche, and Gilles Deleuze. The debates reveal, first, how existential experiments are involved in the consolidation of a spirituality, and second, how a larger cultural context renders some of these experiments obligatory, discourages others, and issues dire warnings in advance about still others. In this instance a large subterranean minority in several European countries ran Spinozist experiments with life. A hegemonic group, led by the Vatican (which sent detectives to the death scene to try to capture the only copy of *The Ethics* before it could be published), some Jewish leaders in Amsterdam, many state authorities, most attentive philosophers of the day, and much of what Spinoza called "the multitude" condemned these experiments. The stakes were high. Was the hegemony of monotheism to remain unchallenged? Or would a visible minority of adventurers cultivate gratitude for being without attaching it to a personal God, drawing courage from these experiments to press for a pluralization of public culture? Spinoza himself was more of a pluralist than any other thinker of that time of whom I am aware.

If one task of those drawn to a tragic vision is to instill in it care for this world, another is to give that kind of voice a more active presence in public life: to pluralize the depth grammar of public life. We do not seek to produce a universal vision. Even if such an agenda could succeed—which is doubtful— the modes of repression that it would introduce would mirror those prevailing in theocracies. We seek to make deep diversity more possible in more places, even while—as part of our tragic vision—we acknowledge the powerful weight of the forces which campaign against this possibility.

Self-cultivation is an essential part of this task, within our creed and others, even though, as we shall see again, it is radically insufficient to it. On the first score, the following enunciation by Nietzsche, the philosopher of immanence, gratitude for being, the spiritualization of enmity, and tragic possibility, invites comparison to offerings by James—the gentle philosopher of abundance and relational generosity through fugitive connection to a limited god: "Out of damp and gloomy days, out of solitude, out of loveless words directed at us, conclusions grow up in us like fungus: one morning they are there, we know not how, and they gaze upon us. Woe to the thinker who is not the gardener but only the soil of the plants that grow up in him."[39]

Capitalism and Tragic Possibility

In *The Rhetoric of Reaction* Albert Hirschman reviews recent economic theories that implicitly link the market to providence, treating interference with it as self-defeating because of its self-equilibrating powers. Sometimes the providence of the market is defended by asserting how *futile* it is to compensate for the inequalities it generates, sometimes by arguing how intervention invariably produces *perverse* effects. These claims are linked to the celebration of free choice in a minimally regulated, self-equilibrating market system. Hirschman argues that these claims express providential assumptions because market self-regulation would otherwise ring untrue in a world where everything is connected to everything else by a thousand cords. The theories depend upon simplifications of economic complexity and uncertainty, simplifications that ignore both internal volatilities and changeable "externalities" periodically flowing or bouncing into market processes.[40] His critique is amplified by the conception of nature-culture exchanges developed in this book. To the extent that natural processes contain volatile elements of their own that impinge upon economic activity, benign assumptions about the market become even less credible. The volatility of nature and the internal volatility of capitalism communicate with each other. The remains of an old theology are discernible within self-balancing theories of the market.

The market theories reviewed by Hirschman are given a new twist in *Wealth and Poverty* by George Gilder, a book published in 1981 when the assemblage between neoliberalism, neoconservatism, and evangelism was being consolidated. It may even be that the Gilder's new twist grows out of a sense on the right that the old theories of market self-equilibration require a supplement. Gilder asserts that the classical demand for numerous firms regulated by a self-equilibrating market poses too stringent a limit on capitalist invention, innovation, experimentation, and progress. He supports large firms with impressive power over the market. But if the market is overrated as an automatic regulator in the short term and if the state, as Gilder also insists, is an impediment when it exceeds its role as police power, military force, and regulator of the money supply, what *does* secure the benign connection between capitalism and human well-being over the long term? Gilder now draws into the foreground a theology that had already hovered in the background of market concepts. Economic advance, he says, is grounded in the very chanciness and innovative power of free enterprise, and in the recognition of capitalist enterprise as the site where divine providence finds its most salient *worldly* expression. Indeed, Gilder skates close to a tragic vision before veering off sharply at the last second:

> Critics of capitalism often imagine that they have discovered some great scandal . . . when they reveal its crucial reliance on luck . . . Chance, however, is not the realm of the anarchic and haphazard but the area of freedom and the condition of creativity. It taps the underlying transcendent order of the universe.
>
> Capitalism succeeds because it accommodates chance and thus accords with the reality of the human situation in a fundamentally incomprehensible, but nonetheless providential universe.
>
> Even relatively simple creative processes require a plunge into darkness—a dependence on incalculable providence.
>
> The crucial rules of creative thought can be summed up as faith, love,

openness, conflict, and falsifiability. The crucial roles of economic inno-vation and progress are faith, altruism, investment, competition and bankruptcy, which are also the rules of capitalism.[41]

Gilder locks together into one system the unpredictability of things, entre-preneurial creativity, unfettered capitalism, and incalculable providence, in the process defining consumer movements, state actions to cushion insecu-rity, powerful unions, and environmental politics as being at odds with this divine combination. His intervention helped to forge an evangelical-capitalist formula built around faith in the providential character of capitalist markets.

God, luck, providence, and capitalism; capitalism, providence, luck, and God. As Gilder understands, but as other celebrants of the market seem to forget, there can be a god who is not providential; but it is difficult to imagine a providential universe without a beneficent god. And since the capitalist system is tied by a thousand ropes and pulleys to forces of nature and civiliza-tion that exceed it, it is unlikely to be self-equilibrating unless the universe in which it is set is protected by providence. So Gilder draws out the element that secular theories of market beneficence suppress: because the market is inter-woven with spiritual life, state policies, climate patterns, scientific practice, resource availability, and so on indefinitely, it is only providential if the uni-verse is, and if it provides a divinely ordained gathering point for these forces. If the story of divine providence were dropped from Gilder's analysis he would become a trenchant critic of unfettered capitalism.

Of course, not all of those attracted to the picture that Gilder draws accept every aspect of his theory. Some support the benign image of capitalism because of the providential god that it glorifies, others because of the eco-nomic entitlements that it justifies for them, others out of resentment against constituencies below them who seek state assistance, others out of hope that a bit of good fortune will catapult them to the ranks of the rich, others out of resentment against liberal élites who would regulate their conduct, still oth-ers out of an implicit refusal to gauge the effects on others and the future of their current practices, and many out of variable and combustible mixtures of these considerations. There is a catch, however. Faith in the equation between capital and providence can easily become transfigured into an ethos of bitter-ness if things don't work out as promised. The transfiguration is less apt to find expression in an outright denial of providence; that would deny the god around whom your life has been staked. It is not highly likely either to find expression in the dissociation of capitalism from providence; that would undermine the worldly identity around which many lives have been built. What expression, then, does it find? It most readily takes the shape of a punitive attitude toward those constituencies and state policies said to obstruct an equation that would otherwise hold. Many capitalist élites, middle-class aspirants to élite status, Catholic conservatives, neoconservatives, media financial reporters, and evangelicals coalesce around this formula, with several occupying a couple of these subject positions. The emergent political formula becomes unfettered capitalism, impressive state subsidies for capital, cultural moralism, a providential god, militarism, and the punitive administration of those outside the sacred fold, with the most fervent adherents making accusations of amoralism, relativism, nihilism, "self-indulgence," and treason against those who challenge this picture. Some participants emphasize certain aspects of the formula, others valorize other aspects. Most of them are on display in Gilder's book.[42]

Things look different if you adopt a tragic vision, without resenting the world for not being providential. Like Gilder, you acknowledge the role of luck, chance, creativity, and innovation in the world, by comparison to those who adopt a deterministic image. But unlike him you do not concentrate creativity and uncertainty in capital enterprise alone; and you dislodge economic life from the promise of incalculable providence. You adopt a tragic vision with meliorist potential, and you work upon yourself and others to overcome resentment of a world with these very possibilities attached to it. You might resent dogmatists who seek to impose sacrifices upon others in the name of their creed, but you do not resent the world for indifference to the human aspirations that you value most. You espouse a tragic vision, as you also seek to mobilize connections with others who resist the human drive to ressentiment without embracing that vision. A spiritualization of enmity. As you proceed, you find yourself warning of dangers that may become more visible when the world is interpreted through the lens of tragic possibility.

Consider one scenario of tragic potential tied to the current epoch of capitalism.[43] Others are possible. Dominant practices of resource depletion, soil erosion, water pollution, and global warming strain the human habitat so severely that the continuation of affluence in advanced capitalist states is squeezed. As unpaid debts to the future come due, regimes that have been closed out of the confined zones of affluence intensify their resentments against affluent states, with the United States the prime object of those responses. These reactions are amplified through an increase in the intensity of floods, storms, and drought in a world in which the United States has both made the most notable contribution to those effects and virulently resisted interstate efforts to mitigate them. The supply of clean water declines, throwing several economies into severe difficulty. A neoconservative regime in Washington, desperate to preserve its advantages and maintain limited supplies of oil in a world of expanded demand and depleted supply, becomes more bellicose yet against some suppliers and competitors. It abrogates more treaties, launches new preemptive wars, treats international agencies belligerently, signs protective treaties with a shrinking number of allies, intensifies divisions at home, fuels tolerance among millions of people elsewhere for nonstate terrorism against the United States, and treats everyone within the state who protests its priorities as being soft on terrorism or engaging in treason. Police, surveillance, border security, and prison budgets skyrocket, while those for education, welfare, medical care, and sustainable practices of consumption languish even more. This set of policies and attitudes in turn inflames tensions between the world's historic religions, with Christianity and Islam taking the lead. The tinderbox in the Middle East explodes, through the conjunction of national divisions, religious conflicts, competition for oil, and the spread of Iraqi sectarian conflicts to neighboring states. Civil wars, some set off by the reckless invasion of Iraq by George W. Bush—despite worldwide protests before it started—help to trigger several of these responses. Once things reach this point, the prospect of falling into a long series of pointless wars against state and nonstate enemies grows too. Eventually investors in countries such as China, who have financed much of the burgeoning American debt generated by cowboy capitalism, engage in capital strikes, placing in a bleak situation the American economy and the capitalist world in which it is entangled by a thousand knots.

In the above scenario several loosely connected contingencies break one way rather than others, creating a destructive result that is not written in the stars. The effect might be compared to the multiple contingencies portrayed in the film *Dr. Strangelove* (1964). The United States and the Soviet Union could have got lucky, after a general went berserk and sent bombers on a nonreversible mission to drop hydrogen bombs on Russia. The visiting general from England *might* have succeeding in stopping the crazy general before the order was issued. The "Russkies" *might* have shot down each plane that entered an attack zone, once the targets were relayed to them by the American president. Every commanding officer on each plane *might* have received the president's message to reverse course. But once things were set in motion, a series of accidents, decisions, and events broke the wrong way, engendering a result that no one wanted except Dr. Strangelove and the general trying to protect his "vital body fluids."

The situation is comparable today, with a potential decline of world proportions waiting in the wings. The globalization and acceleration of capital and communication, the multiplication of minorities unleashed by both, the time bomb of global warming, the growing isolation of the United States from countries seeking to reduce environmental risks, the widespread resentment toward American hegemony during a time when regional inequality has got worse—all of these set the stage of possibility. The prevailing spirituality, economic priorities, and military hubris of the United States could set such a scenario in motion.

Yes, some concatenation of events could turn things around. The outcome is not foreordained by the gods. A new source of energy might be discovered, as cheap, free of adverse effects, and plentiful as nuclear energy was supposed to be when it was first unleashed. And other contingencies could push things in a more positive direction. But why court the risk? Why count on providence or luck in favor of the time and place in which you just happen to live? State Christo-capitalism, built around the promise of a world of abundance, contains the possibility of a decline that unleashes other destructive forces in its wake. This is so because the global dimension of capitalism increasingly entangles everyone with everything. We may stand on the razor's edge of time, in a world in which Fox News is poised to defame any individual or group that delivers the critical message.

As I have been arguing, a series of positive existential orientations, relational tactics, local strategies, academic reforms, microeconomic experiments, large social movements, media strategies, shifts in economic and political ethos, state policies, and cross-state citizen actions are needed to reduce the prospect of such a destructive outcome. Each chapter has focused on one or two initiatives. Today all are needed, both to ward off the worst risks and to pursue the positive possibilities outlined in the previous chapters. More of us must cultivate gratitude for this world in a theistic or nontheistic vein, through engagements with ourselves, church assemblies, films, media events, professional meetings, dinner conversations, local initiatives, and interstate citizen movements, seeking to infuse care for the future into the families, schools, companies, churches, and spiritual assemblies to which we belong. More of us must articulate publicly the dangers facing our time, while simultaneously visualizing positive possibilities of positive interim action in the domains of ecology, consumption reform, reduced inequality, and expanded pluralism. More of us must publicize and participate in microeconomic experiments that reduce inequality, enact sustainable modes of consumption, and return a larger portion of surplus to localities and workers; these experiments simultaneously improve a corner of the world, help participants to apply direct pressure to corporations, and inspire others to apply new pressure to their states. More of us must expose the short time horizon and scandal mongering of the news media, while refining media skills ourselves in a world in which the media help to shape the politics of perception. More of us must participate in direct movements and electoral politics, to press localities, corporations, states, universities, churches, and international institutions to enact new policies. And more of us must participate in targeted cross-state citizens' movements to apply pressure on our states, churches, and corporations from the inside and outside simultaneously.

If action in each zone begins to reverberate with those in others, a positive resonance machine will surge into being. If it lifts off, it will be more potent than the sum of its parts. Of course a new series of injuries and modes of suffering may emerge from its very success, requiring additional rounds of creative action. A tragic vision with meliorist potential, appreciating the volatilities and interdependencies between multiple zones of being, anticipates surprise amid periodic moments of success, without knowing with confidence what the surprises will be.

Would capitalism be transfigured into something else if these activities and movements acquired impressive momentum? I am not sure, partly because of the uncertain volatility of natural and cultural forces that both enter and impinge upon economic life and partly because of the historical plasticity of what counts as "capitalism." Capitalism would surely shift significantly from the form taken in the United States today, leaving the intercoded myths of neoliberalism and neoconservatism in the dust. And it might help set the table of possibility for a world economy more noble than that preceding it. Will economic and political disaster result if considerable success on these fronts is not attained over the next twenty years? That is uncertain too, though the possibility seems real. In a world wound more tightly than heretofore, a series of shocks to the nerve centers of capitalism could usher new waves of fascism into the world, in which repressive political regimes wage perpetual war against underspecified enemies as they bind themselves increasingly to a set of mafia-capitalist operations. This, again, is one of the more dismal possibilities in a larger set, including the positive ones pursued in chapter 4. But it is real and dangerous enough to be included in the list.

Would Tiresias call such a disaster tragic if it occurred? That too is uncertain. The United States is a prime mover in a hierarchical world economy that imposes great suffering on many, so the effect on one country must be weighed against the effects on the current world order. My sense nonetheless is that the scenario would make things worse yet in many places for a long time, though one cannot specify all the ramifications. Beyond that, a tragic *vision* with meliorist potential involves more than periodic attention to dangers in a cosmos not automatically predisposed toward human benefit or mastery. Those who participate in that vision deepen their appreciation of human limits amid the uncertainty of being; they heighten care for the world and the sweetness of life amid the dangers encountered. And they draw upon this fund of positive energy as they struggle to turn things in a more favorable direction. They negotiate the tensions between several components of the same vision. Would that blind, ambiguous seer call upon us to act both militantly and wisely, as if we straddle the razor's edge of time? That seems likely.

NOTES

Introduction: The Spirit of Capitalism

1 Stephen Mitchell, *The Gospel According to Jesus* (New York: Harper, 1991), 106, 107, 111.

2 Thomas Jefferson, *The Jefferson Bible* (Boston: Beacon, 1989). *The Jefferson Bible* was published, at Jefferson's wish, after his death. He was hesitant to see it in print while he was alive. It closes with: "And there laid they Jesus. And rolled a great stone to the door of the sepulchre and departed" (147). Jefferson's Jesus, perhaps like the Jesus in Mitchell's Gospel, is not resurrected.

3 Quoted in Mitchell, *The Gospel According to Jesus*, 278.

4 Ibid., 278–79.

5 Ibid., 279.

6 Jefferson was not alone in his views among the founding fathers. For an account of the theological views of Franklin, Washington, Adams, Jefferson, Madison, and Hamilton which breaks with the accounts we hear regularly on Fox News see Brooke Allen, *Moral Minority: Our Skeptical Founding Fathers* (Chicago: Ivan R. Dee, 2006).

7 Do later doctrines of the Trinity and attacks upon Arianism find support in the earliest versions of the Gospels? Or are they written into them by scribes after the fact? The debate over this question is extensive. Bart Ehrman, in *The Orthodox Corruption of Scripture* (New York: Oxford University Press, 1993), assembles evidence that the virgin birth of Mary and the co-divinity of Jesus with God from birth were redacted into later texts. "Adoptionists," often later known as Arians, held that Jesus became Christ either after his baptism or upon his resurrection. Supporters of the Trinity oppose each of these judgments. We turn to this question in chapter 5.

8 The quotations from Revelation are drawn from *The New Oxford Annotated Bible*, 3rd edn, ed. Michael Coogan (Oxford: Oxford University Press, 2001).

9 Mark Blyth, *Great Transformations: Economic Ideas and Institutional Change in the Twentieth Century* (Cambridge: Cambridge University Press, 2002), and David Harvey, *A Brief History of Neoliberalism* (Oxford: Oxford University Press, 2005), have both been helpful to me. Blyth explores how neoliberals in several countries waged a

war of ideas against Keynesianism, working to embed themselves in academic theory, corporate practices, state policies, and international institutions. Harvey focuses on the role that the capitalist class played in changing a variety of institutions, including international financial institutions. Another early critique of the assumptions that neoliberal theory makes about the relation between the market and the structure of consumption has also influenced me. We will engage *The Social Limits to Growth* by Fred Hirsch (London: Routledge and Kegan Paul, 1977) in chapter 4. Michael Best and William Connolly, *The Politicized Economy* (Lexington: D. C. Heath, 1976; 2nd edn 1983), advances an early critique of Milton Friedman, the granddaddy of neoliberal theory. In chapter 1 we explore a tension between the ethos of capitalism that Friedman seeks to promote through persuasion and the springs of human behavior that he finds wired into economic and political practice. Today we would assert that a neoliberal economy solicits a neoconservative approach to social mores.

10 For a "short history" of multiple territorial and spiritual developments in Islamic history, see Karen Armstrong, *Islam* (New York: Random House, 2002). The very brevity of this book brings out how diverse and variegated Islam has been in different times and places. Armstrong is also alert to the role that European colonization from the eighteenth century on played in defining Islamic resistance to various western currents. The complexity of specific currents in modern Islam is brought out in Saba Mahmood, *Politics of Piety: The Islamic Revival and the Feminist Subject* (Stanford: Stanford University Press, 2005); Charles Hirschkind, *The Ethical Soundscape: Cassette Sermons and Islamics Counterpublics* (New York: Columbia University Press, 2006); and Talal Asad, *Formations of the Secular: Christianity, Islam, Modernity* (Stanford: Stanford University Press, 2003).

Chapter 1: The Volatility of Capitalism

1 Max Weber, *The Protestant Ethic and the Spirit of Capitalism*, trans. Talcott Parsons (New York: Charles Scribner's Sons, 1958), 17, 21.

2 Ibid., 21–23.

3 Blumenberg, *The Legitimacy of the Modern Age*, trans. Robert Wallace (Cambridge: MIT Press, 1983).

4 Weber, *The Protestant Ethic and the Spirit of Capitalism*, 53.

5 Ibid., 181–82.

6 Karl Marx, "Critical Notes on the King of Prussia and Social Reform," *Writings of the Young Marx on Philosophy and Society*, ed. Lloyd Easton and Kurt Guddat (New York: Anchor, 1967), 348, 349.

7 Ibid., 349.

8 See R. H. Tawney, *Religion and the Rise of Capitalism* (New Brunswick, N.J.: Transaction, 1998).

9 Gilles Deleuze and Felix Guattari, *A Thousand Plateaus*, trans. Brian Massumi (Minneapolis: University of Minnesota Press, 1987), 452.

10 Ibid., 453, 454.

11 See Stephen Gould, *The Structure of Evolutionary Theory* (Cambridge: Harvard University Press, 2002), and Brian Goodwin. *How the Leopard Lost Its Spots* (Princeton: Princeton University Press, 1994). Gould comes close to the Nietzschean idea of the moment when he compares his theory of evolution to that of Nietzsche on pages 1214–18.

12 Weber, *The Protestant Ethic and the Spirit of Capitalism*, 67.

13 Deleuze and Guattari, *A Thousand Plateaus*, 453.

14 Ibid.

15 Ibid., 454.

16 Ibid., 455.

17 For a series of essays that break both with structural accounts of capitalist contradiction and neoclassical accounts of smooth economic management, emphasizing the role that cultural forces play in every aspect of economic life, see Ash Amin and Nigel Thrift, eds., *The Blackwell Cultural Economy Reader* (Oxford: Blackwell, 2004).

18 For this thesis see Joseph Ratzinger and Marcello Pera, *Without Roots: The West, Relativism, Christianity, Islam* (New York: Basic, 2006). According to the editor, the book expresses the views that Benedict XVI brought with him to the papacy. In it he praises the new alliance between the Vatican and American evangelism.

19 See William E. Connolly, *Appearance and Reality in Politics* (Cambridge: Cambridge University Press, 1981), chapters 3, 6; *Identity/Difference* (Ithaca: Cornell University Press), chapters 1, 7; and *The Ethos of Pluralization* (Minneapolis: University of Minnesota Press, 1995), chapters 3, 4.

20 The latest stage of this movement is explored in chapter 2.

21 Quoted in Linda Kintz, *Between Jesus and the Market* (Durham: Duke University Press, 1997), 64. I first encountered this theme of the LaHayes in Kintz's remarkable book. The original quote comes from Tim LaHaye and Beverly LaHaye, *The Act of Marriage: The Beauty of Sexual Love* (Grand Rapids: Zondervan, 1995), 23. My interpretation, I believe, is congruent with hers, though its focus may be a bit different. I seek to understand how so many who might identify with the class in which they are located have been drawn away from that quest into a militant politics of individual aspiration, which first makes them identify with classes above their reach and, second, encourages them to neutralize or demonize a series of minority movements. Kintz is also concerned with the second issue.

22 The LaHayes, quoted in Kintz, *Between Jesus and the Market*, 67.

23 Nigel Thrift, *Knowing Capitalism* (London: Sage, 2005), 29.

24 I am impressed with David Harvey's *A Brief History of Neoliberalism* (Oxford: Oxford University Press, 2005). He examines the theoretical and state sources of the neoliberal victory in many places; he shows how the capture of the IMF and the WTO by neoliberalism puts many states under external pressure to conform to its dictates; and above all, he concentrates his critical guns on the redistributive consequences of neoliberalism. But I would correct his general neglect of imbrications between the

right edge of Christianity and popular support for neoliberalism, and I resist his tendency to define postmodernists as allies of corporate slickness. Are Deleuze and Foucault to be placed in that category, even though they fight against many of the same things that Harvey does? It is very possible to be on the left while coming to terms positively with the acceleration of pace, the world as becoming, and some new zones of commodification.

25   George Gilder, *Men and Marriage* (Gretna, La.: Pelican, 1993), 73–74; and quoted in Kintz, *Between Jesus and the Market*, 168–69. In chapter 5 I examine Gilder's equation between capitalism and providence in *Wealth and Poverty* (New York: Basic, 1981). That book is pertinent to understanding the interplay between neoliberalism, neoconservatism, and the evangelical movement.

26   In "God's Casino: The Texas of George Bush," *Dissent*, summer 2006, 37–44, Kevin Task does a superb job of showing how the confluence of new Texas oil money in the 1930s and new twists in local evangelical theology created a "theology of winners." Winners are the ones most apt to celebrate retrospectively the role of chance and risk in life, folding drama and heroism into their own pasts. His essay discusses the Sunbelt sources of a phenomenon that has become more widespread. My concern here is to come to terms with its attractions to those least likely to be winners. One factor involved, perhaps, is the dismantling of critical parts of the welfare state. If those supports are taken away, and there is no movement in sight to restore them, the embrace of gambling and luck becomes more appealing.

27   A recent book that advances this thesis persuasively is by Philip Goodchild, *Capitalism and Religion: The Price of Piety* (London: Routledge, 2002). Goodchild seeks a new piety, appropriate to the new world in which we live.

Chapter 2: The Evangelical-Capitalist Resonance Machine

1   An earlier presentation of the evangelical element in contemporary political economy was presented in the spring of 2005, at the WPSA panel in Oakland organized around the new edition of Sheldon Wolin's *Politics and Vision* (Princeton: Princeton University Press, 2005). That edition adds a part II to the classic 1960 text. While I dissented from Wolin's account of Nietzsche, I drew upon his account of America as "Superpower" in the new edition.

2   This chapter is indebted to Gilles Deleuze and Felix Guattari, "Micropolitics and Segmentarity," *A Thousand Plateaus*, trans. Brian Massumi (Minneapolis: University of Minnesota Press, 1987), 208–31. The authors there invoke the idea of a resonance machine, applying it to the early stages of the Nazi movement in Germany.

3   Here are some pieces that focus on the role that greed plays in this alliance. They do not, however, anchor that greed in anything over and above the normal processes of underregulated capitalism: "Enron's Smoking Gun," Foundation for Taxpayer and Consumer Rights, http://www.consumerwatchdog.org/utilities/nw/nw002172.php3; "Unveiling the Corporate GreedMarket," http://www.consciouschoice.com/cc1709/hightower17

09.html; and "Enron Flew under the Radar," Common Dreams New Center, http://www.commondreams.org/views02/0212.htm.

4 Mark Blyth, *Great Transformations: Economic Ideas and Institutional Change in the Twentieth Century* (Cambridge: Cambridge University Press, 2002), 267.

5 Tim LaHaye and Jerry B. Jenkins, *Left Behind: A Novel of the Earth's Last Days* (Wheaton, Ill.: Tyndale, 1995), 468.

6 This quotation comes from a column by Nicholas Kristof, "Apocalypse (Almost) Now," *New York Times*, 24 November 2004, 27. It is from the last volume in the series. I have not read that one yet . . .

7 There are now large, fuel-eating, dangerous and destructive suvs, and others of smaller, more efficient design. The differences are reviewed in a report in the *New York Times*, 1 April 2005, on the vehicles that Republicans and Democrats respectively buy. In general Republicans favor the larger vehicles and Democrats the smaller. Correlations between party and vehicle are fine. But it would even be more illuminating to study correlations, if any, between existential disposition and vehicle use. This issue could be studied by drawing upon new brain-imaging techniques which, advancing beyond those available for a few decades, can discern specific brain states that bring communicants together. Hummer ads, as we shall see later, are aimed at those who celebrate a bellicose style of life. The suv as an example and symbol of "positional goods" is discussed in chapter 5.

8 David Harvey, in *A Brief History of Neoliberalism* (Oxford: Oxford University Press, 2005), delineates such effects after neoliberalism assumed power in several countries. His comparative study is valuable, particularly if amended to explore the ethos that often infuses the most enthusiastic supporters of the doctrine and their strategies to ward off discomfiting evidence. It is not only predominately Christian countries that are susceptible to this disease. As I will discuss soon, any faith or doctrine can succumb.

9 For a critique of the theological basis in Christianity of George Bush's speeches and policies, see Jim Wallis, *God's Politics: Why the Right Gets It Wrong and the Left Doesn't Get It* (San Francisco: Harper Collins, 2005), particularly chapter 9, "The Theology of Empire."

10 See Max Weber, *The Protestant Ethic and the Spirit of Capitalism*, trans. Talcott Parson (New York: Charles Scribner's Sons, 1958). "Wealth is thus bad ethically only in so far as it is a temptation to idleness and sinful enjoyment of life, and its acquisition is bad only when it is with the purpose of later living merrily and without care . . . The emphasis on the ascetic importance of a fixed calling provided an ethical justification of the modern specialized division of labor. In a similar way the providential interpretation of profit making justified the activities of the business man" (163). These two statements measure both the contact and difference between Weber's analysis of the spiritual element in the formation of capitalism and my more modest attempt to decipher the spirituality of a particular constellation in one country today.

11 Friedrich Nietzsche, *Thus Spoke Zarathustra*, trans. Walter Kaufmann (New York: Vintage, 1966), 99, 140.

12 Quoted in truthout issues, http://www.truthout.org/docs—2005 1/1/2006. The statement was no longer available on Robertson's web site when I reviewed it in March 2006.

13 See Harvey Cox, "Old Time Religion," reprinted in the *Boston Globe*, 9 July 2006.

14 http://www.patrobertson.com/Features/ted—haggard.asp.

15 To read *Zarathustra* as I do is to discern that the drive to "be equal"—which he connects to the will to revenge—is mostly the demand that everyone either be *the same* (e.g., to have the same faith, the same sexuality, the same ethnicity, the same belief in the market) or be punished for not being so. The "overman" is not a separate kind of human for Zarathustra by the end of the text; it eventually becomes a noble voice in many selves on behalf of affirmation. More than Zarathustra, I separate revenge against difference from the drive to reduce economic inequality. The first is a measure of my debt to him, the second of my agonistic response to his unconcern about economic inequality.

16 See Timothy P. Weber, *Waiting for the Second Coming*, 2nd edn (Chicago: University of Chicago Press, 1987). Weber charts the movement from the beginning of the twentieth century to the 1980s. His view that "relative deprivation" only helps to explain its attractions is pertinent to the account here. His attention to millenialists such as former Senator Mark Hatfield of Oregon, who hold the key creedal beliefs but do not embrace the ugly politics, is also pertinent. Once again it is the formal belief in conjunction with susceptibility or resistance to existential resentment that is important. That is why it may be possible to pluralize further the political orientations of evangelists.

17 Frank Ankersmit, "Democracy's Inner Voice: Political Style as Unintended Consequence of Political Action," *Media and the Restyling of Politics*, ed. John Corner and Dick Pels (London: Sage, 2003), 19. Ankersmit's objective is to show how political reality is not exhausted by the articulations of its contestants.

18 Perhaps this is the point to note that existential resentment can be *expressed* without being *articulated* because such an affective disposition is filled with ideas. So to say that people can share the same formal creed while differing in the sensibility infused into it is not to say that a sensibility consists of pure affect. Rather, an idea-imbued sensibility inflects the meaning of a publicly defined creed in this way or that. The explicit creed may say, "Only Jesus can save you." The implicit, affectively charged idea might be either "and you will burn in hell if you are not baptized" *or* "if you are a decent person he will save you." Moreover, two people could share the first disposition but differ significantly in the intensity with which it is felt.

19 Robert Heath, *The Hidden Power of Advertising: How Low Involvement Processing Influences the Ways We Choose Brands* (Oxford: Admap, 2001).

20 Heath's book noted above can profitably be read in conjunction with Mark B. N. Hanson, *New Philosophy for New Media* (Cambridge: MIT Press, 2004), especially chapter 6. Hansen explores experimental art that draws to the foreground *affective* dimensions usually operating in the background of perception. An effective counter-

politics of perception must draw upon such experiments to fashion ways to challenge the media image-and-sound campaigns with which we are bombarded.

21 For an essay that explores the imbrications between media, show business, and electoral politics in England and the Netherlands see John Street, "The Celebrity Politician: Political Style and Popular Culture," *Media and the Restyling of Politics*, ed. John Corner and Dick Pels, 85–98. An insightful book that examines the role of entertainment in politics in the United States is Jeffrey Jones, *Entertaining Politics* (New York: Rowman and Littlefield, 2004).

22 The Basque syndicalist movement, inspired by a Catholic priest, will be discussed in chapter 4; Cornel West's engagement with a prophetic tradition, most visibly expressed in the work of Martin Luther King is in chapter 5. See Cornel West, *Democracy Matters* (New York: Penguin, 2004). For an account of positive currents within the evangelical tradition see Jim Wallis, *God's Politics* (San Francisco: Harper, 2005). For a creative engagement with the theo-politics of John Howard Yoder see Romand Coles, *Beyond Gated Politics* (Minneapolis: University of Minnesota Press, 2005). The larger strategic vision advanced in chapters 4 and 5 of this book is connected to those advanced by West and Coles.

23 James's philosophy of time and meliorism receives its closest expression in *A Pluralistic Universe* (Lincoln: University of Nebraska Press, 1996). I offer a reading of this book in *Pluralism* (Durham, Duke University Press, 2005), chapter 3. We will consult Nietzsche later. Catherine Keller's inspired book *The Face of the Deep: A Theology of Becoming* (New York: Routledge: 2003) reads Genesis itself to present a limited God acting upon a primordial world, before polemical theologies of the second through fourth centuries translated the Christian God into an omnipotent agent creating everything out of nothing. Kathleen Skerrett called my attention to this book, and I have also profited greatly from her (as yet) unpublished essay "Time for Liberal Theology? Towards an Eschatology of Ordinary Time." Again, the affinities of spirituality and ethos across these figures are at least as important as the doctrinal lines of connection across difference.

24 John Sanders, *The God Who Risks: A Theology of Providence* (Downers Grove, Ill.: Intervarsity, 1998), 101–4.

25 Ibid., 108.

26 The Arian controversy will be discussed in chapter 5.

27 "Can God See the Future," *Chronicle of Higher Education*, 26 November 2004, 12.

28 Nietzsche, *Thus Spoke Zarathustra*, 99.

29 It is pertinent to see that the "attachment to this world" spoken of here is not to existing injustices, class suffering, dogmatism, repression of diversity, and the like, but to the human existential condition itself. The wager is that enhancing attachment to this world increases the energy and will to oppose the dangers and injustices now built into it. Why, then, do some equate the assertion by immanent naturalists of existential attachment with attachment to injustice? In some cases, I think, the equation grows out of the idea that the experience of suffering itself, existential and

otherwise, forms the indispensable basis from which to act in support of justice. We immanent naturalists, however, adopt a *somewhat* different view. We think that enhancing attachment to this world amid the differential suffering that accompanies life is indispensable to forming affirmative political energy. I have argued the issue elsewhere and will not rehearse it here. Here the interesting thing to note is the anticipatory structure that some bring to the sentences under consideration. Again, why is such an equation projected by critics into a vision that does not affirm it? Perhaps existential, theological, and ontological issues are simmering here.

30 Deleuze, *Cinema II, The Time Image*, trans. Hugh Tomlinson (New York: Athlone, 1989), 172.

31 The research is summarized in a report from the National Science and Technology Center, Canberra, Australia, 2006, http://www.questacon.edu.au/html/assets/rtf/ strike—a—chord—good—vibrations.rtf. The quotations come from that report.

32 In "Experience and Experiment," *Daedalus*, summer 2006, 67–75, I explore a battery of techniques to deepen attachment to this world, where "this world" includes within its compass a set of temporal experiences that are distinctive.

Chapter 3: Between Science and Faith

1 The study by Stephen White, *Sustaining Affirmation* (Princeton: Princeton University Press, 2002), is pertinent here. White examines comparatively the work of George Kateb, Charles Taylor, Judith Butler, and me. He does so first to bring out the "weak ontology" of each and the role it plays in their different theories, and second to see how effectively each comes to terms with the element of contestability in his or her ontology.

2 Hence I am unable to endorse the view of a variety of academic secularists, Habermasians, Arendtians, and postmodernists who proclaim modernity (and themselves) to be "post-metaphysical."

3 The struggle between Arians and Trinitarians is discussed in chapter 5 of this book. An account of Newton's relation to Arianism, centuries after the issue was supposed to have been resolved, can be found in Maurice Wiles, *Archetypal Heresy: Arianism over the Centuries* (Oxford: Oxford University Press, 1996).

4 Augustine, *On Christian Doctrine*, trans. D. W. Robertson (New York: Macmillan, 1958), 30.

5 As summarized by Donald Green and Ian Shapiro, *Pathologies of Rational Choice Theory* (New Haven: Yale University Press, 1994), rational behavior in rational choice theory is "typically identified with 'maximization of some sort' "; it must be possible for "all of an agent's options to be rank ordered"; and reference orderings are transitive, so that if "A is preferred to B, and B is preferred to C then the consistency rule requires that A be preferred to C" (14–15). As the authors also point out, such a theory treats the preferences of individuals as basic data, rather than exploring how identities and interests are formed through historically specific con-

junctions of child rearing, church attendance, educational experience, searing personal experiences, surprising public events, etc. However, Green and Shapiro test the evidentiary success of rational choice theory against a model of empiricism not itself put up for critical scrutiny. I am also fond of an earlier challenge to empiricism, perhaps comparable to this critique of rational choice theory. "Our review of the areas of contention between Dahl and Mills and of the organization of their respective studies reveals, I believe, that their resulting analyses are in large part self-fulfilling. In each case the focal points of analysis (that is, the political arena vs. The interrelations of the identified elite) and the conceptual decisions made seem to foster the interpretation rather than to provide a test of it. An analysis of the testing operations actually employed by pluralists and elitists will solidify this appraisal; moreover, each reinforces his own position by making favorable assumptions about key (and for practical purposes, untestable) aspects of the system under investigation." William Connolly, *Political Science and Ideology* (New York: Atherton, 1967), 30. What if neither rational-choice theory nor empiricism lives up in practice to the standards to which each holds others in the abstract? The term "ideology" deployed in that early book shares something with the notion of "existential faith" in this chapter. But it is difficult to divest the former of the idea that only others participate in the endeavor, and it is also not commonly extended to those whose interpretations are strongly invested with theistic faith of some sort or other. The Dahl referred to in that early quote is very unlike the Dahl who made a closing address to the Yale conference at which this chapter was initially presented. That Robert Dahl emphasizes how the object of politics is more complex than that of physics, and he concentrates on the role of contingency in political events. He and William James are now kindred spirits.

6 Augustine, *On Christian Doctrine*, 79.

7 Ibid., 87–88.

8 In Harold Bloom and David Rosenberg, eds., *The Book of J* (New York: Grove Weidenfeld, 1993), Bloom argues that the earliest version of Genesis, the J version, is best read as a tragic story in which the serpent warns the first couple against the overreaching of the young God who still has things to learn. In *The Religion of Jesus the Jew* (Minneapolis: Fortress, 1993), Geza Vermes reads the earliest available versions of Mark, Matthew, and Luke to claim that Jesus is presented there as a radical Jewish prophet rather than a divine being.

9 Augustine, *On Christian Doctrine*, 87.

10 Hegel, in *Phenomenology of Spirit*, trans. A. V. Miller (Oxford: Clarendon, 1977), writes that the epistemologist treats the knowing faculty either as a "medium" through which knowledge is received or as an "instrument" by which to test knowledge claims. The problem is "that the use of the instrument on a thing does not let it be what it is for itself, but rather sets out to reshape and alter it." And a medium "does not receive the truth as it is in itself, but only as it exists through the medium" (para 73, p. 46). The dilemma is that each attempt to establish a medium or instru-

ment as final runs into the problem of either introducing another to justify it or repeating the first to justify itself.

11   I pursue this issue in *Why I Am Not a Secularist* (Minneapolis: University of Minnesota Press, 1999).

12   Quoted in Louis Menand, *The Metaphysical Club: A Story of Ideas in America* (New York: Farrar, Straus and Giroux, 1999), 191.

13   Stanley Hauerwas, *With the Grain of the Universe* (Grand Rapids: Brozos, 2001). Hauerwas presents a spirited critique of James, whose theology is too wishy-washy for him. His heroes are Barth, Yoder, and John Paul II, because the God of each is omnipotent and witnessing plays a key role in consolidating faith.

14   The appropriate texts are Stephen Jay Gould, *The Structure of Evolutionary Theory* (Cambridge: Harvard University Press, 2002), and Ilya Prigogine and Isabelle Stengers, *The End of Certainty: Time Chaos and the New Laws of Nature* (New York: Free Press, 1997).

15   Kenneth Boulding, "Expecting the Unexpected," *The Future: Images and Processes*, by Elise Boulding and Kenneth Boulding (Thousand Oaks: Sage, 1995), 7–26.

16   Deleuze and Guattari, *A Thousand Plateaus*, 407.

17   The Deleuzian idea of change through spiral repetition is relevant here. As Jane Bennett summarizes in *The Enchantment of Modern Life* (Princeton: Princeton University Press, 2000,) 40, the "point about spiral repetition is that sometimes that which repeats itself also transforms itself. Because each iteration occurs in a . . . unique context, each turn of the spiral enters into a new and distinctive assemblage." For other works that speak to emergent causation in social and cultural theory see Brian Massumi, *Parables for the Virtual* (Durham: Duke University Press, 2002), and Manuel De Landa, *One Thousand Years of Nonlinear History* (New York: Zone, 1997). De Landa explores auto-catalytic loops that help to generate new forms out of old molds in the formation of granite, the consolidation of ecosystems, and the composition of national languages.

18   Here for instance are some things that Stephen Gould says about the need to rethink cause in evolutionary theory: in Darwin, "the organism supplies raw material in the form of 'random' variation, but does not 'push back' to direct the flow of its own alteration from the inside . . . By contrast the common themes . . . in this book all follow from serious engagement with complexity, interaction, multiple levels of causation, multidirectional flows of influence, and pluralist approaches to explanation in general." Gould, *The Structure of Evolutionary Theory*, 31. Gould also emphasizes how Nietzsche's genealogical mode of analysis prefigures the approach to evolutionary theory that he adopts. See 1214–18.

19   James I. Porter, in *Nietzsche and the Philology of the Future* (Stanford: Stanford University Press, 2000), explores how Nietzsche, in his earliest work, draws upon the atomism of Democritus to address the role of the rhythms of nature in human being. He does not reference Gilles Deleuze, but this early exploration also meshes with Deleuze's and Guattari's engagement with resonance machines.

20   The first quotation comes from Kristian B. Dysthe et al., "Freak Waves, Rogue

Waves, Extreme Waves and Ocean Wave Climate," from the mathematics departments in Bergen and Oslo, www.math.uio.no/-karstent/waves/index—en.html
(July, 2007). The second is from Environmental Literacy Council, "Rogue Waves,"
www.enviroliteracy.org/article.php/257 (July 2007).

21 This is my reconstruction of the reflective reading of Calvin, Geneva, and proto-
capitalism that Alister E. McGrath offers in *A Life of Calvin* (Oxford: Basil Blackwell,
1990). The author resists the idea that Calvinism provided a separate causal factor in
the emergence of capitalism because, his research shows, a certain capitalist spirit
already in Geneva had found its way into Calvin's theology. On the other hand, he
does not want to deny the significance of Calvinism to the shape that early capitalism
took. The inflection given to his findings is mine.

22 Theorists in the neo-Kantian tradition are apt to charge that an immanent naturalist
such as me commits "the naturalistic fallacy" in moving "from is to ought." But the
move is only a "fallacy" if a set of prior assumptions is treated as incontestable. The
assumptions are (1) that morality intrinsically takes the form of law or a derived
principle and (2) that every reasonable person must somehow recognize this characteristic of morality or be deficient *as* an ethical agent. According to Kant, for instance,
the fundamental character of morality as law was something that every ordinary
person recognizes "apodictically." It cannot, he said, be demonstrated by argument;
it must simply be recognized without further fanfare. Immanent naturalists contest
Kant at precisely this point. We construe this "recognition" to be a cultural formation
deeply inscribed in predominantly Christian cultures. I imagine that many who
confess Buddhism or Hinduism share this suspicion with us. We contend that a
commitment to a noble ethic is first grounded in attachment to the abundance of
being, and that obligations, moral laws, rights, and responsibilities are second-order
formations growing out of this affirmation. We thus support an ethic of cultivation
over a morality of command. You can't really be too sure that our practice is "incoherent" until you try to live it yourself. One advantage of our view is that we can
participate in the politics by which new rights come into being without having to
pretend *retrospectively* that those rights were "implicit" in recognized principles all
along, even if nobody had yet "recognized" them. The charge of the naturalistic
fallacy converts the debate between on one side Buddha, Jesus (perhaps), Lucretius,
Spinoza, Hume, Nietzsche, James, and Deleuze, and on the other Augustine, Kant,
and Hegel, into a "mistake" made by the first group, even if many parties to the
second have not really come to terms with these practices.

23 This issue is posed and addressed in plateau 11 of *A Thousand Plateaus* by Gilles
Deleuze and Felix Guattari (Minneapolis: University of Minnesota Press, 1987).
There they seek to show how "rhizomatic" modes of consolidation are just as common and powerful as "arboreal" modes, contending that the latter models of equilibrium tend to prevail when a linear image of time is presupposed. The discussion
of habit in Deleuze's earlier work is also pertinent. But that being said, this is a
domain in need of attention. What makes things hold together?

24 Catherine Keller, *Face of the Deep: A Theology of Becoming* (New York: Routledge: 2003), 80. This book was brought to my attention in a thoughtful unpublished essay by Katherine Skerrett, "Time for Liberal Theology? Towards an Eschatology of Ordinary Time." Skerrett both discusses the work of Keller and carries it into a reflective discussion of the relations between theology, time, and politics.

25 James, *A Pluralistic Universe* (Lincoln: University of Nebraska Press, 1996), expresses faith in a God as an actor in the pluralistic universe. His God, however, is limited rather than omnipotent. It is also projected as a contestable act of faith on James's part. I concur with James on the latter point, except that my contestable projection is different in content from his. The universe does encompass agents of multiple sorts and degrees of agency, including atoms, evolutionary forces, geological processes, tornadoes, volcanoes, snakes, individual human beings, and collective human agents. Again, an agent is a force whose behavior is not entirely reducible to lawlike explanation; it makes a difference in the world without quite knowing what it is doing.

26 Friedrich Nietzsche, *The Will to Power*, trans. Walter Kaufmann (New York: Vintage, 1968), 38.

Chapter 4: Is Eco-egalitarian Capitalism Possible?

1 I say often, because several neo-Marxist approaches take another tack. See for instance David Harvey, *Spaces of Global Capitalism: Towards a Theory of Uneven Geographical Development* (New York: Verso, 2006), as well as the study by J. K. Gibson Graham discussed later in this chapter. In *The Enemy of Nature* (London: Zed, 2002), Joel Kovel argues that capitalism is necessarily at odds with environmentalism. What he sees as a set of interwoven necessities I see as a set of interwoven tendencies, potentially susceptible to redirection. He too evinces a sense of uncertainty here and there, and I understand that the possibilities experimentally introduced in this chapter are difficult to operationalize, in part because of the very structures that he identifies. The difference, perhaps, is whether you think it is vitally important to form images of a positive interim future today or rather wiser to provide an absolute critique of capitalism.

2 An excellent critical engagement with theories which insist that such objectives produce the opposite effect, undermine freedom, or both can be found in Albert Hirschman, *The Rhetoric of Reaction: Perversity, Futility, Jeopardy* (Cambridge: Harvard University Press, 1991).

3 Milton Friedman, *Why Government Is the Problem* (Stanford: Hoover Institution on War, Revolution, and Peace, 1993), 6. I will argue in chapter 5 that this model of the market makes implicit providential assumptions about the world. To put it briefly, since the state, the market, other economies, and volatile forces of nature constantly fold into each other in capitalism, a radical shift in any of these zones will make a real difference in the others. There are no fixed "externalities."

4 For a summary of the research by a team led by the neuroscientist who discovered mirror neurons see Giacomo Rizzolatti, Leonard Fogassi, and Vittorio Gallese, "Mirrors in the Mind," *Scientific American*, November 2006, 54–61. For a discussion of their implications for neuroscience in general see Hanna and Antonio Damasio, "Minding the Body," *Daedalus*, summer, 2006, 15–23.

5 See Elise Boulding and Kenneth Boulding, *The Future: Image and Processes* (Thousand Oaks: Sage, 1995), esp. chapter 6 by Elise Boulding. In a symposium on the mind-body question in *Daedalus*, summer, 2006, 67–75, I discuss how neuroscience can inform micropolitics. The essay in that symposium by two neuroscientists, Antonio and Hanna Damasio, provides insights into how "mirror neurons" work in providing us with a body image and infiltrating the affective dispositions of others through our modes of behavior.

6 See Michael Best and William Connolly, *The Politicized Economy* (Lexington: D. C. Heath, 1976; 2nd edn 1983), chapters 2, 3. I also note the classic study by Jürgen Habermas, *Legitimation Crisis*, trans. Thomas McCarthy (Boston: Beacon, 1975). Habermas's analysis of the sources of motivation and legitimacy deficits in advanced capitalism is still pertinent. He was also the first political sociologist, to my knowledge, to discuss how the risk of climate change could recoil back on the performance capacity of capitalism.

7 Fred Hirsch, *The Social Limits to Growth* (London: Routledge and Kegan Paul, 1977), 3, 7, 52. Some will dissent from Hirsch's approach by saying that he still supports "the commodity form." I support it too, while seeking to change the context in which it is set and to generalize essential commodities. The treatment of labor as a commodity degrades the worker. I would respond to that issue by imbuing the contract form with more participation and more effective protections. For a critical engagement with the theory of commodity fetishism see Jane Bennett, *The Enchantment of Modern Life* (Princeton: Princeton University Press, 2000).

8 For an account that links the suv, nationalism, advertising, militarism, and the electoral demand for a reliable source of plentiful oil see David Campbell, "The Biopolitics of Security: Oil, Empire, and the Sports Utility Vehicle," *American Quarterly*, September 2005, 943–72.

9 Hirsch, *The Social Limits to Growth*, 57.

10 Quoted in Campbell, "The Bipolitics of Security," 961.

11 See Juliet B. Schor, *The Overspent American* (New York: Harper Perennial, 1998). Schor also engages efforts by "downshifters" to break out of these spirals. Such efforts will play an indispensable role in changing the infrastructure of consumption although, as I am sure she agrees, they do not suffice.

12 For Hirsch on these questions see part III of *The Social Limits to Growth*. A valuable counterpoint to this perspective is found in Tom De Luca and John Buell, *Liars! Cheaters! Evildoers! Demonization and the End of Civil Debate in American Politics* (New York: New York University Press, 2005). De Luca and Buell review the relation between the tactics of the right and the increasing inequality of wealth and income in

the United States, as they call upon the democratic left to retune its strategies. A complementary outlook is provided by Philip Goodchild in *Capitalism and Religion: The Price of Piety* (London: Routledge, 2002). After reviewing the ecological crisis simmering in capitalism Goodchild examines the modes of "piety" that currently inhabit capitalist practices, arguing that they must be reconstituted significantly if modernity is to survive.

13   James Gustave Speth, *Red Sky at Morning: America and the Crisis of the Global Environment* (New Haven: Yale University Press, 2004), 208. One thing valuable in this book is Speth's understanding that the United States is the place to start, though not the ending point, in coming to terms with the global environment. The United States introduces the most pollutants, uses the most nonrenewable resources, has the greatest effect on the global shape of capitalism, and is the most resistant of advanced capitalist countries to address the issue. Speth's study could do more to convey the complexity of ecosystems and the role in them of tipping points, fuzzy boundaries, and unpredictability. Joel Kovel, in *The Enemy of Nature*, conveys that complexity in an admirable way. If only he carried that mode of analysis into his rendering of the interplay between the constitutive elements of capitalism.

14   Fred Pearce, *With Speed and Violence: Why Scientists Fear Tipping Points in Climate Change* (Boston: Beacon, 2007), 233. This book picks up where Speth leaves things.

15   Speth, *Red Sky at Morning*, 109.

16   For an account of how General Motors, Standard Oil, and Firestone Tire colluded in the 1920s to unravel the trolley systems in forty-four cities see Best and Connolly, *The Politicized Economy*, 85–101. If recent news reports about how GM has subverted its own experiment with electric cars are correct, these political tactics have not changed.

17   This proposal is advanced by Joseph Stiglitz in "A New Agenda for Global Warming," *Economists Voice*, July 2006, www.bepress.come/ev.

18   I was informed of this policy by John O'Doherty, a reporter for the *Financial Times*.

19   http://www.usgbc.org/DisplayPage.aspx?CMSPageID=147.

20   Beng-ke Ludvall, *Innovation, Growth and Social Cohesion* (Cheltenham: Edward Elgar, 2002), xv.

21   See ibid., and Bruce Stokes, "Europe Faces Globalization," *Yale Global Online*, May 2006, http://yaleglobal.yale.edu/display.article?id=7432 a.

22   The two studies noted above struggle with this issue. My awareness of it is informed by conversations with Lars Tonder, a political theorist from Denmark teaching at Northwestern University.

23   For a defense of the latter move on the part of John Paul II, and the commendation to push it further, see George Weigel, "The Church's Social Doctrine in the Twenty First Century," *Logos: A Journal of Catholic Thought and Culture*, summer 2003, 15–36. The author favors a combination of neoliberal economic practice and the state's enforcement of conservative social mores. Here are a few quotations: The "phenomenology of economic life suggests the possibility that there are economic 'laws'

written into the human condition in a way analogous to the moral laws" (23); "Catholic social doctrine . . . should focus primary attention on questions of wealth creation rather than wealth distribution" (24); and "Catholic doctrine . . . directs us to look first to private sector solutions, or to a private sector/public sector mix of solutions, rather than to the state, in dealing with urgent social issues such as education, health care, and social welfare" (17). Weigel's main answer is private philanthropy.

24 I was introduced to the Mondrogan experiment by J. K. Gibson-Graham, *PostCapitalist Politics* (Minneapolis: University of Minnesota Press, 2005). This book also explores other microeconomic experiments, some of which are listed above. And it examines changes in economic ethos needed to shake down the neoliberal shape of hegemonic economic practices.

25 See http://aflcio.org/corporatewatch 2006.

26 See Michael Best, *The New Competition: Institutions of Industrial Restructuring* (Cambridge: Harvard University Press, 1990), particularly chapter 3. Best also explores experiments with entrepreneurial organization in Japan. America, he thinks, is the country that is least experimental, though he sees movement in this country too. Best's and Gibson-Graham's books can profitably be read together, each picking up themes pertinent to the other.

27 An e-mail message to me from Michael Best in response to questions about recent developments in the Italian sector, 12 July 2006.

28 Joel Kovel, *The Enemy of Nature*, 163. Kovel does not project the kind of interim future visualized here. His judgment is that such a visualization makes people believe that capitalism can be *reformed*, when the relation to labor must be *transformed* to make way for eco-socialism. He also reviews how the actual history of state socialism has been authoritarian, inegalitarian, and eco-destructive. Our approaches touch at the point where the spirituality of the Bruderhof movement meets the element of indetermination in the capitalist axiomatic. I agree that the interim image projected here does not respond sufficiently to the issues at hand. It is a start, perhaps an indispensable start.

29 There are times and places where revolution is necessary, but they usually involve tragic circumstances. In a recent book David Pringle takes the left to task for not proposing specific reforms and for depending too much on the state when it does. I agree to some extent with his first charge—though most of the authors cited here do not succumb to that sin—and plead guilty to the second. Prindle places critics in a bind by this combination of demands. That is because, perhaps, he thinks that a slight softening of neoliberalism is the way to go, and I think that such a strategy cannot succeed in promoting the objectives supported here. Like many others, he ignores the role of religious sentiment in the contemporary American economy. See Prindle, *The Paradox of Democratic Capitalism: Politics and Economics in American Political Thought* (Baltimore: Johns Hopkins University Press, 2006).

30 See the excellent account of the effects of intensified competition on the Grand

Banks by James Petras and Henry Velmeyer, *System in Crisis: The Dynamics of Free Market Capitalism* (London: Fernwood, 2003), chapter 6, "Cod: An Ecological Crisis of Industrial Capitalism."

31 For exploration of the potential of a politics of cross-state citizen movements see chapter 6 of *Neuropolitics: Thinking, Culture, Speed* (Minneapolis: University of Minnesota Press, 2002), and chapter 5 of *Pluralism* (Durham: Duke University Press, 2006).

32 In that respect it is useful to compare the projections that leading supporters of capitalism made about its beneficial effects before it became a consolidated system. Most thought that the expansion of commerce would make the world more gentle. See Albert Hirschman, *The Passions and The Interests: Political Arguments for Capitalism before its Triumph* (Princeton: Princeton University Press, 1977).

Chapter 5: Christianity, Capitalism, and the Tragic

1 Sophocles, *The Theban Plays* (London: Penguin, 1947), 152.

2 I thank Bonnie Honig for calling my attention to the double-edged gender of Tiresias. Here is what one source says. "One day when he was walking on Mount Cyllene, young Tiresias saw two serpents mating . . . Tiresias either separated the serpents, or wounded them, or killed the female . . . the result . . . was that he became a woman . . . His misfortune had made him famous, and one day when Hera and Zeus were quarreling over whether the man or the woman experience the greatest pleasure in love-making, they decided to consult Tiresias, the only individual to have experienced both. Tiresias assured them that if the enjoyment of love was constituted of ten parts, the woman possessed nine and the man one. Hera was so furious at seeing the great secret of her sex revealed that she struck Tiresias blind. Zeus, in compensation, gave him the gift of prophecy and the privilege of living a long time, for seven generations it was said." Pierre Gramal, *The Dictionary of Classical Mythology* (Oxford: Blackwell, 1986), 455–56. This double gender, I suppose, made Tiresias more sensitive to pluripotentialities simmering in the present, and also ready to respond with fury if his wisdom was rejected by someone of single-dimensional gender. The story also calls attention to the ability of the Greek gods to influence events but not to master them entirely.

3 Sophocles, *The Theban Plays*, 154–55.

4 Paul Veyne, *Did the Greeks Believe in Their Myths?*, trans. Paula Wissing (Chicago: University of Chicago Press, 1983), explores this issue. Many of the learned professed either not to believe in them—while often respecting the masses who did—or to believe that the gods were active in the past but not at the time they themselves wrote. Others professed stronger belief, but took prudent action after receiving omens on key occasions in ways that seem to soften the power of belief. Such considerations merely scratch the surface of the issue, as Veyne knows. What does "belief" signify? What are its variations across levels of cognitive complexity and

different contextual triggers in the same person? In *Myth and Thought among the Greeks*, trans. Janet Lloyd (New York: Zone, 2006), Jean-Pierre Vernant explores how the old Greek myths were translated by non-Platonic philosophers into a series of cosmic forces. His account speaks to the "modernization" of a tragic vision by Nietzsche that we will encounter later in this chapter.

5 My thinking about tragic wisdom is influenced by Peter Euben, *The Tragedy of Political Theory* (Princeton: Princeton University Press, 1990), and Steven Johnston, *The Truth about Patriotism* (Durham: Duke University Press, 2007). Euben explores how a tragic bind "disconnects men from some vital center" (72), driving them to acts of hubris that contribute to the worst. Johnston draws upon tragic vision to challenge patriotism and replace it with a reciprocal ethos of civic generosity.

6 Bernard Williams, in *Shame and Necessity* (Berkeley: University of California Press, 1993), considers these two versions. He himself embraces a tragic vision in which he doubts that "there is anything that is intrinsically shaped to human interests, in particular to human beings' ethical interests" (163).

7 Catherine Keller, *Face of the Deep: A Theology of Becoming* (New York: Routledge, 2003). At one point Keller quotes Philo, the Jewish apologist in the Alexandrian school during the Hellenic period: " 'God did not himself form the formless material, since it is unthinkable that he should touch the endless, confused matter' " (45).

8 Paul Ricoeur, *The Symbolism of Evil*, trans. Emerson Buchanan (Boston: Beacon, 1967), 328.

9 Karl Jaspers, *Tragedy Is Not Enough*, trans. Harald Reiche et al. (London: Victor Gollancz, 1953), 38, 94, 87. Jaspers, like Tiresias before him, seeks to cultivate sensitivity to a specific impasse that shapes a tragic situation, so as to increase the chance of forging an "equitable settlement" out of it. The affinities of spirit between Jaspers and Nietzsche across an abyss of creedal difference become clear in Jaspers, *Nietzsche: An Introduction to the Understanding of His Philosophical Activity*, trans. Charles Wallraff (South Bend: Regnery, 1965).

10 Quoted in Richard Rubenstein, *When Jesus Became God: The Struggle to Define Christianity during the Last Days of Rome* (New York: Harcourt, 1999), 135. My summary of these events is drawn from this book; Charles Freeman, *The Closing of the Western Mind* (New York: Alfred A. Knopf, 2003); and Rowan Williams, *Arius: Heresy and Tradition*, rev. edn (Grand Rapids: William B. Erdmans, 2001). As Williams makes clear, the shifts and turns in the doctrine, in conjunction with the limited set of texts available to us now, render it a difficult object of examination. *Archetypal Heresy: Arianism through the Centuries*, by Maurice Wiles (Oxford: Oxford University Press), is also valuable. It shows how Arianism returns in the eighteenth century, through John Locke to some degree and Isaac Newton, William Whiston, and Samuel Clarke to a greater degree.

11 For a wonderful "nonfiction novel" about Julian, written even before the genre was said by Truman Capote to have been invented, see Gore Vidal, *Julian* (New York: Vintage, 1962). Vidal's Julian hides his love of the single god who finds multiple

expressions in the popular Greek gods until he inherits the position of emperor. He seeks to open "the Galileans" to the idea of different creeds operating in the same empire, even as he tries to resurrect and restore "pagan" sites. On Vidal's reading, a double agent inside the army kills Julian during the Persian campaign. But why did Julian find such a campaign necessary? That is another question.

12 Quoted in Rubenstein, *When Jesus Became God*, 233.

13 Quoted in Freeman, *The Closing of the Western Mind*, 190.

14 Quoted in Williams, *Arius*, 4. It is fair to say that Newman might have taken these sentiments back upon experiencing the Holocaust. But would he also have translated that modesty into a willingness to treat Arianism as a worthy doctrine of contestation within and outside his church? It seems wise to read accounts of the Arian controversy alongside the book by Geza Vermes, *The Religion of Jesus the Jew* (Minneapolis: Fortress). One upshot of that book is that when you consult the Jesus of Luke in its earliest available enunciation, it is reasonable to treat him as a radical Jewish prophet. Deep pluralism in predominately Christian countries awaits the day when a majority acknowledge the propriety of Jews, Muslims, atheists, and Christians exploring the word of Jesus through the lens of their respective faiths.

15 Augustine, *The City of God: Against the Pagans*, trans. Henry Bettenson (London: Penguin, 1984), 842.

16 Kathleen Roberts Skerrett, "The Indispensable Rival: William Connolly's Engagement with Augustine of Hippo," *Journal of the American Academy of Religion*, June 2004, 497.

17 Augustine, *The City of God*, 814. The previous two pages make clear that this persecution includes the very *presence* of "heretical" Christians who "cause grief in the hearts of the devout." I admire those who draw sustenance from the abundance of love in Augustine. It is a reserve from which relations of agonistic respect can be cultivated across significant differences of faith. But it also seems imperative, in a country where many campaign against a real diversity of faith, to point to the underside of Augustine's doctrine, finding expression in his orientations to Arians, other heretics, pagans, and Jews.

18 Cornel West, *Democracy Matters: Winning the Fight against Imperialism* (New York: Penguin, 2004), 149. Or again, "Constantinian Christianity has always been at odds with the prophetic legacy of Jesus Christ" (148). "To see the Gospel of Jesus Christ bastardized by imperial Christians and pulverized by Constantinian believers and then exploited by nihilistic elites of the American empire makes my blood boil" (171–72). The distinction between Constantinian and prophetic Christianity does not track neatly that between Trinitarian and Arian Christianity. The connection to Arianism is in the earthiness of Jesus; a difference may reside in the greater distance between humanity and God supported by Arianism. The point is that the resounding defeat of Arianism may have set back for centuries the emergence of a prophetic tradition.

19 See James M. Robinson, *The Gospel of Jesus: A Historical Search for the Original Good*

News (San Francisco: Harper, 2005). Robinson reviews evidence that Mark was the first gentile version of the gospels and the Book of Q the first version by the Jewish devotees of Jesus before gentiles were converted. Matthew and Luke thus represent two diverse attempts to consolidate the two early books. The Book of Q, which is distilled from close, comparative readings of the extant books in their earliest available forms, is rather close to Steven Mitchell's *The Gospel According to Jesus*, discussed in chapter 1.

20 My response to these issues is probably closer to that of Rubenstein than that of Rowan Williams, though both seek to soften the terms of this debate (see note 10, above). The question can thus be posed to me, "But how could there *be* a church if it houses a wide diversity of doctrines?" Fair enough. First, a church could sanction, say, Arianism within it as a minority stance, while not sacrificing monotheism or a special role for Christ. Refusing that, it could acknowledge Arianism within Christianity writ large, though outside its particular sect. Beyond that, it could periodically revisit the issue of the number and range of faiths that should be encompassed either inside the church or under the broader umbrella of Christianity, in a world marked by a persistent diversity of faiths. Finally, it could review the appellations appropriate to faiths outside its confines, in a spiral of broadening possibilities: Catholicism, Protestantism, Christianity, Judaism, Islam, monotheism, Buddhism, and nontheism. Such a review occurred with respect to Judaism after the Second World War. But what about "atheism"? Some defenders of Christianity evince respect for those who confess nontheistic gratitude for being. But many—how many? —continue to label them unbelievers, nihilistic, relativistic, and narcissistic.

21 I say somehow, for if you accept the vision of tragic potential with meliorist possibility embraced here, you accept the idea that this creed or philosophy too is contestable. And that your presumptive care for the diversity of being endows you with a responsibility to overcome resentment of the contestability of your own creed. You are therefore directed to seek worthy allies who embrace providence, human mastery, or a confident meliorism, even as you seek to *inspire* them to come to terms with the element of contestability in the faith they honor. This part of the thesis will be addressed later in the chapter, but I know from experience that it is wise to call attention to it now. For the most blatant way to displace the theme of contestability is to say, "Hey there are people who admit it and are incredibly ruthless." Precisely. That is why both elements are needed in conjunction.

22 William James, *A Pluralistic Universe* (Lincoln: University of Nebraska Press, 1996), 311.

23 I do pursue this question in chapter 4 of *Pluralism* (Durham: Duke University Press, 2005).

24 James, *A Pluralistic Universe*, 299.

25 Ibid., 45.

26 Deleuze, *Difference and Repetition*, 222.

27 I discuss Bergson's image of time in chapter 4 of *Pluralism*. A philosophy of radical immanence is also one of time as becoming, in which time is out of joint with itself.

28 Daniel Smith, "Deleuze and the Theory of Immanent Ideas," paper given at the Symposium on "Experimenting with Intensities," Trent University, Peterborough, Ontario, 12–15 May 2004.

29 Does Deleuze retain in his later work the confidence in the power of transcendental arguments displayed in *Difference and Repetition*? I rather doubt it. Chapter 7 of *Cinema II*, trans. Hugh Tomlinson and Robert Galeta (New York: Athlone, 1989), explores how to restore "belief in this world" under new conditions of being. Belief here slides into faith, and Deleuze is explicit about how it might be secured either through a new recourse to grace or a new appreciation of the chanciness of being. The presentation of these alternatives suggests that the issue is open at the most fundamental level.

30 Ibid., 328.

31 Immanuel Kant, *The Conflict of the Faculties*, trans. Mary Gregor (Lincoln: University of Nebraska Press, 1979).

32 A different version of this section can be found in William E. Connolly, "Immanence, Abundance, Democracy," *Radical Democracy: Politics between Abundance and Lack*, ed. Lars Tønder and Lasse Thomassen (Manchester: Manchester University Press, 2005), 239–55. Tønder and Thomassen focus on debates between Lacanian theories of lack and Deleuzian theories of abundance, as each applies to the issue of democracy.

33 Friedrich Nietzsche, *Beyond Good and Evil*, trans. Marianne Gowan (South Bend: Gateway, 1955), 58. It is pertinent to note that when Nietzsche fabulates a time or a people, formulations that qualify or complicate it usually follow. The fabulation identifies a noble disposition without exhausting the complexity of the constituency in question. Even the "overman" eventually becomes one set of dispositions contending with others, rather than a pure type. The goal of Nietzsche, who recognizes the self to be a complex "social structure," is to magnify noble dispositions in us and to contract others. That is one reason he can imagine a spiritualization of enmity across different constituencies, many of whom have minor strains in themselves that touch dominant chords in others.

34 *Thus Spoke Zarathustra*, trans. Walter Kaufmann (New York: Vintage, 1966), 89.

35 Ibid., 88.

36 Friedrich Nietzsche, *On the Genealogy of Morals*, trans. Walter Kaufmann and R. J. Hollingdale (New York: Random House, 1967), 94.

37 Friedrich Nietzsche, *The Will to Power*, trans. Walter Kaufmann (New York: Vintage, 1968), no. 852, pp. 450–51; no. 1019, pp. 526–27; no. 1029, pp. 531–32; no. 1019, p. 527.

38 Jonathan Israel, *Radical Enlightenment: Philosophy and the Making of Modernity, 1650–1750* (Oxford: Oxford University Press, 2002), 300. Israel devotes a section to this question, evincing his appreciation of the intimate link between philosophical arguments and practical tests. Another relevant book is Matthew Stewart, *The Courtier and the Heretic: Lebniz, Spinoza and the Fate of God in the Modern World* (New York: W. W. Norton, 2006).

39 Friedrich Nietzsche, *Daybreak: Thoughts on the Prejudices of Morality*, trans. R. J. Hollingdale (Cambridge: Cambridge University Press, 1982), 171. I develop a list of possible techniques in *Neuropolitics: Thinking, Culture, Speed* (Minneapolis: University of Minnesota Press, 2002), chapter 4.

40 See Albert Hirschman, *The Rhetoric of Reaction: Perversity, Futility, Jeopardy* (Cambridge: Harvard University Press, 1991): "the perverse-effect doctrine is closely tied to a central tenet of the discipline: the idea of a self regulating market. To the extent this idea is dominant, any public policy aiming to change market outcomes, such as prices or wages, automatically becomes noxious interference with beneficent, equilibrating processes" (27). On the next page Hirschman lists several uncertainties located between the introduction of a minimum wage and the perverse effect that neoliberal theorists predict, showing how the link between intervention and perversity reflects a closed view of economic processes.

41 George Gilder, *Wealth and Poverty* (New York: Basic, 1981), 254, 255, 264, 265. The last statement occurs four pages before the end of the book.

42 A word to the wise. My assertion of a *connection* between a doctrine and a sensibility does not mean that I assert an *equivalence* between them, a point made clear in chapter 2. Here is how a cottage industry, built around accusations against others of falling prey to performative contradictions, works: First you reduce the assertion of a connection to that of an equation. Then you show how the author denies in one place the equation asserted in the other. This rhetorical strategy is only effective when the first misrepresentation is overlooked.

43 My discussion in these pages is indebted to Philip Goodchild, *Capitalism and Religion* (London: Routledge, 2002). Goodchild, while not exploring social movements and state actions needed to turn things around, is more alert than most—except Max Weber and George Gilder—to the internal connections between a spiritual ethos and the institutions of production, work, investment, consumption, and the like. The difference is that the ethos he pursues is close to the one I seek.

INDEX

Adorno, Theodor, 122

Agonistic respect, xiv, 48, 57, 80, 88, 89, 91, 134

Ankersmit, Frank, 54, 152 n. 17

Antigone, xiv, 119, 120; sexuality and, 31

Arian vs. Trinitarian controversy, xiv, 4, 123–27, 132, 147 n. 7, 154 n. 3, 163 n. 10, 164 n. 14, 165 n. 20; tragic vision and, 108–12. *See also* Christianity; Creed; Jesus Christ

Aspirational politics, 32–34, 36

Assemblages, x, 1, 12, 25, 40, 41; capitalist, 9–14, 19, 23, 26, 27, 35, 37, 40, 54; Christian, 13, 14, 35, political, xi, 15, 48, 54; state, 14, 21, 35; time and, 24

Augustine, xii, 2, 19, 121; biblical interpretation and, 71–76, 79, 84, 129; conversion and, 78, 91; diversity and, 89, 164 n. 17; Hauerwas and, 80; providential history and, 126

Bennett, Jane, 156 n. 17

Bergson, Henri, 90, 131, 165 n. 27

Best, Michael, 96, 111, 161 nn. 26–27

Blumenburg, Hans, 17, 18

Blyth, Mark, 43, 44, 147 n. 9

Boulding, Elise, 94, 95

Boulding, Kenneth, 81

Bruderhof communities, 111, 161 n. 28

Bush, George W., 54, 55, 119; Bush syndrome, 49, 50

Calvin, John, 19, 84, 157 n. 21

Calvinism, 31; Arianism and, 127; capitalism and, xii, 17, 19, 50, 84, 157 n. 21; Weber and, xi, 13, 14, 17, 18, 84

Capitalism, vii, viii, 33, 86, 88; Calvinism and, xii, 17, 19, 50, 84, 157 n. 21; capitalist axiomatic, xi, 10, 11, 13, 22–24, 27, 29, 108, 113, 117; capitalist class, xi; capitalist state, 21, 27, 28, 109; Christianity and, x, 9, 13, 14, 22, 28–31, 35, 37, 84, 101, 144; consumption and, 95; climate change and, 101–3; cowboy, xii, xiv, 7, 34, 36, 39, 48, 55, 58, 62, 112, 116, 143; creativity of, 30–34, 36, 140, 141, 142; Deleuze and, 22, 23; eco-egalitarianism and, 93, 105, 160 nn. 12–13, 161 n. 28; ethos of, 110, 111; evangelical right and, 44, 62, 63, 82, 142; future and, 25, 51; microeconomic experiments and, 108–12; nature and, 83; nomadism and, 29; providence and, 140, 141; state and, 36, 35–37; the tragic and, 10; in United States, 14, 28, 114; volatility of, x, 10, 20, 22, 87, 94, 140–42, 145; Weber on, xi, 13, 14, 17, 20, 24, 28, 84, 151 n. 10

William Connolly is the Krieger-Eisenhower Professor
of Political Science at the Johns Hopkins University.

Library of Congress Cataloging-in-Publication Data
Connolly, William E.
Capitalism and Christianity, American style /
William E. Connolly.
p. cm.
Includes bibliographical references and index.
ISBN-13: 978-0-8223-4249-6 (cloth : alk. paper)
ISBN-13: 978-0-8223-4272-4 (pbk. : alk. paper)
1. Capitalism—United States—Religious aspects.
2. Christianity and politics—United States. I. Title.
HB501.C683 2008
261.8'50973—dc22   2007033641